306.87 /AND
Andrews, Paul.
Changing children

D1099144

# *Changing Children*

## Living with a New Generation

## PAUL ANDREWS S.J.

NCAD LIBRARY

WITHDRAWN

Gill & Macmillan

Published in Ireland by
Gill & Macmillan Ltd
Goldenbridge
Dublin 8
with associated companies throughout the world
© Paul Andrews S.J. 1994

0 7171 2138 0

Print origination by Typeform Repro Ltd, Dublin
Printed by ColourBooks Ltd, Dublin

All rights reserved. No part of this publication may be copied,
reproduced or transmitted in any form or by any means,
without permission of the publishers.

A catalogue record is available for this book
from the British Library.

1   3   5   4   2

# Contents

National College of Art and Design
LIBRARY

# Preface

Ireland has changed, its children have changed, and adults try to change them. The ambiguity of the word *change*, transitive and intransitive, runs through this book. Some of the changes in Irish life were brought about by my generation, grandparents now. We changed things, and generally for the better. Within that setting, our children grow up different. It is always a privilege to watch a young person grow and blossom. This generation of parents, probably more than any past generation, has had to face a kaleidoscope of change in the appearance and bodies of their children, in their language, intelligence, values, in their exposure to countless new stimulations and opportunities, in their range of style.

Much of this has been well described and documented. Ireland has been and is researched, and we no longer have to depend on findings from Britain, continental Europe and North America. This is not a summary of research, but a view from a privileged chair. Clearly, names and circumstances are altered in every case, so that there could be no way of recognising any case from either the sex, the location or the family details offered here. My greatest indebtedness is to the people so disguised, the parents and children who have shaped my experience, taught me whatever I know, and given me, a priest without a family, a multitude of children I could love and let go.

A wise doctor, who was supervising my work, brought me up sharply a few years ago with the question: 'Do your clients (aged anything from five to twenty) see you as a father or a grandfather?' Despite reaching three-score years, I had not thought of myself in that way. Age puts me in the grandfather class. When you grow old, you hope that what you have learned will not all die with you. These last thirty years have given me a privileged access to parents and their children, of all ages, but mostly younger than twenty. This access grew out of my work in schools, and developed further as I moved into psychotherapy with young people. The parents and children I met are a limited group: mainly from Ireland or Britain, mainly white, and mainly Christian though with all shades of belief and unbelief.

Those parents have access to good books about child-rearing, some of them listed at the end of this book. None of these, however, quite meets the incessant problems of Irish parents who grew up in the sixties or seventies and find themselves rearing children in a different Ireland, in which the children themselves seem to have changed. These are the questions I have listened to for thirty years, and try to confront in this book. Much of the material of these pages appeared first in monthly articles in a remarkable magazine, which for over a hundred years, without advertising, has commanded a wider readership than almost any other publication in Ireland. I mean, of course, the *Sacred Heart Messenger*, to whose editor I make grateful acknowledgment.

Paul Andrews S.J.
August 1994

# Theory and Practice

People who talk to parents about children risk doing damage. There are stories of lecturers who confidently proposed guidelines and commandments for parents, until they had children themselves; suddenly they lost their nerve. Pontificate about child-rearing and you can be offering hostages to fortune if you have offspring on public view. Jesus could teach 'as one having authority', but few others share that privilege, especially when it comes to making sense of life and people. The revered Bruno Bettelheim, who, having survived concentration camp, founded a famous Orthogenic School for disturbed children, and written wisely on 'the good-enough parent', shocked his friends and admirers by ending his own life with his head in a plastic bag.

There are real hazards — psychiatrists, psychologists and social workers know this to their cost — in being too analytical with one's own children. I can think of an interesting North American couple, the mother a hard-working psycho-therapist from Eastern Europe, the father a talented, disorganised, lazy, heavy drinker from Ireland. They resolved (under the mother's persuasion, as she did most of the child-rearing) to bring up their daughter and son by sweet reason, using no coercion and setting no limits that could not be justified by explanation. The girl grew up like her mother, organised and reasonable. The son grew up like his father, a wastrel of large but squandered talent. The method and

1

philosophy they had consciously espoused for bringing up their children counted for less than their example.

Obviously parents influence their children more by what they are than by what they say. The theories we use for rearing children are constantly falling foul of the unconscious assumptions on which we act all day long. So parents who are determined to bring up their family in a different style from that in which they were reared, may find later, to their discomfort, that they are addressing their children in the tone and sometimes even the words of their own parents.

Repeatedly in the course of writing these pages I have been undermined by the thought that parents know best, and should not be confused with too much theorising. Then the phone rings, and a messed-up family looks for an outside view on their mess; quite simple observations, such as you find below, can often help. So I go on writing.

The research on ways of rearing children has gone on apace, and must take account of different cultures. One promising summary of research[1] described three styles of child-rearing, *laissez-faire*, authoritarian and authoritative. The first and second are disastrous in their effects, the third helpful. Its features are:

(a)   a warm bond of affection between the child and at least one parent

(b)   effective two-way communication between children and parents

(c)   firm but responsive discipline

(d)   tolerance of self-expression

(e)   parental demands for maturity related to the child's stage of growth.

Research can be thanked for producing true but facile formulas. So many other factors enter our dealings with children: sheer fatigue and the need to survive physically; the desire to be loved by children, especially if the marriage itself is under stress; the fear of losing control; financial pressures versus children's demands (if you really love me you will buy me a computer game); conflicting theories about diet, exercise, punishment, picked up from the media. Far be it from me to add another set of theories. Parents are the ultimate experts on their own children. It has been shown again and again that when professionals, whether medical, psychological or any other, assess children, they form a fuller and more accurate picture if they have parents there to prompt and direct them. But parents can be helped by pegs for reflection, ways of thinking about their own offspring and ways of handling them. What follows is just that, pegs for reflection on changing children.

## NOTE

1.  P. Hill, 'Recent advances in selected aspects of adolescent development', in *Journal of Child Psychiatry and Psychology: Annual Research Review,* January 1993, p. 74

# *The Meaning of Children*

My first encounter with a new family is highly charged, with curiosity and expectation and nervousness. There was a time when I would want to gather every detail from the parents before meeting the child. I would try to get a sense of the family over three generations, from the grandparents to the child under scrutiny. I felt one could not know too much, not just about conception, pregnancy, birth and early history of the child, but about family myths, the financial ups and downs, employment of different members, health, conflicts within the family, skeletons in the cupboard in the shape of addicts or unwanted pregnancies or troubles with the law.

There is truth in that, but it can diffuse one's focus. Now I want above all to sense the *meaning* of the child to parents and to themselves. The children I have met stay in my mind with a distinct flavour. They leave an after-taste which is more revealing than any objective facts about them. This is seldom on the surface, and it is often obscure to the parents.

One child may become the conscientious one, who is felt by the others as representing conscience, perhaps in a reproachful way that is resented. I think of Michael, a large and terrifying adolescent, the eldest in a long line of sons. His exhausted mother left much of the 'rearing' of Alan the youngest, to Michael. In Alan's eyes Michael stood for mother (father was an absent alcoholic), for law, for religious observance, for getting homework done on time, for adding punishments at home if young Alan was punished at school for misbehaviour. Alan feared and hated his big brother, and was gently consoled at a later stage when Michael kicked over the traces. The conscientious one often does tire of the role, and envies the younger ones who are allowed more rope, more expression of their instinctual energy, whether for pleasure or for anger.

What is dangerous in a family is the unconscious assigning of roles or meanings: where in mother's or father's mind Jane becomes the family's conscience, Danny the wild one, Deirdre the careful, calculating one, Matt the greedy one, Paul the jealous one, Louise the clown, Peter the cry-baby. Worst of all is when some child becomes the black sheep, carrying the role of scapegoat. This is never stated, so the child has no appeal against his rejection; it is implied by black looks and tone of voice. He becomes the one it is easy to blame, so he easily comes to live up to his reputation. In disturbed families, this sort of control is usually secret and hidden.

Where parents are aware of these meanings, they can control and alter them. There are times when the careful, calculating daughter longs to act uninhibitedly and spontaneously; or when the wild, instinctual child wants to plan his life more carefully, or when the clown of the family wants to be taken seriously. Ideally all the children would have a balance of the conscientious, the controlled, the calculating and the instinctual.

Parents can sense the flavour of each of their children and that flavour can change with the years. Children can taste like a gift, a joy, a loan, a dead weight, a headache, a nuisance, a trophy, a prize bloom, a responsibility, an excitement, a possession, an insurance for old age, a worry, a nightmare.

## THE MEANING OF CHILDREN TO PARENTS

### Jim: Mother's Boy

Mother's boy, mother's possession? Jim was eight when I met him, blond, blue-eyed, alert to a degree that made my best efforts seem sluggish. He looked an angel, the answer to a mother's prayer. In a way he was just that. Erica, his mother, had been clear about her plans. She enjoyed her lovers and she did not want marriage. As she approached thirty, she began to long for a child of her own. She saw her best friend mothering a baby, and yearned. It was not difficult to persuade her current boyfriend to co-operate, and in due course, after a healthy pregnancy, she was delivered of Jim, a lovely, healthy boy, whom she breast-fed till the age of three, when she was pregnant again.

She loved and enjoyed him to the full. They were like lovers lost in each other. Jim became a lively, possessive toddler who for some time had his mother to himself. At first there were no rivals, and their time together was absorbing and rapturous until, when Jim was two, Denis appeared, a fine hulk of a man, who courted Erica, then moved in with her, then beguiled her into marriage, and finally got her with child. They had two little daughters in quick succession, three and four years younger than Jim.

Denis had taken to his step-son Jim — it would be hard not to — but gradually he and Erica began to taste the fury they had unleashed. They had three attractive children, but one of them became a demon, defying his step-father, aggressive towards his step-sisters, and towards all the other children at school who seemed to him like rivals. He was still tender and seductive with his mother, but found it hard to forgive her betrayal of their love. He had had her to himself, and could not agree to sharing her. To his teachers he was rebellious and defiant, in an increasingly clever way. He was intelligent, learned easily when he wanted to, was lovely to meet, but underneath was a volcano.

There was nothing puzzling about it. Jim was furious with his mother for marrying, and with his step-father and step-sisters for taking Erica from him. Most fathers are there from conception, and find it natural to move in on the toddler and save him from his mother. They accept their son's reluctance to give up his place at the centre of mother's life, but the love that binds father to son helps them through the crisis, and normally it leads to a strong identification of son with father, internalising his values and strengths. But Jim had never seen Denis until he was two, and thought of him simply as an unwelcome intruder.

By the time I met eight-year-old Jim, he had been expelled or gently pushed out of four schools. Despite himself he had mastered the basic skills well, but at this stage had a larger investment in wrecking things than in improving his life chances by learning.

It has repeatedly surprised me, how some adults can overlook both the desires and the fantasies of young children. Nothing could be more obvious, you would think, than the passionate attachment of babies to their mother. Jim had learned to be the centre of the universe. For three years he had enjoyed Erica's breast, and the pain of losing it to his little sister, and his place in Erica's bed to Denis, was more than he could bear. He felt betrayed, and the sense of outrage received an extra charge from his energy and intelligence.

The first law a little boy must learn is that you can't keep mother all to yourself — the taboo on incest.[2] Jim saw no reason to learn that lesson, and in refusing that law, he refused all other limits on his desires. Erica had begun by following her own desire, for a child without a husband. She did not think through the consequences. She finished with a husband and a child, who, like her, followed his own desires irrespective of the consequences. Jim, Erica and Denis are still paying a heavy price.

## Lara: A Disappointment

As a man without children, I have often watched fathers with envy, and I am unsure whether the envy is stronger over their sons or their daughters. It is intriguing, almost heart-stopping, to watch them with gorgeous, princess-like little daughters; but it does not last. Many years ago I was invited into a family where the daughter, Lara, was mentioned as a problem.

She was the eldest in the family, and as she turned into her beautiful teens, her father, who had seen her as his princess, was baffled by the change. She would reject his advice but quote what she had heard from some young friend down the road. She obviously preferred to be out of the house than in. From being a dutiful daughter, she seemed to her father to have become something of a monster, looking to a wild bunch of friends for her style in clothes and make-up (tending towards the outrageous), her language (often rough or obscene), her morals (at least as expressed in her conversation) and her centre of gravity.

That at least was how it looked to father. He sat down once with his wife, Lara and myself, and each tried to say what they liked about the other, without ifs or buts. Lara had no difficulty: despite the difference in age and style, she liked her mother for her warmth, her father for being a strong and responsible provider, and for all the fun she used to have with him. But when her father tried to say what he liked in Lara, he could not finish a sentence positively. She can be good company — but she is never in the house. She is bright and intelligent — but she does no work and she's wasting her brains. She is pretty — but look what she's doing with her face and hair and clothes.

In the comfortable suburb where they lived, the teenagers formed a large, noisy, visible group, and Lara found a welcome among them. The old wisdom is that teenagers look to their peers for matters of style and appearance, and to their parents for more lasting values. It seems to be generally true, but it is not always obvious to the parents, because lasting values do not show on the surface, whereas lifestyle does. 'Style' of conversation often means holding forth on matters of politics, morals, religion, in a way that deeply offends parents.

What her father eventually did was heroic. He gave himself three weeks — his wife went along with him on it — in which he would hold back any criticism or comment on Lara, except to compliment her. It meant letting all sorts of annoyances pass unremarked. It gave him a space in which to sort out the trivial from matters of deeper concern. He found that most of what annoyed him was trivial, details of dress, appearance and conversation that changed even in the trial period he gave himself. He saw how much of Lara's posturing was just experimenting with style, trying to find what was really her. He found that she could still be a delight to him, she could still be funny and great company, though her quickness and sophistication often made him nervous.

Lara had in fact given up any hope of pleasing her father. She had unwittingly accepted the role of being a disappointment to him, a thorn in his side, and was beginning to find pleasure in her ability to annoy him. Now she discovered to her surprise that she could still please her father, and in a different way from when she was a little girl.

He could accept her as different. Her meaning for him had changed.

## Patrick: A Prize Bloom

I used to dread meeting Mrs Robinson, but it was quite a while before I understood why. On the surface she was a kindly, attractive, good-living mother and wife with three fine children, who shone in the secondary schools of their country town. They were bright and athletic and biddable, a pleasure to have in class. They were the pride and joy of their mother. That was what made her hard to meet. Within minutes her conversation would have turned to Patrick's grades, or Anne's principal role in the school play. The pride and joy was in their achievements rather than in them. She was ready to lavish attention on them at any inconvenience to herself.

She was like the gardener whose whole concern is his exhibits in the flower show. It was as though she valued Patrick for the size of his bloom, and constantly compared him with others, determined that he should be the best, that his full potential be realised, regardless of the needs and demands of others. She had little patience for the teacher who would pace the classwork to make sure that every pupil was keeping up. Mrs Robinson felt that if they were slowing Patrick down, then they should be moved to another class.

So these fine children grew up self-centred, over-striving, easily depressed by failure of any kind. Failure seldom touched them, but even second place was seen as something you did not talk about. When Patrick finally did his Leaving Certificate, he earned a raft of Bs and As in his results. A prize bloom you might think? Alas, it was not first in its class. His mother heard that another boy in his year had achieved higher points, and in obvious distress demanded from the Principal (who wisely refused) that he arrange for a re-count of Patrick's results.

When you apply a Pharisaical approach to rearing a family, the children are the first casualties. The Pharisees were rebuked by Christ, not because they lived bad lives, but because their intolerance of the less-than-perfect (Pharisee meant The Perfect One) made them blind to people around them. A mother or father who aims to have a perfect family is on the wrong track. Only machines are perfect.

# THE MEANING OF CHILDREN TO THEMSELVES

How does baby Kate start to see herself as separate from mother? How does she develop a sense or image of herself? At first her awareness is a disconnected set of bodily feelings: cold, pain, hunger, weariness. Then at some stage — Jacques Lacan calls it the Mirror Stage — from Kate's first sight of herself as a body from outside, she starts to grasp herself as a unity. She looks at her reflection while mother says 'That's Kate'. It is an illusion, but a compelling one, distracting her from her inner perceptions and feelings. Names, labels simplify the world, make it easier to grasp, but also distract us from the richness of our original sense of it.

Self-image is not just a matter of naming: it is charged with value. Little Kate cannot evaluate herself as good or clever or pretty or lovable. Her sense of herself comes through 'reflected appraisal'. We value ourselves as we are valued, and that first valuation is expressed in the tender or untender hands of parents and care-givers, in the gleam of their eyes, and the tone of their voice, which communicates emotions to us in language long before we can understand the words.

That self-image grows slowly, and continues to grow as long as we are open to growth. Pupils alter the self-image of their teachers and fellow pupils by the nicknames they give, with a sharp-edged perception that reaches to the vulnerable centre of their victim. What has intrigued me in recent years is the genius of children in defining their meaning for themselves. This meaning, caught in favourite images and symbols, may lurk below the surface of the child's mind, yet can be captured by those who listen.

## Rory: The Family Tree

I think of Rory, the eleven-year-old son of a drug-dealing family, understandably unpopular in their housing estate to the point where they had been threatened, attacked and fire-bombed. Rory's delinquent father was in and out of jail. Rory drew more than he talked, and the image that invaded many pictures was of a tree — you might call it a family tree. He drew himself hiding in the branches. It was dangerous enough in the tree — Rory had been abused sexually and physically by his own family — but it was still more dangerous on the ground below, where tigers and alsatians symbolised the hazards to be met away from the relative protection of his family.

## Joel: Images of Potency

More mysterious was the imagery of six-year-old Joel, whose mother had sought a lover to make her pregnant when her impotent husband had failed. Joel, I was told, knew nothing of this. The marriage survived this intrusion, and Joel knew his impotent father as Dad; but he had learning and emotional difficulties. The theme that dominated his talk, his curiosity and his drawing was — potency: images of giants, tractors, JCBs, machines of monstrous power.

## Jessica: The Sharp-clawed Kitten

Jessica was a sweet little girl to meet, with a seductive smile framed in long fair hair, and an endearing way of curling up in a beanbag, comfortable and ready to talk and draw. Her favourite picture was of a kitten, and it fitted; but kittens' velvet pads hide sharp claws, and Jessica's target was her mother, shown as a snarling bitch, the kitten's natural enemy.

## Simon: The Boss

When nine-year-old Simon drew his family for me, he depicted himself as a large, strong figure filling the centre of the page. On either side were child-sized, almost cowering parents. It was an accurate depiction of the family He was an only child and he was the boss. Neither parent had conveyed to him that they or other people had needs. He had never outgrown the imperiousness of infancy. When he shouted, things had to happen. His needs were what made the world go round. In fact, with time the picture changed, because his parents took a hold on their and Simon's lives. Five years later, Simon's self-image had changed, and he could be lived with.

## Johanna: The Invalid

Johanna had been a 'blue' baby, and had needed several blood transfusions during the struggle to survive infancy. It was a successful struggle, carried through by a warm-hearted mother who was not naturally a worrier, but who had to maintain a high level of concern and care for her delicate little daughter. By the time she was four, Johanna was a tough and determined girl, as strong as any of her peers. However she had grown attached to the emotional rewards of being delicate. She was shocked by her first experience of school, at five. She found the school day long and tiring, the classroom cold, the other children inconsiderate, the teacher demanding. She would start the day with pains, and end it with tears and pleas. She continued to think of herself as an invalid, needing special consideration and care.

To accept the status of a normal child was like a second weaning, unusually painful for both mother and daughter. If her mother had had less sense, Johanna could easily have gone on to make a career of being an invalid. Instead, mother regarded her pleas with patience and a firm 'You are OK, Johanna, you will manage. Soon you will enjoy feeling as strong as other children'. And she did.

## NOTE

2. Jacques Lacan has pointed to the Western family, of children with two parents, as the seed-ground for revolutionary and creative people. The setting of father-daughter-son-mother makes for tensions, but they can be creative tensions. In most families they are resolved, as Freud pointed out on the Oedipal model, by the son yielding his privileged position with mother to his father, and accepting the basic law, the taboo on incest.

# The Position of Children

## THE ELDEST CHILD

You who are reading this are either the eldest in your family, or not: a momentous difference, which has been noted for a long time. The Bible describes the struggle of Jacob and Esau to emerge first from the womb, and the later ruse of Jacob to trick his older brother out of his birthright.

A hundred years ago Francis Galton started to put figures on the advantages of being first-born. He found that eldest or only children were disproportionately well represented in the ranks of eminent scientists. Galton's explanation was coloured by his Victorian culture. He thought that since the first-born inherited the bulk of the estate, he (women were not investigated at that stage) would have the leisure to cultivate his mind, whereas his younger siblings would have to earn a living by entering the Army or the Church, or even commerce. Money bought leisure, and Galton took it for granted, as the Greeks did, that leisure would be used to improve the mind. He added that parents treat the eldest child as more of a companion, and accord him more responsibility than the later arrivals.

Later research reinforced his findings. Eldest or only children are more likely to appear in dictionaries of national biography, *Who's Who,* to hold university professorships, to be Rhodes scholars or gifted children. They also tend to be more oriented towards adults than are their younger siblings. They

13

are more docile, co-operative, serious, cautious, anxious and sensitive. There are millions of exceptions, but the *tendency* is clear and significant.

The reasons for the tendency are open to speculation, but they touch the experience of every family. Even though parents often say they made all their mistakes on the first child, that is more than balanced by the fact that they gave him or her the sort of time and energy that none of the later children could hope for.

The eldest is always an only child for a shorter or longer period. Parents talk to him more, play with him more. His father takes a bigger part in the upbringing than with later children. Parents are less relaxed with the first than with the others. They have no model for rearing him except their own memories, and they tend to expect quicker learning, higher achievement, better standards of behaviour, and faster maturing. As can be seen from the tendencies reported above, it often works. It produces a more serious child who relates easily to grown-ups, where the later-born relate more comfortably to their peers (parental authority can be mediated to them through the older children), and are more affectionate, pugnacious, easy-going and friendly than the first-born.

These generalisations have one value: to let us look at ourselves and our children with this dimension in mind. For every Jacob and Esau who are at one another's throats, you find pairs who could not bear to be without their sister or brother. There have been intriguing studies in the Sunday colour magazines of sibling pairs who truly love one another. The passing of years can change things, turn jealousy to deep affection. As a child you fight your big sister and she detests you for putting her nose out of joint by arriving, but half a century later you treasure her and all your shared memories.

**THE ONLY CHILD**

Supposing there is no one to share with? Ireland is full of children who would love to be only children, enjoying their parents' undivided attention. Is this an unmixed blessing?

There was a time when an only child was a rarity in Ireland, the sign of child-bearing problems. Now some parents opt to have only one child, usually for economic reasons: 'We couldn't afford to have any more' or for personal reasons: 'After a terrible birth and two years of sleepless nights and exhaustion with our first, we could not face starting all over again.'

If two children really do make twice as much demand on mother and father as one child makes, then it is as well that the cost is counted in advance. Rather that than have a child who is unwanted or resented. But one may doubt whether several children are in fact so much more of a burden than an only child can be. Burden? I like D.W. Winnicott's comment: 'Children *are* a burden, and if they bring joy it is because they are wanted, and two people have decided to take that kind of burden; in fact, have agreed to call it not a burden, but a baby . . .'

There are hazards with an only child. The point of identifying the hazards is to reduce or avoid them altogether. The first is the obvious one, a lack of playmates. In their early years, children do most of their learning through play (provided they are allowed and encouraged to play rather than being stuck in front of TV).

Parents play with their baby, but that is different from children playing with one another. It is hard for adults to get in touch with the natural madness of children's play, or to stay in play with them for as long as children would like. So the only child may miss the pleasure that comes from irresponsibility, inconsequence and impulsiveness. It is easy for solitary Dara to become precocious, to prefer mother's and father's talk and work and never develop the extraordinary and sustained inventiveness that we see in toddlers who are used to playing with each other. Clearly mothers can help the only child in this, by seeing that he has toddlers to play with.

Dara has missed something else: the sight of mother growing big with another child, her breasts filling for other lips than his, going to hospital, returning to her normal shape, and sharing him with a little brother or sister. There

15

are huge and vital lessons here, which he can never learn from books, lessons that are often painful to learn, but so interesting that they will absorb his mind and fantasy for years.

What he sees about pregnancy and motherhood on TV is not the same. It is on a flat screen, it cannot be smelt or touched, it is not mother, nor does it affect his place on her lap. Dara's real learning is not the superficial stuff that comes in words and pictures, but what he experiences with his senses — smell, taste, touch, ears, eyes — in mother's body and in father's. It is too easy to see the arrival of a sibling as a problem for the first-born. Much more than that, it enriches his life, and the child who misses it is that much the poorer.

A new pregnancy does something else: it confirms that mother and father are sexually interested in each other, drawn together, maintaining the structure of family life. In many houses, the parents' beds are separate. It would be foolish to pretend that the children do not notice, or do not miss the reassurance that comes from the physical closeness of parents.

Because Dara has not had to share mother's lap, he finds it that much harder to share teacher's attention. Whether in playgroup or infant class, he is suddenly surrounded by countless rivals: a much more baffling matter for him than for children from large families. Dara has known mostly adults, stable, loving grown-ups who take him seriously. Now many of his contacts are fleeting and casual, whether with children or with busy teachers, for whom he is one of a group. Only children are all the time looking for *stable* relationships, and this tends to scare off the casual acquaintance. He needs to understand this, and grow accustomed to meeting people on a casual basis. You can help him here.

It may be harder for Dara's mother to allow him to do something necessary: to look after himself and take risks. He will develop faster if mother does nothing for him that he can do for himself, whether it means choosing friends, doing homework alone, using the bus, finding his own way to school, or whatever. I have known girls and boys feel unspoken frustration if they are not free to run risks (reasonable to their age); because they sense that being only children, they may hurt their parents too much if they themselves get hurt.

Other children can feel envious of only children, of the extra resources that they enjoy and the absence of rivals. But they are deprived in some ways, or could be if an alert mother does not work to make up for the experiences they miss.

## THE MIDDLE CHILD

Nobody writes from outer space, especially on family matters. I am a second child, between a big sister and younger brothers. So my ears prick up when parents ask if there is any truth in what they call the 'second child syndrome'. Rather than generalise, look at a case.

### To the Mother of Ruth in the Middle

Nine-year-old Ruth comes halfway between Mary and Anne, and always seems to be the odd one out. She is bright, but little Anne is brighter, and Ruth is the one who always seems to be creating trouble at home.

She is a favourite with teachers, attractive, and competent both in class and at sport. That is not how she perceives herself, nor how she behaves at home. She sees Mary and Anne as the centre of the family and herself as the outsider. She hates wearing Mary's hand-me-down clothes, and does not register that Anne often has to take over the garments that she, Ruth, outgrows. She scrutinises every birthday gift to the others, and compares them with her own with a mathematical eye. She feels every treat for either of the others as an insult to herself, and is especially hurt if the other two do something special with the parents while she is out of the house.

When you give her something special, she gives nothing back, but always wants more, never acknowledges that it has been a kindness, a treat. So from your viewpoint she is the least rewarding of the three children, the one who never makes you feel good and loved.

You can call it 'second-child syndrome' if you want. I do not like labels, because they are easily taken to imply that most second children will go that way. We all know second children who are genuinely fond of their sisters and brothers, who are generous and easily contented.

There are other features of Ruth which have nothing to do with being a second child, but come from her temperament and health history. She was always energetic and determined, always tenacious of your attention, always hard to satisfy. As an infant she would scream for your attention, and if you wanted to move away, she learned to puke all over the cot, to hold you, however exasperated, a little longer. I see something of that steel in your eye when you talk about that time. If I can see the steel, so can Ruth. She no longer screams and pukes, but she achieves the same effect in a more intelligent way, by being provocative and demanding.

How can one change a pattern like this? That is what is at stake: not to change Ruth in herself — those who know her outside the home think she could hardly be bettered — but in her relations with the family, in the jealousy that devours her but which she cannot acknowledge.

Jealousy is not so much wanting what someone else has, but being anxious about what she herself lacks. If Ruth is jealous of Mary's bicycle, it is not because she wants a bike like that for herself, but because she feels it is a love-bicycle, a symbol of the affection and security which Mary enjoys and she does not. You remember that when you had to get glasses for Mary, and later for Anne, beautiful clear-eyed Ruth wanted glasses for herself. *Jealousy is always about feelings, not about objects or events.*

Do not assume that these sisters, each of them lovely, love each other. They have to tolerate each other, but they are individuals, and cannot be assumed to like each other.

Because they are individuals, you never compare them with each other, nor hold them up as an example to each other. As time goes on, if you have to tell them off, do it out of sight of the others.

Most of all, you want this bright Ruth to gain insight into the jealousy that is souring her relations with you and her sisters. Keep your cool when she is provocative. Do not rise to the provocation, nor retaliate. Read it for what it is, a feeling of being an outsider; help her to read her own feelings, rather than hope that she can be weaned from them by special treats. Ruth would sympathise with the older brother in the Gospel parable, who refused to join the homecoming party (choice veal from the fatted calf) for the Prodigal Son. The father there is not merely forgiving, but respectful of the position of those who have not gone astray and feel jealous. He does not offer to kill a special fatted calf for the older brother, but tells him: 'All that I have is yours. No need to feel unloved.'

## Fiona and Susie

Jealousy is not always assertive nor objectionable, but for the jealous one it is always a burden. I remember the quiet burden carried by Fiona in St Declan's School. She was a mouse in class. You had to squeeze words out of her. When she was clearing up with me after school, waiting for her brother, she would chat and chat. One Friday she was going on about her Daddy, what he wears, what he does, what he says, how he plays the piano. I remarked, foolishly, 'I think you are Daddy's pet, Fiona.'

She paused before she replied. She stood there, a plain, slow, straight-haired, pale-faced little six-year-old thinking about something very important. 'Daddy has a curl of Susie's hair in his drawer.' No more, but a crushing repartee. Susie was four, brighter, prettier, and curly-haired. Fiona adores her father, and found it hard to share his love with the next in line. So that treasured curl of Susie in her father's drawer was eating at her.

Some day she'll enjoy Susie, no longer a rival but a sister and companion. Her father was moved and surprised to hear the story of the curl. He had not reckoned on the extent of the power he wields and the treasure he bestows with every mark of affection.

The psychologist Alfred Adler saw birth-order in terms of a power struggle between children. He described the first-born as a power-hungry conservative, unconsciously trying to hold on to the position of dominance with which he started. The second child he saw as the rival, relating to others competitively. The last child, the baby, is the one with secure power, because she has no rival threatening her from behind, and for that reason she often enjoys more of her mother's time and attention.

More recent studies, by Frank Sulloway in the Massachussets Institute of Technology, have thrown up a role for youngest-born children. In the history of science, more radical proposals were propounded and supported by younger sons (something that Darwin, Lenin and Ho Chi Minh have in common). They were opposed by more conservative eldest children. Whether we look at these levels of high achievement, or at the everyday experience of children, it is clear that the family is not a single environment. It has as many environments as members, because each child is interacting with a different set of individuals (i.e. everyone except himself), and parents respond differently to different children.

When Anne O'Connell, a Dublin psychologist, examined Irish children in this light, she found much truth in Adler's theories, but within any one family much depended on the sex and the spacing of the children. A sibling of the opposite sex, or separated by three years or more, seems less likely to loom as a rival. So much depends on the ability of the parents to prepare a place for their baby. Cot and clothes matter less than the readiness of the other children for the new arrival.


## TWINS

Twins run in families, and are more likely to occur the older the mother is at time of birth, and the more children she has already borne. In the past, they were more vulnerable than single babies, less likely to marry, and at a still earlier and more primitive stage they were liable to be killed, on the superstitious notion that the mother had intercourse with two different men. They have been valuable to psychologists studying which traits are inherited and which the results of rearing. It is only quite recently that writers like Mary Rosambeau in non-fiction,[3] and Joanna Trollope in her novels, have explored what it is like to be a twin, or the mother of twins.

More recently twins have been watched from as early as conception, using the ultrasound scans of unborn twins in the womb.[4] Piontelli found that twins often have a different placenta and cord. Most are separated by a dividing membrane, so that noises, pulsations and tactile sensations reach each of them in a different way. Their experiences are diverse from the start, and so are their reactions. Some showed practically no response to stimulation from the twin, others withdrew from contact, and others actively sought contact. Some contacted each other tenderly in the womb, some attacked each other violently, and these patterns seemed to persist after birth. One pair was observed to make what looked like affectionate contact from the twentieth week of gestation: one twin's hand would stroke the other's head through the separating membrane. A year after birth the same twins had a favourite play, in which they hid on either side of a curtain, using it like a separating membrane. One would put his hand round the curtain, the other his head, and the hand would stroke the head. Learning had started early.

## To the Mother of Jerome and Denis

Jerome and Denis are non-identical twins, aged five. You enjoyed the rearing of their older brother and sister, but find yourself exhausted by the twins, who are lovely boys but seem to wrong-foot you all the time.

Jerome and Denis were well used to friends looking into their pram and smiling: 'Twins, how nice.' They have resented people asking them: 'What is it like to be a twin?' How would they know? They have never been anything else. From the beginning Jerome will have found that friends may refer to him as 'the twins' rather than 'Jerome'. One twin said: 'I grew up with an inferiority complex through people staring at us every time we went out. I felt like a thing and not a person.'

You were warned in advance that there would be twins. It does not always happen. Despite modern technology, it still happens that a second infant can surprise everyone in the delivery room, and more than one mother has felt guilty afterwards for crying out in labour: 'But I only wanted one!'

Twins are more at risk in pregnancy, more likely to be miscarried, or to be premature. Before hospitals recognised the importance of initial bonding, and how important the first physical contact is for both mother and baby, twins were more likely to miss it, because, more than single babies, they were likely to be kept in the special care unit for a while.

You will certainly remember the work that started with birth: the major task of falling in love with two people at the same time, and sometimes two little people whom you cannot easily tell apart. You will not forget the task of feeding two instead of one, especially if their sucking was not well developed and they were slow to feed. One mother reported that her twins needed to be fed every three hours, but since feeding took an hour with each baby, it gave her only one hour for everything else that had to be done in the house.

They grew hungry at the same time, and declared their hunger as only a baby can, by crying. So you were regularly feeding one to the accompaniment of the other's wailing. I knew a mother who would put one twin in another room with the radio on loud, so that she could feed the other twin without the background of crying.

You will remember the enormous physical labour of managing two instead of one. If you picked up Jerome, Denis would cry to be lifted too. Later, if you tickled Denis, Jerome would cry: 'Do it to me!' You could not manage two babies and a shopping bag on the bus. Even to fit two carry-cots in the car was a major job. Many mothers of twins complain, like you: 'I had no time to enjoy them. I loved looking quietly at the babies, drinking them in. But if I was gazing at Jerome, Denis would be pulling at me. So I tended to do it less to either of them than to the older, single children.'

The other side of the reports are brighter. Twins show fewer emotional problems than single children, perhaps because from the nature of things, their fathers have to work as joint caretakers; and the emotional stability of twins owes much to the early involvement of *both* parents in their daily care.

Moreover, twins always have company, and thus do not suffer separation traumas. They learn early to communicate with one another, study each other's faces in the pram, use eye-language in an uncanny way, know without words what the other is feeling, put plans into operation without any exchange of language.

Because they need language less, their language development, and with it their verbal intelligence, and later reading skills, can develop more slowly than in single children. It is not enough for twins to talk to one another. Their communication with one another is often non-verbal. They need talkative parents who stimulate them with adult language. One mother noticed how the twins would listen to her, and then practise using her words with one another later on.

Above all, twins need to be treated as separate persons. Address them separately, and by name: 'Jerome, how was the game outside?' 'Denis, would you come in to tea.' Otherwise they may well wait, leave the answering to the other — or worse, allow one twin to dominate and always answer for both of them. How they resent it when at Christmas Auntie brings a present for big Mary, and another for big Jim, and 'Here's a record for the twins'. How they resent it when their school reports are put side by side and compared, though you would never compare them with Jim's or Mary's. They need all the opportunities that you can offer single children, of developing their sense of territory — their own cupboard, perhaps their own room; their taste in colours and clothes. Some schools, with good reason, insist on separating twins into different classes, to save them the pain of competition and comparison.

You are not alone in feeling that the twins demand more time, energy and thought than the other children. Mothers in some countries felt the need for extra support so badly that they formed special associations such as the 'Twins and Multiple Births Association' in Britain or the 'Mother of Twins Club' in the USA. An Irish association — the Castleknock Twins Club — has now been formed and can be contacted at Tel. (01) 8204061/8216859. The Bible mentions the problem early on, in the struggle of Esau and Jacob to come first out of the womb, Jacob hanging onto Esau's heel. Rebecca certainly had her hands full with that pair. They grew up as distinct personalities, and that must be your hope for Jerome and Denis, each with his own personality, tastes, talents and destiny.

## ADOPTION AND BONDING

Legal adoption was introduced in Ireland forty years ago. It has shown marked fluctuations since then, in part due to the tendency for single mothers to keep their babies. The number of children being placed for adoption has fallen from around 1,500 in 1967 to about half of that in 1993. It is a good record. If one compares adopted children with those who went into institutions, by the age of seven the adopted children are about one year ahead in their level of intellectual functioning and schoolwork.[5] They show the same range of brains and brawn and beauty, and the same variety of personalities and problems, as children who have grown up with their natural parents. In fact adoptive parents have now the resource of advice and help from the social services. Yet they appear more frequently in child guidance clinics than their numbers would warrant. Why do they cause anxiety?

One reason must lie in the insecurity of adoptive parents. They have not always worked through all the emotions surrounding adoption: the infertility on one side or the other; the sometimes submerged guilt or resentment arising out of that; the differing level of desire for an adopted child; the choice of boy or girl; the pain of exposing their family life to the scrutiny of social workers.

Moreover there are differences for adopted children at the start of life. They are usually a few weeks old at adoption. It is only in the last twenty years that we have realised how much children learn in those few weeks, and how active they can be. From the research on inborn temperament, and on the learning of newborn babies, it is clear that babies are distinct little persons from the beginning, able, even ten days after birth, to smell out their mother's milk from any other milk, and to react to human voices and human faces in a distinctive way. There can be a wealth of experience and bonding in these weeks for both mother and child.

Twenty years ago Klaus and Kendall popularised the notion that mothers develop 'bonds' with their babies during a sensitive period in the first hours after birth, and that such bonds depend on skin-to-skin contact. As a result, hospitals moved away from a purely technological approach to childbirth to a greater appreciation of mothers' feelings, and a greater reluctance to separate babies from their mothers in the hours after birth.

In these twenty years, studies have shown that while early skin contact and bonding gives a good start to mothering, it is not irreplaceable.[6] Bonding is not an all-or-nothing event. Parents who adopt children well after the supposedly sensitive period not only develop strong love relationships with their adopted children, but they also parent well. It is sensible to make the experience of birth and early care more humane and rewarding for mothers. But what matters is the opportunity for pleasurable parenting, rather than the timing or duration of skin-to-skin contact. Parent-child attachments can develop normally well after the neonatal period, and will change (for better or worse) depending on later circumstances.

Adoptive mothers can make up for the absence of early bonding by their responsiveness once they have their baby. What may lead them to seek professional guidance is a sometimes unwarranted anxiety about having missed the bonding period immediately after birth.

## The Adoptive Mother of Ross

One such was the mother of Ross, adopted at three weeks of age. Though she enjoyed watching him grow into a handsome and brainy twelve-year-old, the enjoyment was shadowed. From time to time, in a temper at being corrected, he would shout: 'You're not my real Mum, you've no right to order me around.'

She was not the first adoptive mother to face such an attack, but it still hurt, because she had invested so much in making him her son. His abusiveness when corrected did not mean that she had failed to mother him, or that he had no bond with her. In his anger and immaturity he reached for a piece of abuse that he knew would strike home. In the same way I have known a nine-year-old girl cry that she did not believe in God, knowing how that would hurt her devout mother. In both cases the child was manipulating arguments rather than speaking the truth. In anger and temper, truth is the first casualty. Piaget, who spent his life watching little children closely, observed 'The mind serves desire before it serves truth'.

In the highly charged question of adoption, two general truths seem to hold good: (a) that the deepest fear of the adoptive parents is that their child may reject and leave them, prove them failures as parents; (b) that the deep, often unspoken fear of the adopted child is that she may be rejected by the adoptive parents as she was given away by her original mother and father.

Ross would scorn this. As with many adopted children coming into their teens, he dismissed it as an issue. 'No, it's not a problem, I've always known about it. I don't worry about the mother who bore me. I'm sure she had good reason to give me away and I don't blame her for it. After all I've got a wonderful, loving mother and father to look after me; they are my real Mum and Dad. It is not an issue at all.'

At a deeper level this turned out to be less than the whole truth. Ross hated talking about adoption, and his reasoned dismissal of it saved him from any painful exploration. It was a sad issue, and one that he was shy of broaching with his parents. He felt that by talking about it, showing curiosity about his natural mother and father, he might hurt the feelings of Mum and Dad.

Freud often found what he called a 'family romance' in the fantasy of natural children at the start of puberty. Feeling slighted by the fact that mother sometimes prefers father to him, the son imagines himself to be adopted, and that he is of noble or supernatural birth; that he is merely placed in this family until bigger and better opportunities come along.

Adopted children feel this with added force. A bright, awakening mind like Ross's sees his copper-coloured hair as unique in the family. He has green eyes where the rest have brown. At an age when his peers are scrutinising their parents as a guide to how tall they may ultimately grow — and growing tall is a hot concern for them — Ross realises he has no guide of that sort. He knows nothing of the appearance of those who brought him into the world. At times he has the feeling about his adoptive family: 'I do not belong here.'

Another, sadder thought may contribute: the notion that he was given away by his natural mother because he was naughty or no good; that he was adopted out of kindness, and has to earn his place in the family by good behaviour. It is a crazy notion. It makes no sense, but it is often there. I have known behaviour in adopted teenagers which could only be seen as the boy testing out this notion, trying out his parents to see how much aggravation they can take before they give him away; testing out his fear that he will be rejected again, and trying the tactic: reject before you are rejected.

Adoptive mothers worry more than other mothers. They sometimes feel that if they helped the adopted son to find his natural parents, it might ease some of his worries. There is an unspoken, unthought guilt at having the child of another woman. But in the fantasies of Ross, the natural mother is often the witch, the one who rejected him; the adoptive mother is the nurturing one with whom he has had the real bond. This is tenderly spelled out in a paperback that teenage adoptees can enjoy: *Find a Stranger, say Goodbye,* by Lois Lowry (Granada Paperbacks).

It can be a huge relief to a teenager to take hold of those unconscious fears and desires. It means exploring feelings, an exploration which is as painful for the parents as for the child. Ross's adoptive parents would fear nothing more than the loss of Ross's love and place in the family. That is precisely what he fears himself, a second rejection. He will be ready for adulthood when he can feel at home in his own history, feel at ease in his own skin, be comfortable with his unique copper hair and green eyes, and know that with all his differences he belongs, irrevocably and for good, in the family he has always known as his own.

## THE GHOST IN THE NURSERY

Family myths are more intriguing than the family itself may recognise. Many of the important emotional realities lie under the surface, but influence the working of the family in mysterious ways. Any experience of life, birth, serious sickness and death, leaves its mark in a family. We are seeing contradictory trends in Ireland in this regard.

There is a new recognition of the trauma attached to miscarriages, stillbirths and cot deaths, partly thanks to the work of ISANDS (Irish Stillbirth and Neonatal Death Society) and ISIDA (Irish Sudden Infant Death Association). Stillborn babies may now be registered, photographed, grieved for, given a solemn burial.

On the other hand we are infected by the Anglo-Saxon reticence about death, the reluctance to attend funerals, to spend time with the bereaved, to talk about the grief and hope that centres on the dead one. One of the most startling cultural differences between Ireland and Britain, is the large and warm support that Irish families receive in a bereavement, compared with the 'Let's get it over quickly and go back to work' attitude of our neighbours. In the controversy about abortion legislation, some extremists try to portray the fetus as little more than a wart, to be removed with minimum ceremony or moral deliberation. It is unrealistic to treat a mother's loss as though it leaves no mark on the family. If she is affected, then so are her husband and children, often in intriguing ways.

### The Mother of Dead Kate and Living Manus

Manus, a troublesome and restless eleven-year-old, always wanted to be out of the house. A year before Manus was born, his mother lost Kate through cot death. The family were shattered by the loss. Could it have affected even Manus who never knew her? Was Manus a replacement baby? His mother had such joy in Kate, such a perfect baby, smiling, a good sleeper and feeder, and with the promise of real beauty. I remember not merely the grief and shock after the cot death, but the different reactions of mother and father. He was at first inclined to blame the doctor, or the nurses, who had seen Kate: 'Surely they should have noticed something,' he used say. Where he was angry, his wife was shattered and guilty: 'Surely I should have noticed something.' It was a difficult time in their marriage.

Whenever a mother hears her baby cry, she feels the overwhelming panic in the child, which has no sense of time. Whatever pains are in that little body, they are much more threatening to her than to an adult, because the baby has no sense that the frustration or pain will ever end. Without a notion of the duration of time, she is caught in a threatening 'Now', in which she seems to be falling apart. A baby's urgent panic and distress gives her crying a quality that reaches mother directly. In those early weeks her ear is finely tuned, day and night, to picking up the reason for baby's distress, absorbing the fear and making it bearable. She does this instinctively, and effectively, repeatedly rescuing her baby from the overwhelming fear of disintegration and death.

With Kate that did not work. The dreadful thing was that mother was given no warning, no cry, nothing she could respond to. They buried Kate, and grieved for her, and within three months mother was pregnant with Manus.

I wonder had she reckoned with the impact of Kate's death on herself? I remember her reactions to Manus in the early weeks. When he cried, there was a double anxiety in the way she picked him up. The cot had been a little palace for Kate, a place where she could be visited and admired, until the terrible day when her breathing stopped. Suddenly it was a cot of death. Perhaps mother had not worked through that experience before Manus arrived?

I knew one little boy who like Manus came on the heels of a cot death. More than most babies, he used to scream when he was put in the cot, and gurgle when picked up. His parents found this resistance to the cot increasingly wearing, and never made a connection between it and the terror they themselves had associated with the cot since the death of their first baby.

The first worry to be faced and worked through after a baby's death is the guilt, the question: 'Could I have prevented it?' Everybody in the house is liable to feel guilty, including the children. The older ones can feel that they should have visited her, spotted something wrong. If, as is common, they resented the arrival of a new baby in the house, then they can feel doubly guilty that their resentment could have contributed to the tragedy.

After a child's death, the whole family needs to grieve and face the mourning together. It is no use trying to spare them. They will feel the grief of the loss through their parents' sorrow, if not directly. They should normally see their little sister's dead body. Children can face death if their parents can, and often more realistically. Where granny may try to soften the impact of a dead body by saying 'She looks as though she fell asleep and never woke up', little children will see the difference and say so. It is dangerous to compare death with sleep, because it adds a terror to falling asleep, if children feel it could easily turn into death.

They are liable to be more damaged by a silence about the death, which leaves questions unanswered. Cot deaths are still mysterious, but it is important to share with the other children whatever the doctor can tell them about the cause of Kate's death. Sometimes a tragic death becomes a taboo subject in a family. Taboo subjects never completely disappear, and children are uncanny in their ability to sense areas that may not be mentioned. Many families have taboo subjects such as the alcoholism of one relative, an abortion in the past, a spell in prison, an unwanted baby who was adopted, a handicapped and institutionalised relative, or a tragic death.

For the sake of the other children in the family, a baby's death should not be taboo, however painful it may be to discuss. Kate has a name, a photograph, an anniversary. She should be an open part of the family prayers and family history, not a secret too sad to mention. Manus is not a replacement for Kate; he can never be. I knew one boy in his position who said to me: 'I feel I am not the child that mother wanted.' He was a boy, not a perfect girl. The dead sister had been idealised by the family: she was too good for this world. Her brother felt inadequate and guilty, as though he was partly to blame for her death.

ISIDA (Irish Sudden Infant Death Association) offers support to families who have lost a child through cot death. They are at 4, Brunswick St Nth, Dublin 7 and can be contacted on a 24-hour help-line: Tel. (01) 8747007. ISANDS (Irish Stillbirth and Neonatal Death Society) also offers effective support and advice to families who have lost a young child. They have produced a wise and useful booklet called *A Little Lifetime* to help such families, available from ISANDS, P.O. Box 6, Dun Laoghaire, Co. Dublin. Since ISANDS was founded in 1983, they have supported hundreds of parents. If one could summarise their wisdom in one sentence, it might be: You can't successfully say 'hello' to your next baby until you have said 'goodbye' to this baby . . . and saying 'goodbye' takes time.

## NOTES

3.  Mary Rosambeau, *How Twins grow up,* London, Bodley Head, 1987. See also Elizabeth Bryan, *Twins, Triplets and More,* London, Penguin, 1992

4.  Alessandra Piontelli, *From Fetus to Child: an observational and psychoanalytic study,* New Library of Psychoanalysis, 1992

5.  Mia Kellmer Pringle, *The Needs of Children,* London, Hutchinson, 1971, pp. 125-6

6.  For a summary of this research, see *Child and Adolescent Psychiatry,* edited by M. Rutter and L. Hersov, Oxford, Blackwell, 1985, pp. 39-40

# The Sex of Children

## NOT SUCH A MARVELLOUS SEX

Since this is written from within a male skin, objectivity is limited. The battle of the sexes may be interesting in one-to-one combat, but it becomes tedious when generalisations are offered, and we could cheerfully do without most of the current wave of books written from a sexually-chauvinist viewpoint, whether male or female. We are not better or worse than the other sex, but different, and the differences have been well mapped by now.

What makes the issue topical is not merely the current preoccupation with sex in the Irish media, but advances in genetic engineering and medical technology. Not only is it now a common option to know the baby's sex before birth, but there are clinics which offer to give parents the sex they desire, sometimes by the brutal expedient of killing unwanted boys or girls in the womb, recalling the primitive customs of tribes which abandoned or killed unwanted boys or (more often) girls after birth. Even if choice could be exercised without killing, it seems hazardous to offer such a loaded choice to the caprices of couples whose own desires may fluctuate from husband to wife and from month to month.

Apart from that possibility of choice, sex differences obtrude on anyone working in a child guidance clinic. Our clientele comprises three or four problem boys for every one girl, and that not merely in Ireland but in the Western world.

More boys are colour-blind, stutter, wet the bed, are seriously behind in reading, are disruptive in class and delinquent in their teens, than girls. On the other hand, in adult life, there are more men than women geniuses throughout history. Now that opportunities for the two sexes have started to level up, we may see in the next hundred years whether women can reverse these statistics, and produce both the heights of achievement and the same problematic extremes as men. At present males occupy these positions, and females are in the middle.

In the battle of the sexes it is easy to be carried away by rhetoric and wishful thinking. In *My Fair Lady* Rex Harrison complained 'Why can't a woman be more like a man?' and boasted 'By and large we are a marvellous sex'. The evidence is against him. We are a delicate sex. Nature produces more boys than girls because boys are more fragile in infancy, more likely to die, more vulnerable to the effects of traumatic events such as hospitalisation. Girls grow faster and at a more even rate than boys in infancy and again at puberty, though boys overtake them later. And of course women live significantly longer than men.

Through all the arguments about sex differences, some things have become clear from research. Girls talk sooner than boys, and use longer sentences. They learn to read sooner, spell better, and learn to count at an earlier age. Boys are more aggressive than girls, and this seems to be linked with hormonal, physical differences, not just with what the adult world expects.

Boys as they grow older show greater mathematical abilities than girls, and girls as they grow older show greater verbal ability than boys, can converse more fluently and explain themselves better. Girls tend to be more consistent in their work than boys, performing as well as they can in all subjects, whereas boys tend to follow their interest and do better in subjects they like.

One striking difference is that girls are less realistic in evaluating their own abilities: they tend to undervalue themselves. If you ask Junior or Leaving Certificate students to forecast their exam performance, girls will expect too little, and be pleasantly surprised by the results, whereas boys are generally more on target in their forecasts. Is this because women and girls think worse of themselves? The answer is not to be found in the statistics but in our reflection on them, looking at the people we know best, ourselves and our families.

Why do boys throw up more problems? Is it simply a natural weakness? There is another explanation, which holds for most families. In the crucial years between two and six, children are learning at their fastest. Boys and girls are discovering that their sex is an important difference, something quite central to them, not just a bodily appendage which the boy has and the girl lacks. In these years, girls have endless opportunities to discover what it is to be a woman. They have their mother in front of them most of the time. They watch a grown woman at work and at leisure and with her friends.

How much of that has a boy? How much does he see of his father at work? He may see him doing the odd job around the house, but many boys have no idea what their father is able to do. He may disappear in the morning to a mysterious place called the office or factory, but what he does there, what it is like, is unknown to the curious son. When it comes to choosing a career, it is striking how much easier the choice is for boys who have seen their father at work than for the majority who can only guess what Daddy does after disappearing in the morning. This is true even for the children of the unemployed. For young children — and the years between two and six are the most crucial here — a father exercising his skills is a working model, whether he has a 'job' outside the home or not.

In these years when he is unconsciously but continuously forming a mental map of what it is to be a boy or a man, most boys do not see enough of the one model who has overwhelming power for them, their father. Other models can help, uncles, friends, big brothers, even the shallow figures on the TV screen. But it is their father who travels with boys through life as an internal model, for better or worse.

In this sense there is no such thing as an absent father. The man who helped to make us is in our fantasy even if we have never known him. Charles Murray in his studies of the 'Underclass' in the USA — that group which feels not merely poor but alienated from society — points to the horrific power of the absent father as a model for his sons. No matter how hard the single mother may work for them, their father remains as a potent exemplar of what it is to be a man, the guy who has his fun and vanishes, shirking personal responsibilities.

Obviously there are many and various patterns: the dead father, remembered with a mix of emotions; the absent, perhaps separated father; sometimes the unknown father, whose picture is filled out by the boy's fantasy. We find our sense of manhood where we can. It is evident how lucky are those boys who have a father close to them, affectionate, competent and interested, during those years from two to six or seven. It gives them the same sort of internal shape and direction that girls enjoy from their mothers. It does not always happen. A survey in Britain showed that one father in three never read to his children, one in four never put the children to bed, and one in six never looked after the children on his own, even for part of a day. Are we any better in Ireland? In view of the higher representation of boys over girls in problem areas, I doubt it.

## WILL BOYS BE BOYS?

One thing has become clear from the immense world-wide research on sexuality: that for any one human being it is not a black-and-white matter but a complicated cocktail, put together from genetic components, the lottery of intercourse yielding XX or XY chromosomes, the contribution of hormones flooding the fetus in the early weeks of pregnancy, the influence on the baby of mother, of father, and of early or late sexual experiences. For any one of us, our sexuality is a unique and interesting personal challenge, part of our endowment that cannot be described simply in terms of male or female, as though they were univocal terms.

The court (of serious research) is still sitting on the question of the origins of bisexuality and homosexuality. The clamour of interested groups outside the court-room, gays or gay-bashers, tends to obscure the occasional messages that emerge from current research. If gays comprise round 1% of the male population, why does it appear to be 0% in black Africa, and 10% in California? That is not our business here. But we cannot escape the questions about the developing sexuality of young people. The commonest of these is: 'Am I gay?' or 'Is my child gay?' — more commonly asked by or about boys than girls.

### Paul: Wanting to be a Star

It is many years since I met Paul, an engaging, sweet-tempered four-year-old. His mother found that he was taking her underwear and putting it on furtively at night under his pyjamas. He had no explanation and she made no great fuss. When we talked it over with her husband, one explanation did occur. Paul idealised his father, and as an infant had revelled in his love. At the age of two he had been displaced as baby by a little sister, who in turn won her father's heart and was called his star and his princess. Paul was not a jealous sort, but he was conscious of moving out of the bright light of his father's attention, which was focussed on little sister and of course on mother. He was still learning what it is to be a male, and was caught between identification with his father, and longing to be the apple of his father's eye. But (and this reasoning was of course below the conscious level) in order to be that apple, it seemed one had to be female.

This never emerged clearly, but a strategy was formed. His father moved closer to Paul, made opportunities to take him off on his own, had him beside him when fixing things round the house or gardening. Paul revelled in it, and the cross-dressing disappeared. Two aspects had been important: Paul's stage of development, still establishing his male identity; and the fact that the cross-dressing concerned underwear, and was furtive. Clinical experience suggests that this type of cross-dressing has some sort of self-soothing function.

## Thomas: Look, I'm Really a Girl

Thomas, another bright and attractive four-year-old with a little sister of two, was different from Paul in one crucial respect. He frankly wanted to be a girl. Nothing furtive about it. He proclaimed it repeatedly, loved to put on his mother's clothes, especially satiny, sensuous slips and blouses, looked for jewellery and make-up, and would show himself off to family and neighbours when dressed like this. In playing with little Anne he insisted on taking female roles — 'I'll be the princess and you can be the prince'. At playschool he mixed only with the girls and shunned rough-and-tumble play. One morning while dressing he stood before his mother, tucked his penis between his legs, and said 'Look, it isn't there any more, I'm really a girl'.

While his mother was seriously worried, his quiet, unassertive father felt it was only a passing phase. Unlike Paul above, Thomas seldom went near his father spontaneously. He let little Anne monopolise her Daddy, while he took over his mother. There was no identification with his father, none of the competition for mother between son and father, which can make these years so stormy but promising. His father tried to change the pattern and spent more time with Thomas, but with limited success. Thomas was clear-headed about his plight, longing to be female, but seeing himself caught in a male body. He could conform to his mother's decisions, that he must not cross-dress, but he would still ask for the jewellery and make-up box as a birthday treat. He was deeply unhappy in his conflict.

Thomas's misery prompts two large and as yet unanswered questions:

(a)  What causes this gender identity disorder?

(b)  What can be done to reduce his misery?

May I refer the reader to one book which tries to make sense of both these complex questions. Dr R. Green in *The 'Sissy Boy' Syndrome*, (Yale University Press, 1987), has tried to put together all the factors that contribute, the genetic endowment, the prenatal flooding with male hormones, the prenatal wishes or expectations of the parents, the child's physical attractiveness, health, and robustness, the reactions of mother and of father to feminine behaviour or looks, and the reaction of his peers.

For a boy like Thomas, deeply discontented with being a male, even the drastic resource of sex-change surgery offers no sure remedy. There is more help to be found in psychological than in surgical intervention. He needs to find increasing comfort in his own sexuality, with the help of parents and professionals. The goal is to reduce childhood conflict and social stigma.

He may find little taste or capacity for rough-and-tumble play; but there are other options apart from being with girls and copying their behaviour. He may build, draw, read, play board games, make music, and play with boys who are not wholly geared to sports and rough-house. If his father uses too narrow a definition of 'masculinity', and pushes the boy into interests outside his scope, he may thereby push him towards his mother and her activities. Such fathers need to accept their son's tastes and limitations, and try to share interests with them which fall outside the macho stereotype.

Obviously sexual concerns take a different colour after puberty. The boy of twelve or thirteen is learning to live with a new sort of body. His sexuality, from being confusing and perhaps self-indulgent, becomes a mode of loving others. It is a journey fraught with worries and questions, and in the revolution Ireland has experienced in the area of sex, these worries can affect parents as much as children.

It would be nice if we could make life healthier simply by getting rid of prohibitions and inhibitions. God knows there have been enough stupid prohibitions and rules in the past; but we do not achieve wisdom simply by recognising their stupidity. We laugh at the Victorians for being prudish about even the names of body parts, to the point of covering the legs of their pianos. However, when we have unwrapped the piano legs, and human legs and torsos, to the point where there is little left to expose, we still have to deal with the self-seeking passions that lead men and women into folly at the least, and often into crime.

What distressed many of our generation about the rules of our youth was not so much the secrecy about sex, as the negative attitude it implied. They left us with a sense of the body as sinful rather than beautiful. There were too many criticisms, too few compliments. Some children grew up in a sexual body, reached their first period, or their first emission of seed, without any idea of what was happening to them, much less any joy in the achievement of sexual maturity.

## Rory Surprises his Mother

I am thinking of fourteen-year-old Rory, who has been reared to feel good about his body. His mother relished his delight in sliding naked around on silky clothes as a toddler. He was and is sensuous in his pleasures. He has always expressed open curiosity about the 'facts of life', and his parents have answered him as clearly as they could.

What has upset his mother now is the discovery of a furtive side to his sexuality. She discovered girlie magazines under his mattress and in the back of his wardrobe she found a pile of her own underwear. He was deeply embarrassed at the discoveries. Mother and son are now afraid he may be gay. In spite of her openness, his sexuality is still complicated. Is this surprising? It is a private matter, and will remain so, no matter how many polls are conducted. In the words of D.W. Winnicott: 'If you ask people about their sex life, you can expect to be told lies.'

What can one make of her discoveries? The magazines are no surprise. At fourteen Rory's body is bewildering him with its eruptions, and the body of the other sex is a fascinating mystery. Girlie magazines are objectionable in all sorts of ways: they are male chauvinist, they debase women and are a cowardly way of viewing the other sex — their readers are usually frightened of females in the flesh. But they are so common under the mattresses of teenage boys that statistically they are not abnormal. They reflect a passing phase in Rory's life, when his curiosity and sexual drive are at their highest, and he feels safer thinking about girls than getting to know them.

What he does with female underwear is probably in the same line. It is a furtive, undemanding way of coming close to the intimacies of the other sex: not as common as the use of pornographic magazines, and raising the suspicion that it may point to a more disturbed sexuality. Cross-dressing in a boy can mean a deep unhappiness in his male skin. If parents see other signs of this, they might look for help outside the family. More commonly this sort of behaviour is a quirk of adolescent development. Where full dressing in women's clothes can indicate a gender identity problem, the use of underwear for sexual arousal is more likely to have a self-soothing function, and need not point to transsexual development. As with the magazines, I would remove the offending articles, see if the embarrassed Rory can talk it through with any understanding; then see it (probably) as an unfortunate blip on the graph of his growing up.

In spite of the enormous change in sexual attitudes among the young, it is as easy, if not easier now for young people to make fools or failures of themselves by mismanaging their sexuality. The power of the sexual drive has not diminished since Plato compared it to a wild, unbroken horse, and it is at its wildest in the mid-teens. If a boy or girl allows the pursuit of sexual pleasure to lead them by the nose, they will spend their days swung between excitement and frustration, and have little energy left for work or play. It is wise and right to control the eyes, the senses and the imagination, so that we are not at the mercy of every sexual titillation from print or TV. One of Rory's tasks in these years is to learn to ride that unbroken horse, to attain the freedom of his own body, to control his own choices and decisions, rather than be led by lust.

What is needed here is a parent with a healthy, positive style, who helps her children to think well of themselves. That is the easy part of changing the pattern of parenting. She will still have to impose limits calmly and with authority. There is a difference between authoritarian parenting (brooking no argument or discussion and producing either spineless yes-children or rebels) and authoritative parenting, which keeps communication open and allows for the differences and separateness of children, but can set limits and make decisions and expect maturity without becoming vindictive or retaliatory when things go badly. This mother learns from watching her children and herself, and seeking where her natural goodness leads her.

## Damien is Worried

Damien like Rory was in mid-puberty, and his mother knew for weeks that he was worried, before he was able to tell her why. He had been called a 'queer' by classmates, and he wondered were they right. It is hard enough in many families to talk about sex, but much harder to talk about homosexuality when it looms as a possibility for one of the children. Not that it is a taboo subject. Sexual behaviour and its variations are the staple diet of the TV soap operas. That is in the imaginary order, at a remove from life. The fact that the airwaves are preoccupied with sex has not made it any easier for young people, especially boys, to gain confidence in their own sexuality as it is becoming evident through the teen years.

On the contrary: the more boys banter with one another using the sexual slagging and double-meaning jokes of the comedies and soaps, the more confused and threatened they may become by their own style and rate of development. For Damien it was no longer a case of feeling his own body grow, listening to his own desires, and discovering how attractive the other sex had become both in fantasy and in real life. That natural growth had been fouled up by the media style that turned girls into sex objects (almost all the jokes are made from the man's viewpoint), and sex into a matter of endlessly repetitive flippancy. Any group of mid-teen boys in a 'slagging' mood will turn the finger on some teacher or boy as gay because of his voice, or gestures, or even because of his shoes or his shirt.

A crowd of boys gathers on the edge of a swimming-pool. One dives in shouting 'Last one in is a queer', and has forgotten the remark before he surfaces. The phrase may stay quivering in the soul of the last one in, who is just at that stage of wondering is he going to grow up straight.

Other memories fed Damien's anxiety. He was close to his mother — but so are many macho boys to their mothers. He once enjoyed dressing up in his sister's clothes at Halloween — but so did a huge number of high-spirited boys. He was deeply attached to his best friend Paul — but best friends can be a terribly important anchor in the early teens when the other sex still seems pretty threatening. At this age even sexual intimacy with another boy need have no significance as regards long-term sexual orientation. It can be alarming for parents when such an incident comes to their notice. But their moral concerns should not be blown into panic by the fear that it turns their son into a homosexual. In this, as in the still more troubling case of abuse by an adult, the situation is helped by calm and under-reaction in the parent.

All these and other factors together, when capped by the 'slagging' (I use the slang word because it describes a huge reality in the lives of many children, much worse in some schools than others) of classmates can cause something approaching panic in a boy who is trying to find his own inner balance, and is expected to make and state an outward sexual choice. The panic can be worse in a single-sex boarding school, where an older boy may find his fantasy preoccupied with some pretty youngster, and feel himself doomed to homosexuality.

'Doomed' is a strong word, but it expresses what is commonly felt by boys in this state of homosexual panic: the fear of orientation towards a life which can carry a terrible burden of insult, loneliness, and a sense of being an outsider. There are no statistics available on how many of those who experience homosexual panic go on to a homosexual way of life. They are a small, probably a tiny minority. There are two dangers: first, that they fail to recognise the panic for what it is, a passing phase, and think of themselves, unjustifiably, as gay; and secondly, that they be seduced into homosexual practices, which could confirm them in their fears and orientation.

Can parents help? Yes, but in an indirect way:

(a)  *Avoid sexual labelling.* Do not read tenderness, caring, artistic interests or a flair for clothes as signs of homosexuality in a boy. He will become a man in his own way, and the ways of manhood are broader than the macho style that some overgrown schoolboys would impose.

(b)  *Avoid sexual teasing.* Many adolescent boys give their best energies to sport or other activities, and are not helped by remarks about the absence of girlfriends. If you tease him as though he is peculiar, you risk making him think that he is.

(c) *Remember* that while we do not know just why some adults are homosexual, we do know that their preference cannot be changed at will nor prevented by exhortation in adolescence. So parents can help Damien with his anxiety when it surfaces, and stay close or at least accessible to him throughout his development.

What about the other sex? Is the 'tomboy' girl likely to grow up with gender identity problems analogous to those of the 'sissy' boy? To judge from the present state of research, the answer is no. One careful comparison of a group of tomboy girls with non-tomboys found that by mid-adolescence, the behavioural differences had practically vanished, apart from a stronger interest in sport by the ex-tomboys. Cross-dressing with a view to sexual arousal appears to be nearly non-existent among females.

## THE SPECTRE OF CHILD ABUSE

It is strange to think that twenty years ago, a book about children's problems might well have omitted any section on child sexual abuse. Children were abused then — witness the sufferings of the victims who are middle-aged today. When a representative sample of Irish adults reported anonymously on their experience,[7] 10% of males and 15% of females had suffered sexual abuse as children, and the proportion was roughly the same in every age-group. It is clear that such abuse often went unreported in the past. In any case, we lacked today's experience and understanding of how to help the victim and treat the perpetrator.

Seven-year-old Clare was described by her mother as deeply upset: not deranged, just in profound sorrow and turmoil. Her mother worried that she might have been abused, but tackling those worries was more complex than seeking help for measles or appendicitis. Professional help may be difficult to find. There are parts of our cities where overworked doctors report that every fifth child they see has been abused; and the services are not in place either to counsel the abused and their families, or to deal, both legally and therapeutically, with the abusers. The day will come when services will exist, as in the case of diphtheria, TB, and other hazards to health. Public health officials worry about hygiene, passive smoking, and other environmental conditions that threaten our health. Unfortunately no inoculation has power over men's lust, and our cultural environment is not sympathetic to the notion of self-control in sexual matters. The germ passes from one generation to the next. The abused can in turn become abusers unless help is forthcoming.

To return to Clare's mother: if Clare has been interfered with, the culprit is more likely to have been somebody known to her, even related to her, than a stranger. In general those who abuse children seem on the surface not monsters but 'nice men'. Most children now are sufficiently warned about the dangers of familiarity with strangers. The little story-book by Robin Lenett, *It's OK to say NO,* has been a great help to many parents as a non-scary form of educating their children against these hazards. So has the *Stay Safe* programme in schools.

Small comfort there. If we assume for these pages that Clare *has* been a victim, then she may well have suffered at the hands of her father, uncle, brother, or familiar friend. You may say that is unthinkable. From Clare's point of view, it is not just unthinkable but unmentionable. Abused children are usually terrified to say what has happened. Sometimes this is because of fierce threats by the abuser: 'If you say anything I'll kill you' or 'I'll deny it and they'll call you a liar'.

Sometimes the abuser has confused her with 'This is a little secret between you and me, just our little secret'. Children need to be clear about the difference between good and bad secrets, as they need to know the difference between good and bad touches, between those that are affectionate and those that intrude where children have the right to privacy.

Most often the abused child feels that the truth is too outrageous for any adult to believe, and that she herself is guilty and stained. She may hold it for years, a stinking mess at the back of her mind, until she meets someone who she senses may be open enough to admit the possibility of such evil.

If that seems hard to believe, consider this scenario. You have just had a row with Clare. You have found her in what looks like sexual play with a neighbour's child, and you are already annoyed because she is so messy and careless around the house. While you are telling her off, she screams: 'You don't care about me anyway,' and goes off sobbing.

If you keep your cool and encourage her to talk, and she implies that her daddy has done things to her, what are your feelings? Horror that she could have suffered in this way? Guilt that you could have allowed it to happen without noticing? Fury at your husband? Large question-marks as to whether Clare is telling the truth or just trying to justify her boldness with a made-up story? Overwhelming anxiety as to the consequences for the family if all this turns out to be true?

You may know that if you involve the health boards or social services in the case, a number of professional people will inevitably be brought into the case, and you cannot foresee the results. You have read about the apparently false accusations in parts of Britain, where families were split up and children taken from their parents.

In situations like this, I have known mothers to turn their backs on the daughter for the sake of keeping the family intact. Sheila, a thirteen-year-old, was abused for half a year by her father, and was showing the familiar after-effects in explosive anger, disruption of class at school, preoccupation with sex, and foul language. Her mother accepted that it happened, but said: 'It's over now, forget about it,' and would not even allow Sheila to talk about it or seek counselling, for fear of the consequences for the family.

It is not over for Sheila. She carries the scars and needs help from outside the family. That help may involve confronting her father, and hearing from his lips two crucial confessions: an exact admission of what he did and when (abusers tend to make their memories vague); and a confession that he was entirely responsible, that it was wholly his fault. Even that will not lift from Sheila the awful sense of dirtiness and guilt which the abused child feels. But it will help, and he owes it to her.

The price that the abuser may face, even in disgrace and prison, is light compared with what the victim pays. When Jesus spoke of the horror of 'scandalising one of these little ones', he may well have been pointing to precisely this. Exposing an immature child to sexual experience, can pervert their sense of their own body and their ability to relate to others. It can awaken unsatisfiable urges in them, lead them to become abusers themselves. It does not have to be like this. I have known victims who re-adjusted, with a lot of help and hard work. Much depends on the nature and extent of the abuse and on the help they can receive.

As for Clare's anxious mother, there are so many possible signs of having been abused that I deliberately did not list any here. The family doctor would be a useful and first port of call. Before that, mother has to prepare her soul for all the questions and agonies I indicated above. If she has to choose between the suffering of children or of adults, then her job is to be a voice for the voiceless, and side with the innocent, the victim.

**NOTE**

7.   IMS Survey, *Childhood Experiences and Attitudes,* Dublin, November 1993

# Appearance and Endowment

## BABIES DIFFER

When I was born, Europe was split between two views of human nature: one, that all healthy humans are born basically alike, and later variations between them are the result of conditioning; and the other, that most of what makes us different is the result of what we inherit from parents, not of any experience since conception. The first view in its most extreme form stemmed from Pavlov's experiments on the conditioning of dogs, and became the official psychology of the Soviet Union. The second found its most extreme form in the racism of Rosenberg and the Nazis.

We have reached a more balanced view now, not by compromise between extremes but by careful study, on many different fronts. Clearly both nature and nurture, both heredity and environment, are important in shaping us; but they interact with one another in an almost unquantifiable way. For parents looking at their twelve-year-old, the question shapes itself in the painful (and futile) form of 'What did we do wrong? Am I to blame?'

There are limits to how far we can change children, limits that are set by their body, and also by the temperament which they bring from the womb. Over the last thirty years it has become evident that newborn babies differ from one another in personal qualities that are likely to persist into later life: in their output of energy, their mood, intensity of emotional reaction, adaptability, reaction to new situations, distract-ability, span of attention and other traits. Babies who are regular in their bodily rhythms (feeding, sleep, evacuation), easy-going, mild in their emotional reactions, and adapt quickly to new situations, are obviously the easiest to rear. Those with the opposite cluster of qualities (i.e. who are unpredictable, with irregular sleep patterns, dislike change, are inflexible, and show intense, often negative emotional reactions) are difficult and make strong demands on parents and later on teachers.

Does this seem obvious? In fact it can be good news for guilt-ridden parents facing a difficult child who is always in trouble at school and finds it extremely hard to fit in with rules and expectations. It is essential, and comforting, to realise that such problems are not always the result of parents' mistakes, or of his determination to annoy you. It may be just the way he is.

Since Galen the Greek divided humans into four tempera-ments, many speculators have tried to categorise human personalities. By contrast, the research on temperament[8] identifies qualities that appear before life has started to form our children. The first people to appreciate these differences are the mothers of newborn babies, noting the traits that mark their children from the start. They can now put more shape on the anonymous prayer: 'Lord give me the serenity to accept what I cannot change, the courage to change what I can, and the wisdom to know the difference.' There are qualities of temperament, like qualities of the body, which form the parameters within which change can take place.

## BABIES ARE ACTIVE

Babies are not passive putty, waiting to be moulded. They are active agents of change, and the detailed observation of infants in the last thirty years[9] has added to our wisdom. Even ten days after birth a baby can smell the difference between milk from her mother and from another woman. She will react more actively to a human voice than to any other sound; to a human face than to any other shape. She grows in intelligence and personality, not by being conditioned passively, but by her experience of acting on the world around her (and that world is essentially her mother); by finding that her cries are heard, her needs are interpreted, and later that her smiles are returned and her gurgles reciprocated with language. Children are spoiled, not because of what we give or do to them but because adults do not value what children themselves can do and give.

Young couples think of themselves as 'starting a family'. In one way it is not the parents who make the family, but the baby. Little children shape the world around them by their dependence. They draw out reliability, intelligence, goodness from their parents. The ordinary couple that brings a baby home from hospital, finds itself lifted to an undreamt-of level of work and responsiveness. As the weeks and months pass, the extraordinary growth of life and intelligence in the infant, and the implicit trust and neediness that it shows, draws from its parents a level of generosity and competence they have never shown before. Small children flatter us by expecting a degree of reliability and availability to which we respond, partly because of our capacity to identify with them. In countless subtle ways children produce a family around them, perhaps by needing something, something which we give because of what we know about expectation and about fulfilment.

Most children contribute to the family situation. Where that does not happen, because of emotional or physical problems in the child, there is a large and unnatural task imposed on the parents, to keep up a family and a family atmosphere in spite of the fact that there is no help to be derived from the individual child. In the new baby, this can arise from a visible problem.

## Living with a Visible Problem

Maeve was born with a cleft lip and palate. Thirty years ago it would have had a profound effect on her development, because so little could have been done for her appearance and speech. Now, no matter where she is in the country, she can have surgical and orthodontic treatment, and speech therapy, which in time will virtually dispose of the visible problem.

That much is possible; but it depends on her parents. The timing of surgery is crucial; parents have been known to delay intervention because they have difficulty adjusting to the reality of the disfigurement. The first sight of Maeve brought shock and grief: mother mourned for the child she had hoped for, and her grief was complicated by the need to respond to the little girl in front of her. So much now depends on mother's self-esteem, and her ability to cope with the trauma. Mothers obviously differ, but research indicates that after the first shock and grief, most mothers of CLP (cleft lip and palate) children recover their energy, and at twelve months, there is no difference in the quality of mother-baby attachment between CLP babies and others.

Baby Maeve is unworried by her appearance. She has never looked in a mirror, and her only sense of herself comes from the reactions of those around her, especially her mother. Her self-esteem comes from reflected appraisal, the experience of being handled and cherished by parents. It is their hands and their facial reactions which tell her that she is precious. Her sense of her value comes from mother's handling of her, from the way she is held and treasured. Later it is reinforced by her father. So love, affection, stroking, letting Maeve know that you are happy to have her around and close to you, will all help her feeling of self-worth. It will always be something solid for her to fall back on.

She will need it. A disfigurement provokes primitive and distressing reactions in those around her. Attractiveness in a child makes for popularity. Pretty children are judged intelligent, friendly, successful, by both their peers and by teachers. A disfigurement carries stigma, and the CLP child may be stereotyped rather than treated as an individual. People may implicitly blame the parents, thinking that because plastic surgery can remove such disfigurement, the parents should be held responsible for maintaining the problem and failing to protect the sensibilities of others.

Reactions to disfigurement can run as deep and be as disturbing as racism. There was for many centuries the practice of deliberately disfiguring criminals. Disfigurement in more primitive times made one a social outcast, branded with the mark of Cain, even the devil's progeny. The old title of CLP children linked them with hares, the devil's familiar, and in Norway even in recent times there was a ban on hanging hares in public, which stemmed from the fear that a pregnant woman might see them and infect her unborn child. Muslims sometimes fear a similar result from a mother cutting or chopping during pregnancy. We have to examine our own reactions; the irrational ones are still to be found. Fairy stories from Grimm's tales right through to *Nightmare on Elm Street* have associated the disfigured face with evil.

A friend of mine, born CLP, used to think in his teens that every time a girl turned down his invitation to dance, it was because of his appearance or speech. Now happily married with a family, he looks back on that as a time of illusion, born of self-consciousness. There was more to him than his CLP, and others' reactions to him were not just to his appearance.

Even to speak of a CLP child is to give the physical defect unwarranted importance. It is *not* central. It is only a part of Maeve's make-up, and has to be kept in proportion. It should never be used as an excuse for opting out of things. One should demand the same standards of Maeve as of other children. The world is not going to spoil her — we should not let her imagine that it will — simply because she was born with a visible defect. She must be asked to do everything she is able to do, so that she will mature and be prepared for life.

In particular she must be equipped to face remarks from other children, and to be able to say something like 'I was born with a cleft lip and palate, and it is being attended to'. The truth is the most disarming answer, and the one most likely to put an end to remarks.

Surgery and dentistry are performing near-miracles for children like Maeve; but improving her speech is a matter more of education than of medicine. It is important for her to see speech therapy as learning skills, demanding her energetic work, rather than have her think 'This is part of me, to speak badly'. Children can learn anything, including to speak properly, but it depends on their effort, not a doctor's.

The good news is that CLP children *do* adjust well. Despite the multiple problems arising from hearing, speech, early feeding, hospitalisations and surgery, they are notable for their lack of psychological pathology, and they display remarkably high self-esteem through having coped with adversity.

Bruno Bettelheim, who knew what it was to cope with trials, wrote: 'Children can learn to live with a disability. But they cannot live well without the conviction that their parents find them utterly and unconditionally lovable. If the parents, knowing their child's defect, love her now, she can believe that others will love her in the future. With this conviction she can live well today and have faith in the years to come.'

## A Less Visible Problem

A CLP baby has a visible problem. Many years ago I worked with Kevin, who was expecting his first child. One autumn he came in to work glowing with happy pride. After a difficult birth, a handsome blue-eyed, blond baby boy had arrived, and Kevin was the proudest of fathers, in love with his first son, who was to be called Kevin. As the weeks passed he became less exuberant. There were questions about little Kevin. He had suffered anoxia in a badly managed birth, and his ability might not be the full shilling. After three months a red-eyed Kevin told me that his little son was brain-damaged and would probably never be able to speak. The prediction of his handicap was correct, and Kevin devoted all his immense energy and ability to providing for his son's future. He enjoyed his later children, born healthy and bright, but he showed his strength most of all in the weeks after Kevin's birth, as joy turned to anxiety and then to horror.

## Frank is Handicapped

I remember another parent, a mother, who felt trapped. Six-year-old Frank was not just slow, but incontinent and cranky. Since his birth, things had got worse between her and her husband Bill. He offered little support, and when I met her, she felt she was running out of steam and exhausted. Frank's demands seemed to grow and grow.

The loudest cry was from herself. Frank would have to be looked after, but his future depended on mother's survival, not just physically but emotionally. He needed mothering as much as — more than — the rest of us, because he would be dependent for longer than most of us. He needed fathering too, of course, and education. But for the moment most of his demands were focussed on mother.

There are state services to help the parents of handi-capped children, but they cannot come close to the meaning such a child has in the family. A baby is born with brain damage. The mother is exhausted after a difficult birth. Suddenly she finds herself responsible for a mite who makes twice as many demands on her energy and concern as her other children. She spends her day cleaning and calming and feeding, and at the end of it she may still feel guilty.

Her other children are showing signs of neglect, and resentment of the baby who has taken over their mother. But you cannot resent a handicapped child, so they show their resentment in other ways, picking on Mum for her cooking, or kicking up at school, displacing their anger onto other targets.

Father is in the same spot. He cannot let himself feel angry with this baby who dirties the house, disturbs his sleep and exhausts his wife. So he does other things with his anger. He turns it on his wife, and blames her for incompetence in running the house. He turns cold and withdraws into himself; maybe withdraws all his emotional investment from the house and family and pours it into his work, or his golf, or his drinking.

I can think of a hundred families which did not handle it like this. Instead the father saw what his wife needed, came to terms with the anger and disappointment he felt at the handicapped baby, and took his share in the enormous burden of work that such a baby brings. He was ready to live with the irrational guilt his wife felt at giving her husband an imperfect child. It was irrational not least because we are all imperfect, but do not show our wounds as obviously as the brain-damaged child.

Jean Vanier has built his L'Arche communities on the conviction that whether we are labelled healthy or handicapped, we are all wounded healers. We all carry scars and need help; but also we all, including the Downs Syndrome and brain-damaged children, can help and heal. In L'Arche, as in the Camphill and other communities, the 'healthy' and the 'handicapped' live and work together, unlabelled.

What does a label say? Stigma arises out of the need of a particular group to isolate the deviant and retain its own image as pure. A label indicates some of the things that the handicapped child does *not* know. But you do not know half of the things that Frank *does* know, or the language in which he might express them, or the feelings that stir in him, mostly unexpressed. Labels are always inadequate.

His mother would like to underplay Frank's problems, and have him schooled in a mainstream class, with normal children. There is a difference of philosophy between the primary teachers' union, the INTO — which includes some of the most devoted and gifted professionals in the country and favours special schools for the handicapped — and on the other hand some professional bodies, such as the Psychological Society of Ireland (PSI), which favour integration. At the moment, children whose IQ falls below 70 are more likely to be in special classes or special schools, because national teachers have not the training or resources to integrate children with enormously diverse rates of learning. These classes and schools are often superb, but they are separate, and mother hates to see Frank pushed out of the mainstream.

Meanwhile, she needs a husband to stroke and support her, and he has turned away. He might say he has not the skills to deal with Frank. That is not the problem. It is his wife he has to help. Before that he must — perhaps with the support of a sensitive and compassionate friend — face his own rage and disappointment, find out what he has done with it.

It is little use wasting energy on getting services for Frank until his father has done something to save his marriage, and help his wife to survive, physically and emotionally, through this period of extreme demand. No two cases of handicap are the same; but they have in common a strong mix of positive and negative emotions in both parents and in the other children. That mix, especially the hidden resentments, must be faced and sorted out if little Frank is to have a chance of growing up well.

## NOTES

8. This research is summarised in Chapter 1 of *Child and Adolescent Psychiatry* edited by M. Rutter and L. Hersov (Oxford, Blackwell, 1985). For a less technical account see *Living with Children 5-10,* p. 40 (London, Open University, 1981)

9. Daniel Stern, *The Interpersonal World of the Infant,* New York, Basic Books, 1985, pp. 38-41

# Parents' Lives and Children's Needs

## THE SEARCH FOR THE RIGHT ANSWER

There is an obsessional side to all of us that wants to know in advance what is going to happen, and how we will handle it. We itch for a set of rules by which to manage the many crises and decisions of family life. It might be nice to have rules of thumb for rearing a family, comforting to believe that:

- at age six they should be starting housework;
- pocket-money should follow the following pattern . . .
- TV not more than forty-five minutes on weekdays, two hours on weekends;
- sleep required according to the following pattern . . .
- homework should take the following lengths of time at different ages . . .

You know that is a fantasy. What you need for raising your children is not a set of rules for new situations — who would be making up those rules anyway? — but the confidence to meet the unforeseen alongside your partner.

Grandparents now would not know what to advise in many of the crises. Who would have thought ten years ago that children would be demanding and receiving computer games that cost £40 and more? That video recorders would be within the reach of families of low income, and seen not as a wild luxury but as normal? There are places where pornographic material is available on computer disc, and will soon be available by modem and telephone, feeding straight into your children's PC.

In other words, one cannot cover all the decisions parents will have to face. Nobody knows the answers, certainly not the preachers nor the grandparents. Yet the family itself is durable, and today's parents, whether in town or country, manage to face unrehearsed pressures. They adjust as their children grow older, learning to accept the children as separate, knowing how to communicate, knowing how to manage their own lives and emotions, and survive, and not being afraid to change the pattern in which they were reared themselves.

## CHANGING THE PATTERN

I have known many mothers express horror at hearing themselves talking to their children in the voice and phrases of their own parents, when they had made up their minds to rear their children differently from the way they were reared themselves.

### Helen's Way

Rather than generalise about changing the pattern, which can sound disloyal or self-willed or even morally suspect, let me talk about it in the context of someone I know. We'll call her Helen. Her parents had stayed together, but it had been a silent marriage, father drinking too much, and mother, if not depressed, at least down in herself and consistently negative with the children.

It left its mark on Helen, but she learned from it. She was determined to break the pattern. She did *not* marry a feckless man like her father. She was sought out by Michael, who saw a strength in her, born of the isolation she had suffered as a young girl. Once married, she was able to articulate to him her fear of being negative like her mother.

The children were a huge joy to her, even the second child Dermot, who had been delicate and difficult from birth. Helen made up her mind that if she had to criticise them or tell them off, the blame would always be outweighed by blessings, by the consistency with which she stroked them and made them feel precious. It became a nightly examination of conscience with her: 'Today, did I criticise them more or bless and stroke them more?'

Her parents had not been physical in their affections, either with one another or with the children. Michael taught her how to touch and be held. So from the first baby on, she enjoyed cuddling the children. They were not all equally touchable. The treatment of Dermot's infantile eczema meant that for a while he could not be hugged and kissed, and he was less comfortable with cuddles than the rest. He liked to be hugged, for the message it gave him, but could not easily touch others with affection. Helen gave him what he could take, and enjoyed watching his body become softer and less rigid over the years.

In this, Helen had in mind one of the few occasions when children featured in the life of Christ (there was an old painting of it in her kitchen). When confronted with children who were probably restless and screaming — at least the apostles considered them a nuisance — Jesus gave them two precious things, time and touch. They responded immediately to this man who was not nervous of them. Adult nervousness is so often shown in bossing children around.

Not everyone appreciated Helen's style. There were times when Helen's mother would be visiting the house, and when she saw Helen with her arms round Dermot, she would sometimes snort: 'You're spoiling that child rotten. Can't you leave him alone?'

She would blame Dermot's sometimes cranky behaviour on the way he was being handled, and intrude heavily in the rearing of her grandchildren. More than once Helen heard the reproach: 'All that boy needs is a good smack.' She knew it would not be 'a good smack' for Dermot, but would only make things worse. But it was not worth getting into an argument with Granny about it.

Granny knew that a pattern was being altered, that her own style of child-rearing was not being copied. She had not the wit to keep quiet about it. Helen did not ask for trouble with her mother, but she was not going to be deterred. At one stage, after her father died, the question arose of Granny coming to live with Helen and her family, in a fairly small house. It was a testing time for Helen, who shared her mother's grief, was pulled by guilt and a sense of duty, but was even more aware of the primary needs of her husband and children.

On one earlier occasion Granny had spent a month with the family: not a happy month. She had moved unbidden into the kitchen, ostensibly to help Helen, but with unspoken criticism of her daughter in many of her moves. She had assumed the right to tell off the children, claiming she was backing up their parents, but in fact confusing them with the presence of a third boss in the house, who had less knowledge of them and a different style of relating. The whole family was caught in the classic bind: 'We must be nice to Granny, she depends on us,' so they could not be angry and shout at her when she unthinkingly moved into what had been Helen's chair in front of the television set.

Helen knew other grannies who could be a centre of warmth and love, a useful extra adult in the household; older women who accepted that they could only enter the kitchen as invited guests, who retained some dignity and independence by contributing to the household costs, who respected the limits of their role and who realised they had no part in the rearing of their grandchildren except as invited baby-sitters. Helen saw that her mother would not be able to adjust to such conditions, and so she painfully, with a sense of unspoken reproaches, made other arrangements for her.

In this generation many parents have, like Helen, broken a pattern, chosen a style that was their own, agreed between husband and wife. It does not mean abandoning values of love or self-control or obedience. But there is a change of style, of tone of voice, of touching, of communication, of readiness to be asked any questions. It cannot be done without a conflict, because we carry our parents' voices and styles about with us. We cannot change a pattern without a twinge of guilt, or at least consciousness of difference. Every generation of Christians is called to do what Christ did, question accepted routines, and push back to the basic commandments of love of God and the neighbour, which have to be rethought afresh in every new family.

## 'YOU'RE SPOILING HIM ROTTEN'

Just as school principals hate to hear the accusation: 'Discipline is going to the dogs', so parents are sensitive to the accusation of spoiling their children, especially if it comes from the older generation. It implies that they have not the courage to do their job. Spoiling has a different meaning at different ages. I remember one mother distressed by the accusation that her nine-year-old Maurice was spoiled and that she was doing the same to three-month-old Ross. What does spoiling mean at different ages?

Baby Ross is a mass of needs: to be fed and held and kept warm and kept clean. His survival depends completely on mother or her substitute. He cannot even perceive the needs of others, let alone meet them. The one gift he can give is his evident contentment when mother feeds or cuddles him. If his cries of need are met consistently, then the world starts to become a trustworthy place, though still more frightening than the warm, nourishing comfort of the womb. The promptness and reliability with which mother responds to his cries becomes part of his consciousness. His first social achievement is to let mother out of his sight without undue anxiety or rage, because she has become an inner certainty as well as an outer predictability. She is becoming an 'internal mother', a comforting sense that even if she is not beside him, he is being looked after.

Penelope Leach puts it this way:[10] 'If you find yourself deliberately withholding attention because your baby is "too demanding", be warned. The slower you are to meet the needs he expresses, and the more you ration your attention to him, the more he will demand, because the more anxious he will become in case those needs are not going to be met. If you leave him to cry alone in his cot because "he has got to learn", he will not learn to play there quietly. Instead he will learn to cry hard the moment he awakens because experience of being left too long has made it impossible for him to be contented there.'

Spoiling has quite a different meaning for Ross than for Maurice. As the baby grows, a lot of his life (from toilet-training on) will consist of postponing his own needs and impulses and adjusting to others' needs. He has to be initiated gently into the realisation that not all his demands can be met at once, if at all, and that other people have needs as well as him. The more secure and contented a baby is, the sooner he is able to wait, to allow for others' needs. That security is built up by the consistency with which mother responds to his needs in the first year of his life.

A spoiled child — and Maurice may well be such — is full of unsatisfied *needs* and intolerant of others' *demands*. He is selfish, and unable to tolerate frustration. The way that spoiling comes about varies at different ages. Rigid disciplinarians of young babies breed spoiled, unhappy children with no confidence in themselves or their parents. Ross could be spoilt by a mother who will never leave him alone when he is not wanting attention, or who in other ways is *unresponsive* to him. Grandparents can sometimes spoil their children in this way.

After the first year, a child is spoiled by over-protection, by never being allowed to do things for himself, by never being allowed out of his mother's sight. Some children grow up with a strong internal need to achieve, a satisfaction in managing their own life that makes them happy, well-motivated students. The sort of parents who produce this inner motivation are deeply involved with their children, watching them every step of the way, but not doing things for them that they could do for themselves. They take more pleasure in seeing the child try than in doing things for him. They love to see him feed and dress himself, choose his own friends, go on messages, use public transport, manage his own home-work, make his own mistakes and correct them, rather than go out with perfect homework for which he feels he can take only half the credit.

Apart from over-protection, children past the toddler stage can be spoiled in the obvious way, by lack of discipline for fear of 'repressing' him. He is spoiled by being allowed to wreck the furniture, walk on the table, draw on the wall, ride round the living-room on his tricycle. This is certainly happening more nowadays, where parents are less sure of their standards because so many contradictory messages are shouted at them, and they may fear seeming old-fashioned or harsh.

Fashions change, but there is no change in the old law that a two-year-old wants to be boss, and protests at being thwarted in any way. In babyhood his needs *have* to be met. In childhood he begins to make allowance for others' needs and demands. In the period between the two, management is never easy. There is nothing sadder than to see a household where a nine-year-old has been allowed to go on imagining that he is the boss, that the world revolves around his needs, and that what he shouts must be heeded. At that stage it will take a concerted effort from both parents to bring him back to a sense of others' needs.

However, a heedless child is not always a spoiled child. Some marriages become a dialogue of the deaf, not for want of talking but for want of listening. In the same way mother and daughter can find themselves talking without communication.

## To Maria's Mother: Talking to the Wall

You find your nine-year-old Maria difficult. She doesn't seem to hear when you are speaking to her, just looks away till you are finished, then goes on pleading or denying or whatever. You might as well be talking to the wall. You just do not seem able to communicate with one another.

In the interviewing business, there is one useful rule. If you want to find out who is interviewing whom, just work out *who does most of the talking?* That is the one who is being interviewed. It would look as though in your conversations, Maria is interviewing you, not the other way round.

You and Maria have a long history of conversations, going back to when she reached up and smiled at you as a baby, and you cooed and murmured back to her. You were responding to one another and enjoying it. There was more communication then than now, when after nine years you find that the conversations have become like a pair of monologues, one consisting of criticism and instructions, the other of denials and pleading.

She comes home an hour late from school, dashes into the house, muddy shoes doing a job on your carpet, throws her half-open school bag across the room and makes for the fridge, looking furiously for food. You are angry about the carpet, worried about her lateness, and fairly miffed that she went straight for the fridge instead of greeting you. If you start with any of these issues, there will be a shouting match. You may be worked up. The signs are that she is too.

Later you learn that she was set upon by some other girls on the way home, had to run across fields to escape — hence the mud and the delay in reaching home. When she burst in your door she was scared after the fight, angry with the other girls, guilty about coming home late, and wanting to be mothered — hence the dive for the fridge: food so often stands for mother. How do you receive her?

You're spreading mud all over my clean carpet!
I've been sick with worry waiting for you!
You look as though you've lost half your homework from that bag!
You might at least ask me before you raid the fridge!

When Maria is in the middle of strong emotions, she cannot listen to anyone. She cannot accept advice or consolation or constructive criticism, much less a scolding. She wants you to understand her, to sense what is going on inside her at that particular moment. And she wants to be understood without having to disclose fully what she is experiencing.

It is a moment that tests you. Are you so swallowed up by your own emotions, of anxiety, anger, rejection, that you cannot get in touch with her anger and worry and need? So much depends on your opening remark, not so much the words as the tone: one of acceptance, understanding, identifying with Maria, or one of exasperation.

Maria will not hear what you are saying unless you first reach her feelings, and let her register not so much what has happened, as the anxiety and anger and need she feels now. The event itself is less important than the feelings that possess her. You have to let them surface, and accept them without moralising or preaching or giving out. Then she will probably reach her own wisdom, seeing the danger of mixing with certain girls, or of delaying on her way home, and regret what she has done to the carpet. The wisdom she attains herself is more lasting and precious than the advice you may lavish on her. Remember again: if you do most of the talking, then she is interviewing you.

If you want a useful exchange with Maria, look not so much at the event itself as at the feelings and relationships it implies. It is easy to moralise about coming home promptly, about watching who you mix with, about care for the carpet. None of that is news to Maria, and none of it touches where she is at. She is concerned about those girls and how she is going to get on with them, or avoid them, in future. She is frightened, and longing for a bit of mothering. She is angry at her tormentors, but they are gone, so she vents her anger on you, messing your carpet and ignoring you as she bursts in.

Can you start with something like 'Maria, you look so upset!' and as she launches into her story: 'You didn't think those girls would turn against you like that.' Help her to know her own feelings by serving as a mirror to them, without flattery or detraction. If you can help her to bring to utterance her strong emotions, her anxiety and anger and guilt, she will have a chance to plan for tomorrow knowing that she is understood by you.

## DON'T ASK WHY?

Understanding does not come through asking 'why'. Of all the questions parents ask, this is probably the commonest and the most destructive. Think of a few examples:

- Maria, why can't you be home at the time you were told?
- Why don't you do your homework first?
- Why don't you tidy your room?
- Why do you have to turn the music up so loud?
- Why are you going out with that skinhead?

Parents' 'whys' have a completely different flavour from those of a child. The 'whys' of children are part of their education, a reminder of what natural curiosity is like:

- Why is the grass green?
- Why is the moon sometimes round and sometimes not?
- Why is Mrs Kelly so fat?
- Why hasn't Daddy got breasts?

These are questions that need accurate and informed answers. They grow out of puzzlement, and a desire to understand, and they lead us into areas that we had either forgotten to mention or had repressed. When Dr Sam Johnson said 'Questioning is not the mode of conversation among gentlemen', he was referring not so much to this search for understanding, as to the veiled accusations that are masked by the 'whys' of adults.

Children generally hate parental questions starting with 'why' because the question does not really expect a straight answer. If your teenage Grainne answers the first question above with 'I stayed on at the disco because I would have been the first to break up the group', it may well be an honest answer, but does it win her a fair, unbiased hearing? Children learn that adults only ask 'why' when they disapprove or are doubtful about what you are doing. The result of their answer is not going to be enlightenment for the adults, but a prohibition or a criticism of what they are up to.

Children who are constantly asked 'why' learn another thing: that adults simply do not understand children. Otherwise there would be no need for what seems like incessant questioning. Inside, Grainne is thinking: 'If you would just try to understand me, you could easily answer your own question. The reason you ask me is that it doesn't seem worth the effort to you to think it out for yourself.'

Grown-ups may believe there is no sting in the word 'why', that it is a neutral word. Children sense otherwise. The *Oxford English Dictionary* gives as its second definition for the word 'why', 'Implying or suggesting a negative assertion'. It implies that you, Grainne, can have no valid reason for what you have done. It also implies the adults' conviction that you owe them an explanation, perhaps a justification of your thoughts and deeds.

The reverse is not always true. It may not be in order for Grainne to ask 'Why are you in such bad form today, Mum?' or 'Why does Daddy drink too much on Fridays?' There may be helpful answers for both these questions, but it is not every family that grants its children the right to question as well as be questioned.

Because the question 'why' is often more of an accusation, children learn to be cautious in their answers. As Goldsmith said: 'Ask me no questions and I'll tell you no lies.' An honest answer may be disbelieved, or it may draw fire on them. An answer is demanded, so Grainne learns to produce one that will minimise the damage, at the same time resenting the fact that Mum could not work out the true reason for herself. Wasn't she young once?

It can also happen that Grainne does not know the true answer herself. The reasons we do things are not always at the top of our minds. Why is Grainne jealous of one sister and not of another? Why does a child with plenty of money start to steal? Why does a girl prefer other girls to boys? Why does a boy grow angry or fearful if he finds dirt round the house? There are unconscious reasons hidden in our history and in the family's dynamics. If adults press their interrogations on the children, they may be given some rationalisation, but be no nearer to the truth, because the child herself does not understand.

What is the alternative to this questioning? Empathy, putting ourselves in the child's skin, working to understand her priorities and worries. This is not the same as indifference. Disobedience may still call for sanctions if it is real disobedience. Still more, if we can show that we approve of her motives (in Grainne's case, not spoiling the party by breaking away early) while criticising some of the consequences, the way is open for more honest exchange the next time. If we want to criticise our children, let us do it straightforwardly, not by unreal questioning, and only after we have made a serious effort to get inside their skin and to understand.

Nobody really understands me; nor do I want them to. I am quite prepared to accept sanctions justly imposed by those whose job it is. That does not give them the right to judge me and blame me, to ascribe motives or point to the malice or foolishness in me. Even the most truculent and difficult children can show a surprisingly generous readiness to accept just sanctions, but a fierce resistance to being blamed or judged.

National College of Art and Design
LIBRARY

## WHOSE JOB IS IT TO JUDGE?

The Gospel tells us not to judge, not to pass judgment on others. But even in Christian countries we seem to consider it a right and proper thing to apportion blame to people, even when we are neither judges nor Gardai nor have any responsibility for maintaining the law. In marriage disputes, or in trouble with children, we are constantly seeking to decide who is to blame. Christ would tell us we are all guilty, and the only ones who will be judged harshly by God are the Pharisees, who deny having any responsibility for the world's evil.

### Disruptive Denis

Denis was a sullen thirteen-year-old, bright enough, but doing badly at school, because he was inattentive and disruptive in class. His father was an intelligent, hard-working and sober man, in many ways an admirable husband; but not an admirable father. He wanted perfect children, and of his three sons, the eldest and youngest were just about good enough, but Denis, the middle one, was noisy and messy, and his father could neither understand nor tolerate it. All he could see in Denis were his bad reports from school and his messiness around the house. He reacted by alternately ignoring and scolding him.

Denis pined for his father's approval, and without it he shifted between quiet, almost suicidal despair, and outbursts of acting up at school which always got him into trouble.

His mother could see what was happening, and grieved for it, but could make no impression on her husband, who could always produce more evidence of Denis' blameworthiness and reach vindictively for further sanctions against his son.

Denis was a good footballer and hurler. On the field he could forget his grief and work off some of his anger in action. At one point his father banned him from games on the pretext that this would make him work harder. By taking the one joy and outlet from Denis' life, he only made things worse. He considered himself a mature man, and ran a large business efficiently. He could not see it as his business to understand his son, only to moralise, judge and blame him for not producing results.

The story has no happy ending. Denis and his father still share the same house, but the despair and anger of the son are deepening. Faced with rejection by the man who fathered him, he has internalised it, and is deeply convinced of his worthlessness.

If things are bad between children and adults, it is up to the adults to take a lead in putting things right. They should be calm enough, secure enough and perceptive enough to see what has to be done and make the first move themselves.

Does that sound like a judgment itself? Suppose the adults are barely surviving, and are themselves on the edge of panic?

## ON THE EDGE OF PANIC

When I watch mothers of young children, what I admire most is their ability to absorb panic. Young babies who are hungry, or in pain, or soiled, or tired, cry as if there were no tomorrow, as if they were falling apart. It is the urgent edge of their scream that touches us. They have no sense of time, of before and after. It is no use telling them to wait, or that things will soon be comfortable. They are caught in the 'now', with no notion that the pain will ever end.

What mother does at these moments shapes the trust of the baby for the rest of his life. She picks him up, makes soothing noises, diagnoses with a practised eye what is causing the panic, holds the baby, absorbs the fear, sharing it and changing it into something the baby can handle because mother can. From the reliability of mother's response, from the fact that she is there when baby panics, and can read the signs and meet the crisis, baby develops an internal mother, an inner confidence that his cries are heard by what is outside him, and that the world makes sense and is not a hostile place.

The need for such containment does not end with infancy. When children have been seen through that phase, and are all in touch with mother by language, they think they can tell her what is going on in them. But panics still occur, and when mother is tired or unwell, they touch her in a painful way. It is still true that in most crises — and they seem to multiply — she cannot solve the problem, but can live with it and change

67

the situation by containing the intense feelings her children arouse.

An example: Tom tells you about some sex-play among the boys down in the fields, and your heart is in your mouth — had he been abused? What was happening? In fact Tom is cheerful enough about it, and has told you the full story. You talk it over with your husband, take a couple of wise precautions and calm your fears. I have known cases where the emotion triggered by a slight sexual incident did more damage than the incident itself. The children could handle what had happened, but the anger and fear of adults blew it into a local war. Obviously parents need vigilance in this area, but also need to watch their own emotions, and remember that the adult duty is to remain calm, to absorb the panic that may be in the air, and to say less rather than more.

Then there was the time you talked to Fergal's exhausted teacher after school, and in answering your questions she mentioned that Fergal had been rather 'disruptive' — one of the panic button words in communication between teachers and parents. This time you got really agitated, cross-questioned Fergal, extracted promises from him, revealed your fear that he was going to be a problem in school. He went back into school puzzled and angry. The incident that sparked off the 'disruptive' remark grew out of a row with his friend, which deeply upset Fergal. Instead of understanding it, the adults had blown it into a minor revolution, with implications for his future character.

Teacher's remarks are always liable to trigger strong feelings in parents. They hit you where you are most vulnerable, in the children you love. I have known parents, in a panic after hearing the exasperation of an exhausted teacher, decide to change school, or bring the case to the Board of Management. So a small matter, which needed only minor negotiation, was blown into a local war, because the mother (and the teacher) could not contain their own emotions and keep things in proportion. We all learn at some stage the dangers of over-reaction:

When in danger or in doubt,
Run in circles, scream and shout.

For parents, the greatest danger in over-reaction is that it heightens the anxiety, and often the misbehaviour, of children who feel that if grown-ups cannot keep their cool, what hope have children?

To contain all this emotion — and children rouse it in us all the time — mothers need some support themselves. Psychotherapists are in a similar position. In their work they absorb the most intense emotions, of despair, desire, jealousy, anger. Their clients are implicitly inviting them to jump into the river of emotion, and share it with them. In order to be useful, and maintain a professional stance, therapists need to stand back and think about what is happening in therapy sessions. They do this by regularly talking over their work with an experienced supervisor whose job is to pick up and interpret what is happening between therapist and client.

The mother of a young child, to whom she is passionately attached, is facing emotional crises all day. For her, the support of a husband is not a luxury but a lifeline. Others may substitute for him to some extent: relations, friends, a support group if she is otherwise isolated. But nothing can really substitute for the support of the other parent, who has a similar stake in the child. Without it, both mother and child will be to some extent deprived.

## LOOKING FOR HELP

Suppose the family mess has gone to the point where you have exhausted your own resources? Suppose the whole household is at war because of Ciaran, who is in everyone's hair, quarrelling from breakfast all through the school day to TV programmes at night; and who has just been suspended for disruptiveness at school after several warnings?

Why do parents look for help? They are inviting a stranger to poke into one of the few areas of their life that is totally their own, namely the rearing of their family. It is like undressing in public. They feel embarrassed and vulnerable. What they are saying is: Things are in such a mess that we do not know where to go next, and the embarrassment of sharing the mess with a stranger is less than the pain of living with it any longer.

The statement of the mess is only a first step. That first step can be therapeutic by itself. I can think of many cases where the decision by parents to look for help outside the family marked the beginning of change inside the family. For the child in trouble, and for his parents, it was not just a recognition of something deeply wrong, but also it signalled the mother's or father's change-over from hopeless bewilderment to hope. Usually one parent is more anxious than the other to look for help, and here the waters grow muddy.

### Timid Finbarr

A father brought me six-year-old Finbarr for educational advice, because he was too timid to talk in school. Mother said it went back to the time when Finbarr spent a week in hospital at the age of one. Fair enough, hospitalisation at that age can be traumatic, if mother is not allowed to stay with the child.

It was only many months later that another reality emerged. Mother disappeared one day, simply walked out on the family and stayed away for three weeks. She had done this five times before in the course of Finbarr's life. In presenting Finbarr, the parents felt that hospitalisation was a more clear-cut and safer explanation to offer, and simply kept silent about the can of worms, the festering ulcer of conflict, which lay behind those periodic walk-outs. Did they really believe that Finbarr was to blame, that with a little more courage or resolution he could be cured independently of his parents? Probably not, in their heart of hearts. They could not talk to one another about it — that was a large part of Finbarr's problem — so it was easier to plonk the problem onto Finbarr's little head, and seek help for him.

Back to Ciaran: there were muddy waters here too. The school was baffled, because he was a bright, competent, athletic boy who you would think could have enjoyed most aspects of school life, but instead seemed bent on destroying his chances. One Saturday his father — a rare occurrence — watched him at football, and Ciaran played an exceptional game, scoring twice. A teacher was there when Ciaran walked over to his father after the match. Dad was reminiscing about his own football days. Ciaran joined them in silence. The teacher congratulated him on his game. Ciaran looked at his father, who under the pressure of his son's gaze said 'You don't tell people if they've played a good game'. Ciaran walked away, and the teacher had a first inkling of why the boy was always angry, always destroying what he had done. He could not please his father, was constantly put down by the one man whose approval counted for him. He was caught in a bind: hounded by father to do his duty and be good at school, but baffled by the difficulty of pleasing his father, who was more easily aggravated than satisfied, and whose moods changed in a terrifying way.

Of course there was more behind it than that: a cranky marriage; some heavy drinking on father's part; mother suspecting he was an alcoholic and he in turn accusing her of having problems; drunken rows that sometimes ended in the beating of wife and children — a regular can of worms. But for the outside world, even for those whom they asked for help, Ciaran was the problem. Wasn't he disruptive in class, and didn't the teacher suspend him after many warnings? No doubt Ciaran was hard to live with. He had accepted an angry role inside and outside the family, and had given up trying to please Dad. Now in a sort of adolescent despair, he was just waiting until he was old enough to escape from under the feet of adults.

In the event, both parents stopped denying reality, and tried to look at themselves. An alcoholic problem was recognised, and Ciaran received the needed help from Alateen, an organisation of young people whose lives have been affected by a parent's heavy drinking. In a way, his disruptive behaviour at school had served its purpose. It had driven his parents to the point where they had to seek help, and their first question, about Ciaran's boldness, had led to questions about other ugly realities in their own lives. The truth had started to set them free. Like every liberation, it was bought with pain.

A parent's addiction was part of that mess, as it is of many cases brought to child guidance. It is not always part of the presenting problem. But does any parent seriously believe that children could be unaffected when the centre of a

parent's gravitation is no longer towards the family but
towards bottles or pills?

## Kate has Stopped Working

Kate's mother looked for help on the grounds that in the last
two years, her affectionate and clever twelve-year-old had
given up working at school, though she was still as lively as
ever. Between that and her husband's drinking, mother was
at her wit's end.

Part of her knew that the two belonged together, Ian's
drinking and Kate's nose-dive at school. She was tempted to
try all the remedies that had nothing to do with Kate's
problem: test her eyes and her ears, test her for allergies and
watch her diet, have her 'assessed', set up weekly contact with
her teacher, use rewards or punishments for schoolwork, sit
beside her at homework, get her extra help, give her a quieter
place for homework, tell her off at home for idling at school,
buy books on study habits, talk about changing school, or
changing to another teacher, threaten her with boarding
school, etc. As she tried the remedies which implied that Kate
was to blame, she knew that the real problem was outside
Kate.

Ian's drinking habits had changed in the last two years.
Under stress at work, he began to go for a drink on the way
home, and gradually this had taken over his evenings. He
could not see, but his wife could, that his life was becoming
unmanageable.

He was powerless over alcohol. He was lying on in bed in
the morning, looking for an early drink to clear his sore head,
grumpy at breakfast and at work, sometimes late for work, no
longer interested in the small problems of the family,
defensive about his evenings, ingenious in thinking up
excuses for having a drink, prickly about any suggestion that
he had a problem.

At the same time he was keeping up some appearances,
fairly faithful to his St Vincent de Paul meetings, though they
always ended in time for a jar; on good terms with the parish
priest, but with a garrulous affability that his wife knew was
false.

Alcoholics Anonymous have charted the pattern clearly,
but Kate could not see any pattern. She could see that the
father she loved, who was devoted to her, and reliable, was

no longer reliable or devoted. He was always making excuses for not going to functions like the Feis or concerts where she might be singing — that would interfere with his evening's drinking, though he did not give that excuse.

He could still be his old funny self in the evening before he went out — he was in good form at the prospect — but there was a false note about it. When sober, he was mawkishly sentimental, and lavish with promises of treats to come. When full of gin, he was a different person, an ogre, abusive and violent towards his wife, bad-tempered and impatient with the children, shouting, blaming, unpredictable, and, for Kate, terrifying.

His wife was worried enough watching this, seeing the household money disappear in the pub. It was much worse when Kate, her most promising scholar, started to bring home disastrous reports from school. It was tempting to try to solve her school problem as though it had nothing to do with Ian's drinking. That would be missing the cause of her idleness.

Kate was using most of her mental energy below the surface of her mind, worrying about home. She was preoccupied, absent-minded. She still loved to lose herself from her worries at a party or some activity, like a concert, that drew her energies totally. The dull routine of school could not do that.

Could you imagine a Bosnian girl, in a Muslim town under Serbian bombardment, settling down to learn irregular verbs or tackle Maths problems, as the bombs crash around her and her homeland is destroyed? The underlying fear absorbs all her energies.

Kate's anxiety was like that. At some level she knew her world was coming apart. She could not confront her father, because she had not the evidence, but she knew she had somehow lost him. She saw her mother's stress and found her short-tempered. Because mother seemed to blame her for bad work, she blamed herself.

What could be done? The root of the trouble was Ian's destructive, out-of-hand drinking, and that would not change till he acknowledged it. He needed help in achieving this: help from family, friends, priests, business colleagues, AA or other; above all, as AA constantly stress, help from God, who is our strength when we are weakest. Even then the job was only beginning; Ian had to work at his sobriety even harder than at his drinking.

If mother had gone to Kate for comfort and support against Ian, she would put her in the uncomfortable position of being an ally against her father. What she needed was to share mother's recognition of where the problem lay, stated not in anger but in love; and to have some hope of remedy.

Children of alcoholics suffer from a terrible isolation, and from anxiety at the sudden changes of mood in someone they love. This is not a rare experience. Most families in this country could count at least one relative who is an alcoholic, either recovered or still sinking. Kate's mother identified her problem, not in Kate's working habits, but in Ian's drinking habits. Once that was faced, she could shed her guilt and start to cope.

## PARENTS AT WAR

There are other children in the front line, where the parents are not alcoholic but are in conflict. Children react in different ways, depending on their temperament and history. Generally they stop using their brains for schoolwork.

### Is Alan really lazy?

Alan had brains to burn, and was always lovely to talk to. But he simply would not work in school. It was baffling. All the sanctions that the teacher could use — reports to parents, spending his break doing the missed homework, tellings-off, time outside the door — made no impression whatever. Alan did not seem to mind them. He was always polite but never contrite. Work did not matter to him, though he was intelligent enough to realise that it mattered to grown-ups.

He had been in the school two years when he came in visibly upset, and told his teacher quietly that there had been an awful row at home, Dad had thrown things at Mum, and hit her; she had fled the house after leaving the children with their grandmother. 'Has anything like this happened before?' 'Oh yes', said Alan, 'on and off they have rows and Mum goes missing.'

A lot of misery could have been saved if, when he first came to the school, the parents had been able to trust the teacher or the Principal with an intimation of what was wrong.

Obviously they did not want their conflict known outside the family; but normally one can trust a teacher to accept information in confidence, and it is extraordinary how a child can be helped by the knowledge that his situation is known and understood by somebody who sees as much of him as does his primary teacher.

Shouting matches at home will leave their mark on a child's work at school. Parents may feel that with the tension between them, there is no avoiding the rows. But some ways of handling conflict are less damaging for children than others. They recover from traumatic bereavement, such as a parent's death, more easily than they get over persistent conflict. When you look at conflict, some sorts do more harm. There are families where parents are unhappy or tense with one another, but not quarrelling within sight of the children; in these cases the children can be practically unaffected. The parents' conflict has almost no effect on their behaviour because they are not exposed to it.

The more noisy and violent the rows, the worse is the probable effect on the children. Some will react by fury and rebellion at school, others by being withdrawn and switched-off. If the parents work to keep the quarrels out of the children's sight and hearing, they may well spare them the worst effects of conflict. Obviously it is better to tackle the roots of the conflict. Meanwhile it is worth remembering that it is a service to children to keep the conflict under wraps, not exposing them to the sight or sound of it.

Children do not grow used to rows between parents. They may survive the occasional blow-up, especially with support. When the rows go on and on, children in general get more and more upset.

'Conflict' does not mean the disagreements that are part of every day in every home. What is important is how these disagreements are resolved. Warring parents try to resolve disagreements by aggression, and in doing this they are teaching their children something bad. If they can listen, yield on non-essentials, compromise, keep the love flowing, they are teaching something precious.

Sometimes the conflict is about the children, about household rules or questions of management. These rows are the most likely to affect children's behaviour badly, because they feel responsible and guilty. They may work out a strategy for surviving, but they will show the hurt at school in all sorts of ways.

Children are learning from parents every day how to deal with disagreements; badly, if they grow angry and aggressive; well, if they can listen to one another, especially in what concerns the rearing of children, and meet somewhere in the middle. The hardest and most important thing in all family matters is not to win victories but to keep the love flowing.

It still remains a painful question: how much do you tell the children? Although they may be shattered by parents screaming and out of control, they can be reassured by parents who can talk about their worries in a controlled way. As little animals can pick up the signs of a coming earthquake even before the seismograph, so children can sense a movement in the foundations of their world before they can put words on it.

How can you help them? Obviously, stop the earthquake, if you can. If the tension and conflict persist, children will generally cope better if you talk about it to them. By putting words on the situation, you spare them some of the unnamed terror, the unspeakable fear that they will be left without parents. What do *you* fear, when you think of talking about marital conflict to your child?

- He'll be upset. Yes, but he is probably upset already, and showing it by moodiness, rebellion, withdrawal, loss of concentration, or in some other way. Putting words on what they instinctively perceive can help them to cope with it better.
- He'll blame me. He may well be angry with one or both parents, because the foundations of his world are shaking. Quite possibly he feels guilty himself about the conflict, and feels he is somehow responsible for the unhappiness. He needs a reassuring parent rather than a defensive one.

- He may side with my partner against me. Children should never be put in the impossible position of having to choose between parents. They want their parents together, not split up. It is painful to risk hearing a child express preference for one parent over the other; but the overshadowing fear in his mind is of losing both.
- He will play up. This is realistic. Some children under stress give vent to their confusion and unhappiness by misbehaviour and flight from work, like Alan above. It is worth alerting the school to the fact that the child is under stress. Teachers too can make allowances.
- He'll think we don't love him. Quite possible, and all the more reason for talking it out and assuring him that you do. If your child thinks that he was partly to blame for your conflict through his naughtiness, you can help him enormously by relieving his mind of that guilt.
- He'll worry about the future. In all likelihood he is worrying about it already, and is desperate to be told that somebody is thinking about him and not just about adult wars.

If two tense parents come together to explain such worries to their children, the conversation is likely to be difficult and inhibited, and may end in an argument between adults. It works better if mother and father talk to them separately, but without trying to make a case or score points off the other. It needs to be done in a leisurely way, without fear of interruption, and with time for questions and objections, especially for the menacing fear in every child's mind, that his parents will split up and leave him. One may be a warring wife or husband, but one can still be a good parent, keeping the children out of the conflict, and helping them to cope with it.

Putting children first is an unpopular, politically incorrect notion in today's Europe. We need to rediscover the truth that those who bring children into the world have no personal rights which override those of their children. In the misery of marital conflict, there is often a collective wish not to look at children's pain.

The pain is not remedied by separation. We have outgrown the illusion that children do better if quarrelling parents split. Clearly we owe these children, like all the deprived, whatever help can be provided in therapy and support, just as we offer medical help to children who suffer because of exposure to infection. But just as we know the risks from exposure to infection, so we know now that children from single or separated parents have the odds stacked against them, in physical and emotional health, in education, and the prospect of founding a stable family themselves.

**The Saturday Parent**

Children are not the only ones to suffer in family breakdown. A father put it to me: 'I feel I was pushed out of our home by a neurotic wife, and have not merely cut my standard of living in half, but lost contact with my children. I pine for them, and often wonder what arrangement can do least damage to my three — Emma who is fourteen, Damien eleven and Brian three.'

**To the Father of Emma, Damien and Brian**

You think she is neurotic. She says she cannot live with you. I do not know which of you is right, but I know some of the answers to your big question. Children and parents caught in the pain of a family break-up feel that nobody could ever have gone through such suffering before. No two families are the same, but much is known now about limiting the damage — and in these messes, children tend to suffer more than adults. To see it through the eyes of a ten-year-old boy, read Roddy Doyle's *Paddy Clarke, Ha, Ha, Ha.* There, as with you and with nineteen out of twenty such break-ups, father leaves the home and children see him less.

You want to see them, and despite all appearances, they want to see you. They need to know that the end of mother-father love is not the end of father-child love. Telling them is important, but showing matters more. They are right to be wary of adult language about how you care for them. They had implicit faith in you as they had in their mother. If that faith is broken, all words lose some of their strength to reassure.

Each of your three children wants to know that he/she still has a place in your mind; and that is shown if you remember not just their birthdays and Christmases, but their teachers and subjects at school, their friends, hobbies, games, tastes in food and clothes, all that makes each of them unique. In your isolation you may well feel de-skilled by the break-up, an outcast in the family's eyes, unworthy of the children. But you are the only father they have, and much of their future depends on how well you can continue to love them and be a father to them, seeing them regularly, making no promises you cannot keep faithfully, telling them nothing that is not the truth.

If you cannot speak well of your wife to the children, it is safer not to talk about her at all — but that is a big loss. It would be best if Emma could chat to you about her mother (and to her mother about you) without feeling you were disapproving, or quizzing her, or spying on her, or liable to use information in a hostile way. Emma, Damien and Brian need to know that you still want them to have their mother, and that mother still wants them to have you, without risking the love of the other parent. I think sadly of a sixteen-year-old girl who could not visit her father without being pulled into a critical discussion of her mother, and being questioned in a way that felt to her like spying. Despite her protests, father persisted, and in the end she broke off contact with him.

Can you see the children often enough, and informally enough, to keep in touch with their everyday lives? For a young child that probably means at least once a week. This is where things become really difficult. If the separation is legal, then the law has not much place for informality, and yet it is the way children relate to father and mother.

The least damaging separations are those where children can walk, cycle or take the bus to Dad when the spirit moves them. That is easier with older than with younger children, and it means that you and your wife live not too far apart. If we listen to children, that appears to be closest to the ideal arrangement, even though it is hard to fit into a rigid agreement. It saves children from the constraining feeling: It's Saturday, that means Dad, McDonald's and a film. Formal, rigid agreements are foreign to children's lives. I have known parents take endless pains to ensure equal access to both parties, splitting the children's time exactly between father and mother, yet seeing this meticulous fairness become a major irritant to the children, who, every day had to work out 'Where are we sleeping tonight?'

Young children need parents who will talk to each other, even if it is only on the phone or the doorstep; and they need parents who can bear to be together on important occasions — for instance accompanying children to see the other parent in hospital, or going together to big occasions, like Confirmation, the school play or an important sporting event. The worst cases are where an estranged couple are unable to make even the simplest arrangements with one another, and use their children like scouts travelling between the battle-lines carrying written messages.

This is discouraging stuff, and the absent parent is constantly tempted to discouragement, feeling 'maybe it would be best for Emma if she just forgot about me'. After visiting the absent parent, children often come back emotionally upset — just as children in hospital are often upset when their parents leave at the end of a visit. At one time hospital staff used to feel that children would 'settle in' to hospital better if they were never visited.

That was as mistaken as thinking that children would be better forgetting about the separated father, because they are upset after visiting him. It is painful for them to be reminded of the Dad they are missing. But it would be much more painful for them to think they had no place in his mind and heart. They need more time with you, not less.

If you are to continue to be a parent, you do need somewhere to bring them. Fast-food cafés are no substitute for a base that is yours, which your children can start to make their own. What they need from you is not toys or money or gifts, but a share of yourself, a chance to waste time with you, and for that you need a place where you are not paying for the time.

Even when you have such a base, you will certainly find at times that your children resist visiting you. Little Brian may resist from fear of separation from mother, or from an awareness that you are not as good as mother at managing the hour-by-hour problems he presents. Emma and Damien, moving into the busy teens, may find the routine of weekly visits boring, or resent carrying out arrangements which have been made for them by parents, or miss the excitement they might be enjoying with friends or hobbies.

Do not let this put you off the effort to keep in touch. Nobody can tell a parent how to get on with his own children; but I have seen quite a few teenage children lose contact with their fathers because of their resistance and his discouragement. Father suspects them of cupboard love. They are irritated by arrangements that become rigid and boring. Real contact can often be saved by more flexibility — and for that the wife must co-operate.

Even after the tragedy of a break-up, children can emerge who feel loved, who are well reared by both parents, provided the two adults can manage to talk to one another, and the children know they have a place in the heart of both their parents.

## THE FACTS OF DEATH

Death, like marital conflict, can be a taboo subject with children, because we want to spare them as long as possible from consciousness of the harshest realities of adult life. Children often ask about what are called 'the facts of life'; but seldom about the facts of death, because they and we think they know them. Ordinary conversation today is tending to make death more vague (and sex more explicit). In the Gulf War they talked about 'body counts', meaning numbers of dead soldiers; and about 'collateral damage', meaning massacred civilians. I hear children saying someone 'passed on', avoiding the name of death, as though it was the ultimate failure, the Great Unmentionable.

Yet one of the healthiest things in our Irish culture is the community support for a bereaved family shown at and after the funeral. Where in Leeds or Boston they send flowers and try to forget a death, Irish people take time off to call to the house, share the grief which they can do nothing to assuage, and help the sorrowing family in practical ways.

## Worried Stevie

Stevie is four, and worried about death. He has just lost a loved Granny, and his mother, equally bereaved, has been too upset to comfort him. For Stevie the funeral is over, and he is left with unspoken fears. He will handle them easier if they are spoken about. When a child faces death — and his first experience is usually the death of a loved pet — some parents protect him with lies, pretending the dog has run away. 'But I always thought he loved me — how could he run away from me?' Or they hide the corpse and get a new dog immediately, only to hear the child say 'That's no good to me'. Why would it be any good, any more than a substitute child for the one you have lost?

Or they speak of Granny 'going to sleep', only to find that they have added a new terror to the child's experience of sleep. If Daddy falls asleep in front of the TV, Stevie wonders has he gone for ever. If his sister is being 'put to sleep' for an operation, he wonders will she ever wake up. And if Granny is spoken of as going to sleep, he may wonder will she be coming back like he does from sleep.

Stevie must be clear that death is final. Everything that lives, dies, and is gone for ever. Our hope of heaven includes the hope of seeing again those we loved, and the assurance that life after death is a fuller, though a different life from anything we have known before. Stevie needs to realise that once Granny died, she could not feel or see any more. We take it for granted, but it is hard for Stevie to accept. Many of his worries may centre on Granny feeling cold or abandoned, boxed in her coffin. If he sees the coffin, he needs to know that the shrouds and fine materials around the corpse are for our comfort, but that Granny is beyond feeling or seeing them.

How much has Granny's death altered the daily pattern of Stevie's life? Children often register a bereavement especially in the details of daily or weekly behaviour: a visit to Granny, games with her, presents from her, and so on. Mourning can more easily be carried through where the other aspects of

Stevie's life are unchanged, because then grief is not mixed with distress over the disruption of familiar routines.

Should you take a four-year-old to the funeral of someone close? We have a strong urge at these times to protect children, because we hate to see them unhappy. I remember a perceptive nine-year-old who lost his mother suddenly, through cancer, and after the funeral told his father: 'You should have brought Clare [who was four] to the funeral. She would have liked being the centre of attention, and she would have been able to say goodbye to mother, and see that she had really gone for ever.'

Being sent away from a house of mourning may exclude rather than relieve. It may even seem like a punishment — and for what? Children very easily think that a tragedy is their fault, even the tragedy of death. That sense of guilt can sometimes show itself after the death of a brother or sister in goody-goody behaviour, as though trying to make up for what has happened. Brothers and sisters often wish each other dead — and then are terrified to find their momentary wishes come true. Or the anger they may have felt towards a parent may return to torment them if the parent dies.

That sort of anguish is more than a child can handle alone. Parents of a child like Stevie may be so lost in their personal grief that they underestimate their child's suffering, which is different, more mixed with anger and guilt, but equally in need of support and talking out. Children may show the distress of bereavement in different ways from adults: not so much in tears, loss of appetite or sleep, as in angry behaviour, attention-seeking, or cheerfully denying that they feel anything at all.

If everyone puts on a brave face 'for the children's sake', it may deprive them of a feeling of usefulness and mutual support. Even young children can consciously work at comforting their parents. They are deprived, not so much because we do not give them things, as because adults do not value what children have to give — even in moments of major stress like a bereavement.

Here at the frontiers of life and death, a child's growing faith, his sense of a heavenly father and life after death, can be nurtured; but only if we are ready to let him taste the truth of death, share our grief, and if we can value the comfort that children can offer us in these dark hours.

## Lucy and the Mid-life Crisis

It is not always the adults who successfully broach taboo subjects. Children can force an issue in startling ways, the result of sophisticated but unconscious planning. A mother — call her Joan — once talked to me about her fifteen-year-old daughter, Lucy, who was acting like a slut. The previous week she had been seen on the street of her country town in a prolonged, intimate embrace with her boyfriend during the school lunch break. Joan was at her wit's end because, as she added, 'My husband is also going though a bad phase.'

There was more here than met the eye, as we brought to the surface the two themes of the underlying plot, Lucy's sexual acting out, and her father's 'bad phase'.

Joan told me what the 'bad phase' meant in practice. At the age of forty-eight, her husband was in a florid mid-life crisis. He had been a good footballer but had finally hung up his boots. His son could outrun him and beat him at tennis. His view of his toes was increasingly obscured by a bulge at his middle. His hair-line was slowly receding, and his jet black crop was showing quite a few grey streaks. Recently he had gone for promotion in his firm, and the coveted job went to a younger man.

He was taking Joan for granted, not communicating much, and his patterns were erratic. He was coming home late, out at the pub or elsewhere most evenings, and Joan had come to realise, through the grapevine of a middle-sized country town, that he was acting as though he was God's gift to women. She was not sure how far he had gone on his evening excursions, but she knew that he was making a fool of himself with younger women. He had been frequenting a nightclub where sad middle-aged men flirted with girls in an atmosphere where drink lowered inhibitions and amplified disco music made real conversation impossible.

If Joan knew it, then so did Lucy. The grapevine of a school is richer and more merciless than that of the parents. If another girl or boy wanted to hurt her, she was acutely vulnerable through the antics of her father. Lucy had the sexual curiosity and appetites of her age, and her boyfriend was not slow to take his chances.

There was something about the behaviour Joan described — exhibitionistic necking in a time and place where she was sure to be seen — that was not like Lucy. Joan was surely right in linking it with her husband's crisis. Lucy saw the marriage at risk. She felt the whole family was being made to look foolish and worse. She saw the damage her father was doing to Joan. It would be an under-statement to say that she was furious with him, perhaps also with Joan that she had let this happen.

So part of her sluttish behaviour could be heard as a scream of anger: 'If he can have his fun, so can I!' Also a scream of revenge: 'If he can bring shame on the family, so can I!'

More than either of these, however, her behaviour was constructive. She was pushing things to a point where Joan had to do something about it. This was hardly a conscious intention. Children have ways of working on their parents' lives with an instinct for survival, but with deadly precision in their choice of weapons. Lucy was sharp enough to know that her public necking would be observed. Her first reaction to criticism might be that Joan was a prude, that things are different now, everybody's doing it, did she never watch TV, was Joan forbidding her to have a boyfriend, and so on.

All beside the point. Joan could not tackle her alone. Her husband had to be brought in on the scene, and the reality of his own life had to be faced. Of course he denied any connection between his behaviour and Lucy's. He allowed his righteous indignation full rein about the sluttish behaviour of his daughter. He wanted to preach to her, treat her on a purely moral level, as though either she did not know right from wrong, or was just giving in to herself, or letting her boyfriend use her.

Lucy did not let him away with this. She quoted chapter and verse about his own philanderings, and if some of the details were embroidered by school gossip, there was enough truth in it to make him both furious and ashamed. Joan was able to stick with it, showing her love for both of them, but not allowing the truth to be obscured. It was like that scriptural drama when the adulterous King David was confronted by the prophet Nathan, first with a story of the rich man exploiting the poor, then with the accusing phrase: You are that man.

If children are deprived, it is not because they are not given things, but because adults do not value what children have to give. In a curious, dramatic way, Lucy was giving her parents a vision of truth. I have known younger children keep quarrelling parents together by giving so much trouble that the parents had to forget their own conflict to cope with the child. Lucy had a more difficult task, but with Joan's help she actually succeeded in pushing her father to weather his mid-life crisis in a less destructive and foolish way.

## WHEN ONE PARTNER IS OFF BALANCE

Unfortunately the energy and ingenuity of youth is not always enough to save a situation. Now that medication can bring psychotic patients to a state where they can live in the community, some families find themselves living with a father or mother who is incurably fragile, but well enough to live at home.

### Living with Neurosis

I think of Maura, whose husband had been in hospital twice with obsessional neurosis, and was now sufficiently recovered to hold down a job. He let out all the stresses of the job on Maura and their teenage children, Naomi and Denis. He occupied the bathroom for over an hour every morning. The day was so punctuated by his wild explosions of temper that they dreaded seeing him come in the door. Maura could not afford boarding school for the children, and wanted to save them from their deteriorating father whom she described, with some justice, as mad.

There was more than a clinical diagnosis in the phrase. There was fury and resentment at being trapped. Her plight is common enough. Many of us have to live with neurotics who could do with therapeutic help. Worse than that, we see our children grow bitter and angry under the lash of a parent who seems sane enough to pass muster, but who in family life can persecute everyone close to him (or her).

Obsessional neurosis is a sickness, but not one that yields easily to drugs. If Maura's husband tortured all around him, he was at least as badly tortured himself, by deep fears and anger that tore him apart. He tried to keep his life together by rigid rituals and carefully devised controls. He feared contamination by germs, dust, dirt, ink, excrement, so washed himself and his clothes endlessly. When these controls were threatened, by someone leaving a window open, or touching his jacket, or keeping him out of the bathroom, the anxiety rose to panic and an explosion followed, out of all proportion to the incident that triggered it.

They had tried unsuccessfully to cure him. The worst of obsessional parents is that they dress up their madness in morality, accuse their household of carelessness and stupidity, and project their anger on any target within reach. Maura could detach herself from these rantings to some extent, but the children could not. They internalised their father's accusations, while half knowing how non-sensical they were. The basic morality for a Christian is 'Judge not that you may not be judged'. It is the one commandment that obsessionals ignore. They are judging and condemning all the time. You see such parents being vindictive with children, imposing tasks or punishments that are simply retaliatory and an expression of the parent's anger. I have known an exasperated father set hundreds of lines for his son to write out, or keep him at homework till after midnight, all in the cause of morality and discipline, but in reality bubbling up from an unacknowledged resentment in the father.

What could Maura do as she watched her children growing cynical and furious at living day by day with injustice and harassment? She could not take them away because she had no means of support, and her husband owned the house.

For the moment Maura and the children had to live with a sick man. While she looked for a cure for him — or perhaps for him to realise what damage he was doing to the family which basically he loved — was there any way of making a bad job better, or at least no worse? What could one usefully say to Maura?

● 'First, remember that it is a sickness, from which your husband suffers too. While his obsessions are dressed up as morality, they are in fact as uncontrollable as a rash or a high temperature. One should not impute to him more malice than he deserves. Judge not.

- 'Secondly, keep the emotional temperature as low as possible. If you or Denis or Naomi lose your cool, or if you tease or provoke your husband, he will grow more upset and feel more threatened. It is possible to make things even worse than they are now.
- 'Thirdly, try not to be caught in the same inflexible, unsmiling rigidity as seizes your husband. When he lays down stupid rituals about cleanliness or shutting windows, remember what is important and what is trivial. Do not counter him with obsessions of your own, but be flexible. Keep a sense of humour and as much detachment from the nonsense as you can manage.
- 'Fourthly, in order to be calm and flexible, you need someone to stroke and soften you, and the children need all the tenderness you can give them. Have some trusted friends to whom you can talk out your plight; not that they can cure it for you, but they can at least listen and support you.
- 'As Denis and Naomi grow older, they may be able to stand back and see what is happening to their father. Meanwhile, since loading their frustration onto father would be too dangerous, they may well vent some of it on you.'

## GOING OUT TO WORK: MAKING THE DECISION

Is there any point in discussing working mothers? Is it like arguing about whether the tide should come in? Ireland is living through a social change. The skills and aspirations of women, the labour-saving resources in homes, the high price of mortgages and the financial demands of rearing a family have all contributed to a growth in the number of mothers who go out to work. It is like a flowing tide, yet many decisions lie within the freedom of the individual mother, and it is worth considering the impact on children.

First, though, the impact on mothers. There are rewards in having children, but how they pay for those pleasures, with interrupted sleep, incessant work, impoverishment, loneliness, dependence. Germaine Greer remarked that if men had children they would drive a harder bargain. 'They would demand financial commitment from the partner, insist upon guaranteed maintenance for themselves and their children, and force employers to provide day care and/or the state to invest adequately in the socialisation, education and training of their children.' (*Sunday Times,* 8 August 1993.) Fighting words from a feminist, but with the focus on adults. Here I want to focus on children.

The question is a minefield for a man to address. Emotions run high in both directions: in those who resent the assumption that a mother has to bury all her gifts and qualifications, carry the child-minding and house management alone, and leave her husband to do all the money-making for the family; and in those who feel furious that married women are taking jobs that other people need more. Let's risk a look at it.

You are making up your mind whether to take a job outside the home and wondering what effect it would have on your three children, aged four, six and ten, and on your husband. No matter what you decide, you may be criticised, to your face or behind your back. It is your decision, and it is the harder to make now because every year attitudes and possibilities are changing in the matter of mothers working outside the home. Shared jobs, flexitime, and using a computer to run a job from home, have all added to the openings for working mothers; but the organisation of the working place is still heavily biased in favour of the male.

What factors should go into your decision? *First* that children differ hugely from one another, and some — even in your own family — need you more than others. Some children, for a number of reasons, need more than just mothering. There are times when they need something like special therapy, extra attention. You are the only one who knows them well enough to read their special needs.

*Secondly,* in their first three years of life, children's development is speeded up by the attention of one person who knows them, loves them, and responds to them with an eye and care that nobody else can show. That one person is usually a mother, but it can be a father, granny, aunt, or somebody else to whom the baby is the most important being in the world. There is no hired 'expert' outside the home who can do the job as well as a mother figure.

Child-minders and crèche workers can help; but if the job is left to them, baby's development, of personality and abilities, will be that much slower. It is the mother's gift for reading the baby's language that brings him on. From sheer familiarity she can read the meaning of his cries and whimpers and quivering lips, and by responding, teach him that the world is attuned to him, that the world makes sense. In these first years, when the child does not understand his own needs, mother's presence as the primary child-minder has a particular power. The Irish proverb holds here: *Ní féidir leis an gobadán an dá trá a fhreastal*— The sandpiper (*gobadán* also means a very clever person) can't cover two strands at the one time — no matter how clever she is.

This does not mean that she has to be on the job twenty-four hours a day. It is the quality rather than the quantity of mother's attention that counts. Nearly all babies get used to someone other than mother looking after them at times, and both mother and child are the better for this.

Your youngest is four, probably able to explain herself, maybe even going to school. In deciding about work, you need to look into your own heart. Know what you really want, before you start planning. Do not mind what your neighbours and friends tell you. Do not mind what your husband expects. He is part of the decision, but only part, and sometimes (less so in the 1990s) men are old-fashioned enough to feel threatened if there is a another wage-earner in the house.

Be brave enough to ignore that, and see what your heart tells you. You may find the making of a home, and the hobbies that go with it, vastly more satisfying than a nine-to-five job with less responsibility or creative openings than home-making, but more attendant pressures.

Or you may be conscious of energies unspent, and abilities unused in the long days at home. You know you would be more contented if you had more to do. There are mothers driven to depression and boredom at home, who would find contentment in the stimulation of a part-time job. An interested working mother, who can still be available to her children, is of more use to them than a miserable house-bound mum.

If the *third* factor is your contentment, then the *fourth* must be your availability to the children if you are working. That needs thought and planning. You will have less time at home. Make sure you still have time with your husband and children, time to talk and listen and enjoy them. If something has to suffer, then let it be the housework. Better still, share the housework, so that everybody comes to understand what it takes to keep a home running.

The key factor in all this is that children grow and blossom in their parents' attention and responsiveness. They survive less responsive or present parents, but their development slows down. It would be doing them a poor service to earn more money so as to 'enrich' their lives with computer games or bicycles, if in the process you are taking from the emotional and intellectual quality of their development. In infancy that calls for full devotedness. Later it means being available and in touch with their experience, and sufficiently free in yourself to love them. That can be compatible with an outside job, especially one that leaves you more contented.

### Barely Surviving Sam

Sam's mother Anne stayed at home, but I found her at the end of her tether. Nine-year-old Sam was ruining the family with his temper. Every meal was a battle to keep him from bossing the three younger children. Under correction, he would burst out in angry reproaches that nobody loved him. His father was supportive, but was only there at nights. Anne was near defeat.

Sam was delicate, the survivor of several serious operations. Anne was conscientious and had high standards in the matter of control. She tried isolation (he screamed and banged the door down), slaps (both parents felt bad afterwards), holding him (he yelled the house down).

We shifted the focus from Sam to Anne, the one who was most at risk in the house. Sam was not enjoying life, but he was indulging himself. Anne was the main sufferer, and near the end of her resources. If she had to choose between her own survival and good order at table, she would certainly be right to choose her own survival. Unless she could function as a mother, everyone suffered, and grievously. She had to be able to enjoy something in her day and week, have something to look forward to. Nobody can operate as a mother in a state of unrelieved tension.

Her husband was a good partner as far as his work permitted him. But Anne engaged his help mainly towards managing Sam. His main task should be to ensure Anne's good health and spirits, to guarantee her survival as a mother. Money spent on this was more important than money spent on Sam.

This was not particularly welcome talk to Anne, because she suffered from a chronic sense of guilt. She was too conscientious, and had a conscience that took on itself everything wrong that happened in the house. In the lifelong tension — we all experience it — between the desire to control on the one side, and the forces of joy and exuberance on the other, Anne's balance was too heavily weighted on the side of control and quiet.

Every good family is a mess to some extent, and has its periods of chaos. All mealtimes are liable to involve some squabbling, as five or six people try to make their voices heard, their presence accepted. Much depends on the ability of parents to keep their own cool, to enjoy the exuberance and diversity of the children, not lose themselves in trying to shout down the bossy ones, but rather focus hard on those who would not be heard without that bit of extra encouragement. Anne started to give her precious attention to quiet Barbara, and ignore Sam's determined efforts to break in on her.

She had suffered so much to bring Sam to this point where he was a reasonably healthy and vigorous nine-year-old. He had needed two life-threatening operations, long periods of intense care, and even now, a higher than average vigilance on Anne's part in case of infections or over-fatigue. He had been handled, as it were, in cotton wool, and had become accustomed and attached to the emotional rewards of being delicate. It had been his privilege for so long, to be treated as though he was *the* special one, that he was reluctant to accept his position of one of a group of four.

In a way he was only being weaned now, years later than the normal child. He was learning that he is not the centre of the universe, not the boss, and that the world did not revolve around his needs. It was a hard lesson for him to learn, and he played on Anne's vulnerability, her highly developed skill in sparing him pain. She winced when he shouted 'You hate me! Nobody likes me!' It was not a statement of fact, but a blow struck at Anne's most sensitive point, a crude attempt to recapture the special emotional rewards he enjoyed when his very survival was in question.

Anne knew that in fact he suffered in school because he was a natural target for bullies, and found it hard to make friends. Some of that difficulty came from his history. Other children do not take kindly to a boy who feels he should be the centre, the special one. Because he was going through a bad time at school, despite the care of his teacher, Anne found it hard to apply at home the ordinary wisdom for dealing with attention-seekers: seek them out with attention when they are being good, and starve them of attention, positive or negative, when they are acting up.

Sam was not a bad child. He could be generous and thoughtful. He recovered from his temper and apologised. He was learning a hard lesson in those months, and Anne had to be the main teacher. She allowed him to express his feelings verbally, but did not shout back. He had to learn to control these outbursts, these feelings of hate. When Anne made firm decisions and stuck by them, she was helping him to control his rage. If she flew off the handle, she was adding to his sense of isolation, bewilderment and powerlessness. She stopped falling for his threats or attempts at blackmail ('I won't love you any more'), knowing that she would be paying off the instalments for a very long time. If he won every time, he would have no brake on his own powerful emotions.

That year, while Sam was going through a hard lesson, Anne ensured that there was some joy in his life. He loved drawing, and it was a blessed relief for the family when he could lose himself with paper and pencil, and work out some of his feelings through art.

Anne needed a resource like that herself, an area where she was not just coping with pressures, but expressing herself; a space of her own, free from feelings of guilt and obligation. Only she could know where best to find it — and it was not a selfish search. Unless she could survive and relish life, at least occasionally, not just Sam but the whole family were the losers.

## Surviving for What?

In a cosy bungalow near the centre of Ireland I met Eileen, another survivor whom I will never forget. She was nearly fifty, and the youngest of her eight children had turned ten. She loved them, but they had exhausted her, especially the handicapped one. Her husband could not face bad news or problems, just grew irritable and blamed her. Anyway he was out at cards seven nights a week. So she carried the children's problems on her own, and worked a full-time job because the farm was failing and the bank was threatening to repossess the house. As the children moved out one by one, she wondered had life passed her by. The children had her to worry about them. Who would worry about her?

You know the story of the priest, the parson and the rabbi arguing about when human life begins. The priest held out for the moment of conception. The parson thought it might come later, when the personality starts to form. The old rabbi differed from both: 'I know when life begins, he said. It begins when the children leave home and the dog dies.'

The story says something about Eileen's plight. Parents, especially mothers, differ so much in their reaction to the children leaving home. Some feel their life is over. Others, like the rabbi, feel that life is just beginning for them.

The Lord gave us our face looking forward, not back. We are meant to live life in forward gear, not in reverse. You do find people whose ideal is somehow the reconstruction of the home, often idealised, from which they started. I know middle-aged people, some of them nuns or priests, who at the back of their minds feel that happiness consists in 'getting things back to the way they were'. Religious people often see nostalgia as a respectable emotion.

Christmas is the time when this is often attempted. It is one reason why psychiatrists are extra busy in the approach to Christmas. Grown men and women feel pressured to go back to their parents and sit around the table like children. They revive the pain of old jealousies and rivalries between sisters and brothers. They feel again the old resentments of father or mother and feel they are playing a charade of happy families.

One recent Christmas I met a single woman in her thirties who was near breaking point. Her mother had died a year before, and her widowed father and two bachelor brothers expected her to leave her Dublin friends, go down 'home' — meaning her father's home, not hers — and prepare and serve dinner for the men of the house. She was being torn in two between feeling she could not refuse her father, and fury at re-living the role of the exploited daughter.

Most families live with one or two taboo topics, or truths which may not be mentioned, such as one parent's heavy drinking, the dominance of a bully in the family or the manipulative helplessness of one member who continues to be dependent on the rest. When you have left home you can face the reality of these taboos, and even see them as serving a purpose. But for a grown woman or man to go back home and live with them again is depressing, even infuriating, especially at Christmas when everyone is supposed to be happy.

In Eileen's case the taboo topics were obvious. Nobody mentioned the absence of her husband, who passed himself off in public as a good provider. In fact the farm was losing money, father could not face problems except by blaming, he absented himself with his cronies every night of the week, and the only thing that held the house together was the fact that Eileen was able to earn money and at the same time take the hassle of eight children.

Perhaps that is a one-sided view. The husband was indeed an incompetent farmer and an absent card-player. He certainly dodged any sort of emotional stress, and to that extent he had never grown up. He was de-skilled as a father; and here one can feel sympathy for him. At the age of fifty he was waking up some mornings well aware of these realities. He loved Eileen but did not recognise how dependent he was on her. He was fond of his children when they were good and affectionate and gave no trouble. What he could not take was their human failings. They could forgive him for being weak, incompetent and cowardly. What infuriated them and Eileen was his lying about it, and pretending to be the strong man of the house and father of the family. Unless he could come to terms with the truth, they would hold this against him.

Meanwhile, what about Eileen? Her contribution was heroic, especially the fact that she was not pitying herself or acting the martyr, but trying to sort out her present and future. If there was a Nobel Prize for ordinary living, it should go to the likes of her.

She was not looking for a medal or a prize. She was fighting with the suspicion that life had passed her by. She will soon have succeeded as a mother, in that she will have made herself redundant. Her nest is not empty yet, but that state is within sight. Ireland has too many full nests, homes with several reluctant chickens, young adults torn between the desire for independence and the comforts of a home where everything is paid for. Birds can teach human parents a lesson: when the fledgling is not sure he can manage, the mother gives him a little push that makes him stretch his wings and find he can fly.

Eileen's problem was not so much the reluctant chickens — she could give the discreet push quite effectively — as the mid-life crisis. For twenty and more years, her children had kept her busy. What will occupy her when they are gone? The next generation? Some women are so geared to children that they long for the arrival of grandchildren, to give them more babies to mind. Eileen was not one of them. She will be a warm and considerate grandmother when the time comes, but does not need baby-sitting chores to fill her life. She needs to be stroked, not just as a mother, but as a woman.

I think of a mother of eleven children, many of them artistic. She started to paint when they were all grown and struggling to make their way. Before long she found herself exhibiting and selling her creations, and had the satisfaction of doing even better than her children.

All over the country women like Eileen, aged forty-something, are looking around for chances of further education, or occupations which will keep them growing. Good luck to them. Like their children, they are moving into the future, not the past. They have done their mothering, not perfectly — only machines are perfect — but well enough to launch a family Now they are able without guilt to stay in forward gear, and plan a life in which they can receive as well as give.

## WHAT ARE FATHERS FOR?

Some years ago, in a boys' secondary school, I met a hall full of fathers, drawn by the topic: *What are fathers for?* He was a brave headmaster who arranged the meeting. The mothers, who form the majority of most parents' meetings, were curious and miffed at not being invited. A meeting which affected their sons was being held without them. They felt excluded. More often it is the other way round. Fathers often feel excluded from the life of their children, because they miss the intimate association with the baby and toddler that mothers have.

That is where the exclusion started, in the months of pregnancy, when mother's concerns began to centre around the baby, before and after birth, instead of around her husband. Even her language changed. She talked about Daddy (father and protector) rather than Joe (husband and lover). There was another male in her life, and much as the husband loved both of them, his status had changed.

In describing God's continuing care of us, Saint Augustine used a phrase that has stuck with me: 'God did not just make us and then go away.' The same is true of fathers. In one sense they cannot go away, though many of them try to, namely those men who make girls pregnant and then disappear. In those families, which in some housing estates form the majority of households, the mother and child may be furious at the absent father, but he is not really absent. For the mother he is the object of anger and maybe yearning, when she needs more support in rearing the child and surviving. For the child, especially the son, the absent father remains as a model of what it is to be a man: somebody who has his fun and then vanishes, refusing to shoulder responsibility.

## Bill's particular problem

That was not the case with my friend Bill, who once talked to me about feeling shut out from his only son Manus. He did not go away. He loved the baby even through the sleepless nights of his infancy and his messy destructiveness as a toddler. Unlike his own father, he learned to change nappies, feed Manus and take over when his wife was sick. He read to Manus, showed him that reading books can offer pleasure and excitement. For a while Manus was very possessive of his mother, and correspondingly resentful of his father. He once told Bill to 'get lost' when he came home from work and interrupted Manus' enjoyment of mother. That resentment was mixed in Manus with a fear that his angry wishes might come true, and he would be left without a father. At that stage Bill was able to absorb his frustration, fury and fear, and teach Manus that he could love his mother without eliminating his father.

Bill's wife Anne was so tolerant of Manus that at times he took advantage, and if she did not give him what he wanted, he would abuse her verbally and even hit her. If Bill had not intervened strongly, Manus might have grown into a habit that in fact made him very anxious as well as causing pain to Anne. Bill protected her from an abusive child.

He also had to save Manus from an over-protective mother. She loved babying him far beyond infancy. By contrast Bill showed Manus a love that was not just sheltering but also liberating. His presence and confidence showed Manus what it is to be a man, showed him that he was not merely lovable but competent. He enjoyed the skills Bill taught him, because they came from Daddy, to swim, draw, ride a bike, kick a football and mend things. Bill was more willing than Anne to let Manus experiment with independence, use public transport, go on messages, choose his own friends, manage homework on his own, and face the consequences of his own mistakes or carelessness if he brought bad homework back to teacher.

All through those childhood years Bill learned and practised a father's trade, and enjoyed it. Then what went wrong? In his mid-thirties he lost his job, and spent nine months at home while looking for work. He took over from Anne in the house so that she could do part-time work. His own discouragement and depression made him irritable with Manus. He could not see how much Manus loved having him around. Instead he felt he had failed his wife and children, because he could not earn a living or give a straight answer when friends asked:'What are you doing?'

He is a tidy, orderly man, and Manus' messiness annoyed him. Bill liked to keep things under control, and was admired as a decisive and fair football referee. But while his whistle could control thirty bruisers on a pitch, he seemed ineffective in getting Manus to do what he wanted in trivial matters. That period of unemployment sapped Bill's confidence in himself as a father. During it he said things to Manus that hurt him and caused Bill regret, though he never apologised.

I have been close to some fathers in this sad state, and been close to their sons at the same time. I would say two things to such fathers. First, though you think yourself irrelevant and unimportant to your son, because he seems to take so little notice of what you say, you are huge in his fantasy, still enormously important as a source of approval. Second, the key question for both of you to answer is: 'How can Manus please you?' He feels that nothing he does can please you, because you are so ready with criticism.

The change has to come from you, in this way. For three weeks — bring Anne in on the plan as well — deny yourself the right to criticise or blame Manus except in cases where Anne requires your help. Turn a blind eye to behaviour that annoys you but open both eyes to anything that Manus does that could please you. Take nothing for granted. Register every kindness, homework done, snappy dressing, success at games. Show that you can enjoy him as he is. Enjoy him in the ways he is different from you as well as the ways in which he resembles you.

## ALL HE NEEDS IS A GOOD SMACK

Smacking, like sex, grips our attention. Most of my generation have long and rich memories of different forms of corporal punishment. The last twelve years have seen a considerable change in our children. Since the Department of Education, in 1982, banned corporal punishment in schools, children are more critical of smacking, whether at home or school. They pick up from US-based comics and TV the notion of 'suing' anybody who hits them.

In fact, as I understand it, parents still have a legal right to use 'reasonable physical punishment' on their children, and teachers still stand in the parent's place, so they share that right, even though regulations (as distinct from the law of the land) forbid smacking. I do not know of any case that has been tried at law.

In a recent survey, six out of seven Irish adults said they had been smacked at some stage, and a large majority rejected a suggestion that corporal punishment should be banned by law. So smacking is still, and is likely to remain, a legal option for parents, even though the climate of opinion about it is changing. Religion is quoted on both sides, but the springs of Christianity are found in the attitude of Jesus, who brought the noisy children to the front of the crowd (Mark 10,13) so that he could bless them and spend time with them.

What does smacking do to us, and to the children we may smack? There has been enough dispassionate research here and in other countries to help us make up our minds.

First, there are countries with children at least as well-behaved as our own, where it would be unthinkable to strike a child. Two contrasting examples are the former USSR and Spain. It is not that they did not use punishment. In the USSR there was a carefully developed system for correcting children who misbehaved, through their companions as well as their parents and teachers and even their parents' employers. They had a whole array of effective sanctions, which did not include hitting them.

Parents smack their children because they feel angry at what looks like persistent disobedience — for instance, Brendan has repeatedly messed with the gas fire, or hurt his little sister. If punishment is to be an effective deterrent, it has to be used carefully, soon after the offence, and in such a way that little Brendan associates it with what he has just done wrong. The trouble is that what triggers the smacking is more likely to be exasperation and strong emotion in the mother (most corporal punishment at home is administered by mothers) than a careful plan for eliminating a specific misbehaviour.

In general, children cannot remember the reason they were smacked, so they are unlikely to avoid that behaviour in future. Smacked children are generally not sorry for what they did; they are so overwhelmed by indignity and pain that they are angry rather than remorseful. The only reason they do not retaliate (as they would to a brother or sister) is because of their parent's overwhelming size and power. There is clear evidence that smacked children tend to take it out on smaller children. Whatever else they learn, they do tend to remember the lesson that is modelled by the parent: if you are really fed up with somebody doing something you dislike, you hit them.

One other finding must be mentioned. An unexpectedly large number of children who are repeatedly smacked, end up with actual injury. Shaking a baby can cause whiplash. A light blow from an adult catches Brendan off balance, and he hits his head off something. A smack aimed at his bottom hits his spine instead. A clip on the ear can burst an ear-drum (in fact Irish law has made a definite ruling here: a clip on the ear is one form of smacking which has been found 'unreasonable punishment' even from a parent, because of the danger to the head).

You sometimes hear from older people the phrase 'All he needs is a good smack'. If only it was as simple as that! The smack may be good at venting the grown-up's emotions. For the child it is seldom good, and seldom an effective way of learning to behave.

So what is effective? Many of the misbehaviours of children carry their own sanction. You warn Brendan that if he bosses or bullies his local friends, they will not play with him. He goes on bossing them, and they melt away. You may help him to draw the lesson from it. He needs no further punishment. You watch him playing roughly with his new toy car and warn him it will break. He does not heed you, and it breaks. He is sad, and with your help he will learn from the experience.

Discipline means literally a way of *learning*. It is concerned with teaching, rather than winning victories or getting control. Its aim is for Brendan to learn to control his own behaviour, and much of that learning can come from the sanctions that are built in to misbehaviour. There are plenty of sanctions other than smacking that are used by Irish families: such as giving Brendan extra chores in the house, or confining him in a dull isolated place for a few minutes, or withdrawing a privilege, or grounding him. But most mistakes of discipline are made because they focus on punishing bad behaviour rather than rewarding good.

## Stefan: Father's Obsession v. Baby's Needs

It may need an extreme case to demonstrate a basic attitude in a parent, and the ambiguities inherent in the notion of parental love. Love entails allowing for separateness and difference, and few parents would say they fall down on that. It may take a happening on the brink of one's normal existence to show where priorities lie between a parent's selfish desires and the needs of children.

One such story was unfolded to me by Anne, an Irishwoman in her sixties, who lived and married in North America. Her only child, a bright and promising girl, started dating a Chinese fellow student in medical school. Stefan, Anne's husband, objected: 'Why couldn't you go out with a white boy? I don't want to have slitty-eyed grandchildren.' The fact that Stefan himself was of mixed race added an irrational vehemence to his objections.

Stefan and his daughter both stuck to their guns. Eventually the daughter moved out of home, and the father made his own plans. Unknown to his wife (though she soon found out), he fathered two children by white women, who each received $10,000 while another $10,000 went in each case to the lawyer who arranged the deal.

The first part of his plan succeeded. He found himself with a healthy white baby boy, followed six months later by a healthy white baby girl. But where and how to rear them? His wife had by now confronted him and he begged her to act as mother to his two babies. Anne deliberated and prayed about it seriously. She knew that if she once met the children, and picked them up, she would grow attached to them, and all other potential helpers would melt away. But she, in her mid-sixties, would probably leave them in the lurch by sickness or death before they were properly grown. With the warm heart and hard head of an Irish countrywoman, she told her husband: 'You have made your bed. Lie on it. We have a good marriage, and I am staying with you, but not as a mother to these babies — it would be unfair to them.'

Stefan saw children as possessions, there to serve a parent's needs. When he realised that his alienated daughter was not going to be there to care for his old age, he thought that $40,000 of his hard-earned money could buy him a substitute. He had not thought through the rearing of his bought babies, and soon discovered that money could not buy what a child needs if it is to grow into a human being.

The other angles of the story are intriguing. How could a man of markedly mixed race be so intolerant of his daughter's mixed race choice? How could a father be so unaware of his daughter as a separate person, and imagine her as something between his princess, his servant and his health care investment for old age? Once the babies were born and delivered to their father, what plan could have best served their interests?

The end of the story vanishes into the western mist. I never met Anne again. She was determined to keep the marriage intact, but to let her husband look after his children. I was left with a clear sense of her wisdom and strength, but also with large questions about a culture which could allow such production of children simply to serve a man's racist whims.

## NOTE

10. Penelope Leach, *The Parents' A to Z*, London, Penguin, 1983, p. 246

# *Daily Stuff*

The daily texture of life with children has changed in many ways. Eating, sleeping, work and entertainment are still there, but today's parents face decisions that my parents never knew.

## A Finicky Eater

Eleven-year-old Raymond was presented as a finicky eater. He demanded a different menu from the other three children. His mother did not mind the extra work, but wondered if it was the right thing for her son.

She touched me on a raw spot. As a child I was like Raymond, so I know his angle. At home I was faddy about food, and Mother indulged me, although that generally meant I was allowed to fill up with bread and jam instead of vegetables. The first time I played truant was in order to avoid having to eat a cooked meal (instead of Mother's sandwiches) in a primary school. I was healthy until I went to a boarding school where they stood over you to see that you ate every last bit of fat, every spoonful of milk pudding, both repellent to me. In another boarding school, I was allowed to starve rather than eat the wartime menu, which included horsemeat and moist bread with lumps of potato in it. This time it did affect me, in arrested growth and frequent sickness.

So I have thought a lot about children like Raymond, whom I meet often. Faddiness has different meanings at different ages. In a toddler it is one of the first ways of establishing independence, of saying No to Mother. Family

104

meals are a perfect battleground for him; his mother cannot ignore him, because she worries about his nourishment, and she cannot really win the battle, because she cannot force-feed him.

Wise mothers avoid a battle using their cleverness and experience to refuse to be drawn into a struggle they cannot win. They try from the very beginning to treat eating as a pleasure, are more concerned about baby's enjoyment of feeding than about the mess, and help him to take over responsibility for feeding himself as soon as he wants to. If he has never been forced, as an infant, to eat more than he wants, or anything he dislikes, he will enter the toddler stage with only positive feelings about food and the business of eating it.

A friend in the USA adopted a Guatamalan boy of three, who had been out on the streets of his rural village as soon as he could walk. She was struck by the assurance of José about his needs. He would look for food when he was hungry, stop as soon as he had had enough.

He had learned early to look after himself, and had none of the faddiness of his neighbouring Californian toddlers, for whom food was a way of getting at mother. They would ask for ice-cream or sweets to see if mother loved them, not because they were hungry. José, old for his years, could not understand them. Early on he had learned to forage for food. But in most homes, mother makes all decisions about who eats what. She was the original provider, with milk from her breast or a bottle. For most of us there is a tight link between food and mother, and how we relish our food reflects to some extent how we are getting on with mother at the moment.

From early on it is important to encourage mealtime independence even at the expense of manners. The first lesson must be that mealtimes are pleasant: not a time for prolonged imprisonment in a high chair, not a time for quarrels, or repeated corrections about table manners; nor yet a time for showing your disapproval of mother by turning up your nose at what she provides. If baby faces the approach of 'one more spoonful for Mummy', he will quickly learn that this is an area where he can exercise power over her.

Fourteen million children die every year of malnutrition. Raymond will not be one of them, even if what he wants to eat is nothing. His appetite will save him, and if he is offered food, not forced to eat it, but barred from eating between meals, food can remain the pleasure and privilege it really is, rather than the miserable duty it can so easily become.

This does not mean that Raymond should enjoy a special menu. He had in fact been checked for allergies. It is important to avoid what damages health, but one child's meat is another child's poison. Some children react badly to foods of a certain colour or texture or sweetness, while others thrive on them. Many children are made giddy and restless by white sugar, sweets and soft drinks. I have known parents improve the calm and concentration of their five-year-old by removing fizzy drinks from his diet. Allergies are individual things, and it is only the parents who are close enough to observe the effects of each change of diet.

If a toddler learns to look on an apple, or piece of cheese, or celery, as a treat, he will not regard sweets as the only sign of mother love. If children are offered some variety of food, they will generally eat enough to keep them healthy. Their own felt needs are a better guarantee of health than their parents' dietary theories.

The taste for sweet things in particular can grow and grow, and the range of junk food now available has certainly complicated parents' decisions. So has the possibility of 'grazing' in some better-off homes, where there are virtually no sit-down family meals, and children survive by raiding the fridge, or heating a commercially prepared snack in the microwave, then eating it in silence while watching TV.

What have the grazers lost? They have lost a chance to meet the family, listen to them and tell them what is happening in their lives. They rapidly lose the taste for cooked food with a flavour, in favour of the bland and almost flavourless confections of the microwave. They have certainly saved time, which they use looking at visual pap, as bland and forgettable as the stuff they vacantly push into their mouths while viewing. Convenience and time-saving — for both parents and children — are quoted to justify the grazing habit. But a price *is* paid, in the chance to talk and listen and know what real food tastes like. You do need to ask: what is the time saved for?

By the time he is grown, Raymond will need to be able to plan and cook healthy meals for himself, to budget and shop for himself and maintain a reasonable weight. Spells away from home will almost certainly teach him to experiment with foods which he claims to hate. In fact his mother weaned herself from the job of preparing his special menu, by teaching him how to prepare the special things he wanted himself. It became clear then that it was not the food he wanted, but her extra attention. For both their sakes she moved him, without forcing, but by means of his own hunger, into a more catholic appetite.

## GOING TO BED

One third of our lives is spent in bed, and the rituals surrounding it make up much of the daily stuff of family life. Just as food is not merely nourishment, but carries the overtones of mother love, so bed often has deeper connotations. For most of us it is sweet nature's second course, releasing us from weariness and recharging us for the next day. For the depressive it is more than that, a blessed release from the oppression of conscious existence. For the lover it is the place of heightened existence, of climax. No two children will think of bed in the same way, but it is striking how many find it a place highly charged with tensions or pleasures.

Going to bed can seem to them an arbitrary separation imposed by their parents. Take the extreme case of thirty-year-old Denis who still lived at home with his elderly, rather fussy parents. They had not really noticed, in the daily routines of home, that Denis was now a man. He did not get on well with them, but could not gather the energy to move out. When his father would say 'It's time for bed', that was a signal for Denis to reach out for another paper and mutter 'I'll be up soon, Dad'.

Resisting bedtime had become such a habit for him that at thirty he was regularly spending most of his nights in an armchair, where he had fallen asleep over the papers. He would wake in the early morning cold and stiff, tumble into bed, and then oversleep the alarm, because he felt that getting out of bed, like getting into it, was something his parents were doing to him. He lost two jobs through being consistently late, before he realised that he was treating bedtime as something imposed on him by parents, not as part of his own responsibility.

Now there was more to Denis' case than reluctance to go to bed, but it shows how big a price can be paid for bad sleeping patterns, and how important it is to avoid the pitfalls. Children are so different from one another in temperament. They differ in the regularity of their habits — some babies have a lovely rhythm about their time for eating, sleeping, evacuation, while others are unpredictable. They differ considerably in their need for sleep, as adults do. Parents are the ones who know those needs. Tiredness shows itself in baggy eyes, in marked reluctance to rise in the morning, in daytime sleepiness and unscheduled dozes. Usually this is because they have stayed up too late, which in turn points to using television unwisely. (Some families do not think of 'using television'. They feel used by it, as though they had no control over it.)

Most children fall asleep within twenty minutes of 'lights out', and while individuals vary in their needs, the *average* sleeping pattern of different age-groups has been established: nine hours for six to seven-year-olds, eight hours for those of 10–11.

The research does more than establish averages.[11] It points to the pattern of management that prevents trouble arising: a standard, unremitting pre-sleep routine, set by the parents, and allowing only very rare exceptions; a period of progressive settling down. Children learn best if they are put into their cots/beds while still awake and are encouraged to soothe themselves. The parent tucks up the child and retires, proof against any delaying tactics. And the baby or child grows accustomed to reasonable levels of household sounds, so that the house is not required to be bound over into a hushed state.

If this pattern has not been established, and problems arise, much depends on the ability of parents to use practical advice, such as the use of 'systematic ignoring' of children's protests.

Jim Horne comments: 'It is remarkable how the behavioural problems of children's sleep can be resolved so quickly by the right approach, and frequently to the amazement of parents who over months of anguish may have become desperate for "a good night's sleep" for themselves as well. Parents easily forget that infants and children are usually much more adaptable than themselves, and very forgiving of what may seem to be short but harsh treatments.'

Between the ages of twelve and twenty, children should gradually learn the ability to choose when to go to sleep, and when to wake up. They should be increasingly in charge of this part of their lives, as they are able to manage their own patterns of eating and drinking and exercise.

One of the important boons of bedtime is that it leaves the parents free for one another, or free to be on their own. The hardest lesson for any child is that mother does not belong exclusively to him; there is another man in her life, who has claims on her time, affection and bed. Parents have needs too, and a right to time on their own. They need to fight for their rights, because they will not be easily ceded by children who want to sit at the fire, or TV, as long as Mum and Dad are there. From early on, children have to learn that parents require their own privacy and time. Even if children are being sent upstairs before they are ready to sleep, they can read or listen or talk. Part of the issue is not their needs but those of their parents.

With older children it is wise to separate bedtime from sleep time, so that if your Louise actually needs less sleep than you do, she is content to spend extra time in the privacy of her room. She will usually welcome this kind of 'private time', provided she has a place which feels like home and provided that you do not come barging in saying 'Why isn't your light out?' when she had planned to read. Privacy is two-way. You can have it for yourself by offering it gradually to growing children.

I remember one Louise who started sleep-walking in her third year at secondary school, when she had just started working for her first public exam, and was anxious about it. She would get out of bed — usually early in the night when her parents were still up — and wander around the house, showing an accurate sense of where the stairs and furniture were, but acting like a robot. The first night her father told her to get back to bed, and when she did not respond, gave out to her for disobedience, which woke her into a wild and distressed state.

This could have led to a vicious cycle of worry and reproach, but fortunately both parents realised it had been a mistake to wake Louise, and instead gave her extra attention and showed their concern over her adjustment in school. The sleep-walking soon disappeared. It is a strange habit, as Louise could remember nothing of it the next morning, and was quite unaware of what was going on around her. The danger came from the panic of her parents, and from Louise picking up their anxiety which would then have added to her own.

A difficult part of bedtime is competition and comparisons between children. The youngest often become impatient for the privileges of older children. Staying up is seen as a privilege, where for grown-ups it is a privilege to go to bed. From early on, bed needs to be seen as a pleasant place, not just for sleep, but for being secure and warm, a haven for the child's own possessions, safe from disturbance, with her personality stamped on the colours and furnishings and decorations; not a punishment cell but a personal castle, with all the special things, books, teddies, posters, that are precious as she grows.

For some children sleep remains frightening, a time when you lose control, and people the darkness with the fearful shapes created by your own fears and imaginations, and sometimes with the terrifying things you have seen on television. Little boys may have a fascinated appetite for horror films, but little tolerance for them.

Why do parents allow children to watch horrors? I know how urgent the demand may be from your children. 'Everyone in the class is allowed watch', they say. Never believe it. Phone around and ask. Except for the producers, there is no profit in such films, nothing human, only fuel for fear, as directors become cleverer and cleverer in their use of music and special effects to surprise and frighten even the most hardened viewer. Children have too many unresolved anxieties, angers and fears, ready to take over the imagination. Their nightmares often show vividly how the imagination meshes these fears with the horrors of the small screen, to make sleep and darkness a place peopled with terror.

For all children, bedtime should be a time of blessing, when parents and children are reconciled after the rows or differences of the day, and the needs of the family are placed firmly before the heavenly Father. It is a proper time for prayer together, between light and darkness, between waking and sleeping, when we are surrendering control in a moment that is at once sweet nature's second course, and a foretaste of death. They need not be long or burdensome prayers, but a confident commending of ourselves and our family to the one who loves us.

## The Problems of Sleep: Control and Wetting

There are other hazards in sleep. Because we surrender conscious control, the body is sometimes slow to wake us when the bladder is filling. I think of a nine-year-old who still wets the bed five nights out of seven. He has been handled gently, and is quite embarrassed about it now, especially if other children hear about it. The doctor says he has no physical complaint, and his mother wonders has she been too soft with him.

Not too soft, no. Brian does not enjoy his state, and scolding only makes it worse. Nobody likes to wake up wet, cold and smelly, with the awkwardness of looking after pyjamas and bed-clothes. By Brian's age, nineteen out of twenty boys have learned to be dry at night, so he is something of an exception.

Up to the age of five, one cannot speak of bed-wetting as a problem. Children learn bladder control at different ages, girls faster than boys. Many normal five-year-olds are only beginning to be dry at night. They have occasional dry nights, or at least their bed is dry for some hours each night, and they occasionally wake and go to the lavatory unbidden.

Between five and seven years of age about one in ten children is still wetting at night though maybe not every night. By ten years of age the proportion of bed-wetters is down to about 3%, and by fourteen only 1%. The time to start looking for help is in the sixth year of life, if there is no sign of the child beginning to be dry at night.

There are of course practical ways of helping, by managing the type of bed-clothes in such a way that laundering is easy and unfussy, and ensuring that Brian is able to wash well in

111

the morning, and that the bed is not allowed to become smelly.

Bed-wetting runs in families, in the sense that parents who were themselves late to train, will tend to have children who are slower than average; they may also tend to use the sort of unsuitable and stressful methods of toilet-training which produced their problems.

There may be a physical abnormality, such as a small or oddly shaped bladder, or an obstruction of the urinary tract: a rare condition, and one that a doctor should pick up. Kidney trouble and urinary infection are common in bed-wetting, but they are not the whole explanation. In fact sometimes they can be an effect rather than a cause, and curing the infection will not put an end to bed-wetting.

There is often a history of stress in the first four years of life, the loss of or separation from a parent, or brother or sister, or hospitalisation in the early years. Where this is the case, parents will usually be able to report other signs of distress as well as bed-wetting. The child will register unhappiness during the day as well as in sleep.

Many mothers report that their bed-wetting child is a deep sleeper. In fact there is no evidence that the pattern of sleep, or of brain-waves shown in the EEG, has any connection with the complaint.

Obviously if there was an easy cure for Brian's complaint, he would not have survived this way to his tenth year. At this stage he needs professional help — and quite a few professionals are in a good position to help: family doctors, psychiatrists, community nurses, psychologists. The one you approach will want first to assess carefully the history of the bed-wetting, all aspects of how Brian sleeps, how his wetting has been handled, and whether it is associated more with schooltimes, or sickness — all the circumstances in fact.

The treatment of choice will vary. Many children are cured by the prospect of the first appointment or tackling of the problem. Some may be helped by lifting during the night and restriction of fluid intake in the evening hours; others by the use of tricyclic anti-depressants, which, while they have the disadvantages of all drugs, may be useful in obtaining a rapid relief from the symptom, as when the child is about to go on a holiday, or when his wetting has become the focus of hurtful and hostile reactions from others.

Of the regular methods, the most effective and safest is the 'bell-and-pad', essentially a systematic way of conditioning Brian into dryness after first enlisting his co-operation. It is not an automatic cure, and needs to be combined with explanations, a progress chart, and encouragement. One needs professional advice in setting up the treatment, and the apparatus has become more efficient and less intrusive over the last few years.

Prior to that, the family should avoid anything that could be punitive or shaming for Brian. That is unChristian and counter-productive, and postpones the time, which will certainly come, when he can be securely dry at night.

## HOUSEWORK: SHOULD MOTHER BE A MARTYR?

In eating, sleeping and bladder control, one can map the progress of children from dependence to taking control of themselves. The same is not always true of housework. Some children grow into their teens without any awareness of putting out the bins, ironing, shopping, budgeting, cooking, cleaning, de-frosting the fridge. If asked about it, they say 'Ask Mum'.

Let's imagine an upset. Mother develops acute appendicitis tomorrow, is totally out of action for three weeks, and has to take it easy for at least another month. What will happen to the house? What are the minimum jobs needed to keep the household going? Would father and children be *able* to tackle them? Have they learned the skills of shopping, cooking, cleaning, and managing all the machines and gadgets that help mother? Would they feel dreadfully put-upon if they had to work in the house? Does mother always have to call on a relation or neighbour in an emergency? If so, then it is time to start involving the family in the running of the house.

Here is a project I sometimes set for children on the edge of their teens. It may require a couple of weeks, but it is full of interest for the household. Get each of the family to fill out the following table.

The project may demonstrate that mother is carrying nine-tenths of the household burdens without anybody noticing; that household jobs are seen as ways of 'helping mother', and that mother thanks the helpers as though *she* should really be doing all the chores.

| Job | Hours spent per week by: | | | |
|---|---|---|---|---|
| | **Mother** | **Father** | **Children** | **Others** |
| Shopping | | | | |
| Organising household | | | | |
| Keeping records, bills, etc. | | | | |
| Preparing/cooking food | | | | |
| Washing/drying up | | | | |
| Cleaning house | | | | |
| Looking after car | | | | |
| Repairs in the house | | | | |
| Gardening | | | | |
| Washing/ironing/ mending | | | | |
| Physical care of family, baths, hair, etc. | | | | |
| Any other tasks | | | | |
| Total: | | | | |

If mother is doing everything *for* her children, what is she doing *to* them? She is teaching them that children do not have any responsibilities around the house. They are learning nothing about how much time, effort and skill are needed to keep a household going from day to day. They are taking a great deal for granted, and probably have no idea how much effort mother and others put into looking after them. They are missing out on the feeling of accomplishment of a job well done. There are several skills they could learn but do not: to cook, clean, mend fuses, handle machines, and so on.

Of course there are mothers who enjoy acting the martyr, and their families have grown used to leaving her suffering in the kitchen while they watch TV or disappear. There are mothers who are convinced that they can do all the housework better and more quickly themselves, and do not like handing over work to others.

If they carry all the burdens like this, they are actively teaching their husbands and children a falsehood, namely that they have no responsibility for the home, and deserve to have everything done for them.

The other option, of sharing the work, obviously requires planning and teaching. Little children have to be taught to tidy their bed and room, clean their shoes, care for their dirty clothes, hand out the washing, clean the car, lay the table, hoover, dust and polish, not to speak of more complex tasks like cooking, mending and managing machines. Teaching means pacing the work to the ability and age of the child, explaining why the work is needed, allowing for their feelings and frustrations, making all criticism constructive and specific, and accepting that in the end the job may not be done as well as mother would do it.

Where children are reared in this way, they are not doing things for mother. She is doing something very important for them: not just imparting useful skills, but instilling the basic conviction that we depend on one another, and can never afford to take one another for granted. It is one lesson that Irish men, in particular, need to learn from the beginning.

## LEARNING THE VALUE OF MONEY

Money is an emotional topic for old and young. Adults work hard to earn it, and maintain the discretion in how to spend it, when so many envious or dishonest people want to do that for you. Children cost money; and though we are happy to spend it on things we know they need, it can be aggravating to see them go through it as though it grew on trees.

Families differ enormously in attitudes to children's pocket-money. It is generally not true that the more the father earns, the more the children receive. In fact, the reverse would seem to be nearer the truth. It is hard to suggest guidelines for any family, but a couple of questions have to be answered first.

(i) Do you see pocket-money as a regular and consistent allowance, which little Liam will claim as a right, with no strings attached? Or do you regard it as a reward for good behaviour, which can be withdrawn as a punishment, and which remains, week by week, at your discretion? If you want Liam to learn how to budget and use money wisely, then it should be regular and predictable. He is not likely to learn to save if he is not sure if and when the next allowance is coming.

(ii) Are you and Liam clear about what expenses it should cover: buses, sweets, club subscriptions, toys, hobbies, school books and stationery? When Liam tells you how much his friend Seán is getting every week, does he also know what Seán has to pay for? As they grow older, children can cope with larger sums, and can budget for their transport, or save for bigger expenses. Obviously you retain some control on how Liam spends it: you will not let him ruin his teeth with endless sweets, or his health with junk food. But unless you leave him some discretion and control, the whole point of pocket-money, i.e. learning how to use it, is lost.

(iii) Do you allow Liam extra earnings, such as tips for doing jobs? If so, do you keep an eye on his standard of performance, and rule out sharp practice? If children share responsibility for all the work of the house and garden, yet are paid for washing up, cleaning their room, or polishing the car, you are implying that these are extra for them, jobs that by rights you should be doing yourself, and are hiring them to do for you. That is not a healthy road to go

116

down. It is difficult to decide what should be paid for and what not, and it needs to be a joint parental decision.

In parent-teacher meetings, pocket-money is a topic parents are loath to discuss, a delicate, emotionally charged topic, on which differences between families are vast. I would suggest working on these lines:

(i) Let pocket-money be regular, starting small and increasing regularly with age, but with the understanding — and children have to understand the reality of poverty — that if times are bad, it may be cut back. The purpose is to help Liam learn to manage money. For that, the allowance must be regular, not capricious. Set your own standards, immune to the blackmail of comparisons with other children. It is no shame to be worse off than other people.

(ii) Encourage saving for a purpose such as birthday presents, but do not expect little children to do much saving. Their ability to postpone satisfactions varies hugely.

(iii) Discuss money with Liam: the point of bank accounts (as a teenager he should start one), the hazards of borrowing, hire-purchase and credit cards, the folly of buying now and paying later, despite the bad example of politicians and 'businessmen' who over the years have led their followers or employees like lemmings over the cliff of bankruptcy.

(iv) Blessed are the poor in spirit, who do not believe the lies of advertising, nor think a man good because he possesses much. This is the other side of teaching our children to manage money. In a world saturated by advertising, we need constant reminding that some of the best things in life cannot be bought with money. Children may learn some of this by listening to us, but much more by watching our lives.

# INTRUDERS IN THE HOME: THE SMALL SCREEN

Most thoughtful parents have at some stage considered throwing out their TV set, as the only way to cure children's addiction. What bothers them is not just the programmes, but what it does to the family to have the set always as a competitor to conversation. Is there anything to be said for it?

The way you use TV is every bit as important as the school you choose. The question is not 'What does TV do to us?' but 'What do we do with TV?' Can anything be said for TV? In some families it is like asking 'Can anything be said for food?' It is the staple way of filling the idle hours, it is on day and night, and life would be unthinkable without it.

In one way it is like bed. When people are depressed and their life is empty, they often retreat to bed. I notice the same about television with both children and adults. If they are bored with life, or depressed, or in a down phase, then they will slump in front of the set almost uncaring about what is on, but anxious to keep control of the programme buttons. If they are interested in the people around them, and in living, then they may pick out the odd TV programme they want to watch, but otherwise they have too many active things to occupy them, and they cannot afford the time spent in front of the box.

Like bed it is addictive. Even in the middle of sparkling company or lovely scenery, eyes can be drawn to the flickering screen, no matter what is on it, in the hope of titillation. If we allow it, it does things to us. It startlingly reduces conversation between children and parents.

An English speech therapist has shown the link between speech problems and unselective watching of TV in young children. The years from two to six are so rich in possibilities. The mind is developing and learning faster than at any other time of our life, moving from silence to the capacity for speech, which gives us access to reading and all other human learning. You cannot read until you can understand speech, and you learn to understand and use speech through conversation, above all with parents.

They can make sense of the first utterance of the toddler, and gradually build up their vocabulary and confidence in

118

talking. Why cannot TV do this? After all it is a talking medium. But it is not a listening medium. Little Mary cannot answer, she just sits dumb, and if she were to mutter back there is no sign that she is heard, which is the only incentive to go on talking.

This is equally true of computer games, which are said to be 'interactive'. The only interaction possible is the child's manipulation of the mouse or joystick, not speech. Our experience of computer games is still too fresh to allow for serious research on their effects. In the four years since they first featured seriously on the Christmas lists of Irish children, they have swollen to a £7 million market. They are deliberately addictive, eliciting alternately frustration and boredom, which keep young fingers on the joystick (though some children are more liable than others to enter this addictive slavery).

However like television, computer games are here to stay. Until there is legislation to rate them according to their level of violence, parental vigilance is all-important. The concerns of parents — at least of those who can see beyond the attractions of an electronic baby-sitter — centre round the addiction, which keeps children from more active and creative occupations; and round the violence which is built into most of the games. Children are conditioned, at least temporarily, to think, feel and plan like the actors (Super Mario, Sonic Hedgehog or whoever) whose destiny they control in the games. The conflicts they face are commonly resolved by bombs or bullets, kicks or punches; and it is hard to believe that this programme for success does not affect the player.

Fathers have intervened after watching their sons carry out screen executions, or act as sadistic warders whipping prisoners into submission. The limited research on the impact of games suggests a worrying link between addiction to them and violence. Parents have worried also about the stereotyping in many games — women as victims, Orientals as enemies. Intervention need not mean banning games, but selecting them and the conditions in which they are used.

What conditions? That children have a balance in their lives between solitary games with the computer, and social activities and sports; that they limit screen time to an hour at a stretch, and ensure that children do not sit too close to the screen; that the computer is placed in a social area of the home, to avoid the worst scenario, of a child playing alone in a darkened bedroom for five hours.

If children are to learn the uses of a computer, it is wise to spend money on an IBM-compatible PC which can take them forward from games to word-processing, accounting and other computer activities, rather than confine them to a console for video cartridges (the console market is dominated by Sega and Nintendo) that plugs into a TV set. There are mail-order firms that specialise in selling games that mix education with entertainment. There are programmes and magazines that offer useful reviews of the games in a market where prices and products are constantly changing. The danger for many parents is that they know so much less about these games than their children do, and allow themselves to be bullied into purchases which they quickly regret. They need to play the games, know the choices available, and select as carefully as they would choose a school or a teacher for their children. Games are as powerful as parents allow them to be. Like drink, TV, food and all the rest of creation, they are good things that we can learn to use well or foolishly.

While those who play computer games are active and involved (though not creative — the creative minds are in the inventors who design the options from which the player can choose) children who view TV are passive. If they turn on the set without questions or curiosity, view unselectively and switch programmes frequently, they remember practically nothing, any more than they remember the individual drops after standing under a shower. (You can easily test this by asking them on a Tuesday morning about Monday evening's programmes.) Children are often hosed with TV in an unselective, passive way that leaves them soused, unthinking, but heavily dependent. In a study of North American four-year-olds, one third of the children would more readily have done without their father than without the TV set!

The children at risk are easy to recognise: they watch more than ten hours a week, go straight to the set when they come home, demand from the parents the sort of instant gratification that they experience in channel-control, a variety of delights at the press of a button. They relate more feelingly to TV characters than to their own family and friends; and they gradually lose the capacity to express themselves.

If this happens in a family, then communication between parents and children drops sharply. Children lose the capacity to entertain themselves, and the ability to express ideas logically (the quick switching of cameras and scenes in a TV programme is no training for logical thinking). What about the emotions? There is much sentiment in TV plays and soap operas, but the effect is a stereotyping of emotions. Children live through the predictable and shallowly-drawn feelings of the familiar characters on the screen, and lose touch with the range of feelings they experience themselves, delight, loneliness, anger and tender love. Unselective viewing is paid for by damage to communication, to thinking and to feeling. Grant Noble in his study of TV and Irish children[12] found that pupils' schoolwork suffered if their viewing was unplanned and unselective, so that they became passively dependent on spoon-fed, over-simplified mush, and lost the ability to think, write, create or feel for themselves.

Some parents feel helpless against TV, and they *are* helpless until they decide to *use* it instead of being used by it. They give much thought to choosing a school and following up school reports, but have no strategy for managing the alternative education from the box. The key to using it lies in being *selective*, choosing programmes in advance, picking some films or documentaries that can be watched by parents and children together, a shared experience that can bond a family, showing one generation how the other thinks and feels. When that happens, children have been found to view TV through the filter of their parents' values. With father or mother beside them, they can cope with stories that might otherwise bewilder or upset them. The box is no more powerful than you allow it to be.

## NOTES

11. Jim Horne, 'Sleep and its Disorders in Children', in *Journal of Child Psychology and Psychiatry*, Vol. 33, p. 472, March 1992

12. Grant Noble, *Children in front of the small screen*, London, Constable, 1975

# *How They're Shaping*

You cannot pigeon-hole children. They cannot be described with an adjective, much less summed up as a problem. All the same, there are times when a mother, watching her child intently, feels that there is one focal issue in his development which needs tackling. This chapter is shaped by such issues, and comes as a set of letters to mothers.

## To the Mother of Speechless Jean

In the exciting years between the ages of one and six, when a baby is learning faster than at any other time of her life, perhaps the most exciting development is that of speech. In this, as in most other areas of development, girls move faster than boys. As little Jean learns to put names on people and things, and then to combine those words into ever more complex sentences, her own interior life, of thought, fantasy, emotion and memory, takes off like a rocket. From day to day parents see dramatic advances in talking and understanding.

Baby-watchers have charted the progress of language in average children: three words spoken with meaning at twelve months; three-word sentences at twenty-one to twenty-four months; the appearance of pronouns (I, we, you) at twenty-four months; non-stop chatter by the age of three. That chatter is not conversation but monologue. It is only gradually that children develop the ability to listen, and later still to give and take conversation in a reciprocal way. We all know people who never learned it, and whose marriages are a dialogue of the deaf — but that is a different problem from yours.

The average child is just a statistic. Any number of children develop faster in some areas and slower in others. When Thomas Carlyle was ten months old, and had not uttered a word, he heard a fellow baby crying and suddenly said 'What ails thee, Jock?' From then on he spoke in sentences. The understanding of words is of greater importance in assessing a child's intelligence than the ability to say them.

If Jean is slow to speak, it may be that she is working hard at some other skill, such as walking. When that is achieved she may make a quick breakthrough in speech. At the moment her energy is being used elsewhere.

Or perhaps she is getting less than her share of attention because of a sister or brother near in age, who draws most of the interest of the adults in her life. It is from their attention that Jean will learn to speak. Sometimes it is the adoring attention of big brothers or sisters that delays a little one's speech. They interpret her needs, answer questions for her, so that she has little need to speak for herself. Their chatter at table may be so continuous that Jean has little chance for face-to-face chat with her parents.

One important possibility to be explored is loss of hearing, in particular high-frequency deafness. I once knew a boy from a silent farmhouse with elderly parents, who reached the age of eleven before his teachers noticed that he was very hard of hearing. An observant mother or father will normally notice whether a child reacts to ordinary noises; initially by crying or blinking, and after four months by turning his head towards the source of the sound.

A boy with high-frequency deafness will respond to passing cars and clapping hands and other low-frequency sounds, but miss some of the pitches used in human speech, such as consonants, particularly 's' and 'f'. Obviously the least suspicion of hearing loss should be followed up as soon as possible with your doctor.

If there is no hearing defect, and if young Jean shows her intelligence in other ways, such as recognising the names of things (even though she does not say them), then it is a matter of stimulating her and having patience. A low level of intelligence will show itself in late development all round. Jean is not like that. Keep talking to her, pointing things out to her, communicating with her in all the ways a mother and father know how. One of these days, like Thomas Carlyle, she will ask you what you were worried about.

## To the Mother of Clumsy Andrew

He is ten, and has always been clumsy. He writes slowly, is poor at games, and it took him ages to learn to tie his shoe-laces (you have resorted to slip-on shoes for him). He is left-handed and right-eyed, and you want to help him in any way you can.

You can help him enormously. About 10% of children are cross-lateral like Andrew — their preferred eye and preferred hand are on different sides. They may need more help than most in learning left-right orientation and hand-eye co-ordination. Andrew, when reading or writing may tend to move from right to left of the page, or may be simply unsure. When you see that uncertainty, you can tackle it in various ways.

Tie a coloured ribbon to his left wrist, or a piece of wool to his left finger: 'That is the side of the page we start from.' Without badgering or pressurising him, make sure he knows left from right. 'Show me your right ear, your left hand, your right elbow... Touch your left ear with your right hand...' Ring the changes on these games. Play them with him on his own, away from the possible remarks or mockery of other children. As with all teaching of your children, if you find yourself impatient or irritated, give it up till you are fresh again.

Apart from that, any left-handed child needs a little more help when writing, to wean him, if necessary, out of the awkward position known as 'the hook', where his arm is curled round the paper, and his pencil is tilted towards the body. This style tires him more quickly, and with pen-users, often results in smudging the words he has just written. Move him instead into a comfortable position with the top left-hand corner of the paper slightly higher than the right, and the paper placed slightly left-of-centre of the body. Andrew sounds as though he needs more practice at writing. You can make it more fun if you work with him, for maybe fifteen minutes a day. Dictate something simple (easy to spell) and interesting to him, and make a graph from week to week of the words he writes in a given time, to give him a sense of how his speed and control are improving.

Children like Andrew may have difficulty too in sequencing, remembering things in order. You can help him by working over the commonest sequences, days of the week, months and seasons of the year, letters of the alphabet, important telephone numbers. Again it has to be done as privately as possible, and as a game rather than a pressurised lesson.

There is still the clumsiness. As a parent you learn to live with it without adding to Andrew's embarrassment. Remarks like 'Watch you don't drop that', or 'Let me do it for you', are not a help. They sap his confidence. The sort of help he needs is to have lots of time to learn and experiment for himself, with your encouragement. He may need extra time to dress himself, make his bed, manage his dinner with knife and fork.

A sympathetic teacher will arrange that he has extra time for writing down his homework, and even for completing a test.

The way out of clumsiness is practice, lots of it, using both the large muscles (running, skipping, swimming, hopping, dancing, throwing) and the fine muscles (work with pencil, paint-brush, computer joystick, scissors, jigsaws, Lego and so on). Get him to help you in the kitchen, even if it slows you down. Provided you have the patience and calm for it, you can be Andrew's best teacher, and offer him ways of developing into a handy boy. That sort of teaching is impossible in a large school class, but quite manageable at home.

## To the Mother of Restless David

Your seven-year-old David is so restless that he gets on everyone's nerves. He can't sit still, and his teacher is always complaining about his lack of concentration. You wonder does he need a doctor for his hyperactivity?

Our parents had not heard the word 'hyperactive'. Perhaps you have read *The Myth of the Hyperactive Child* (by P. Schrag & D. Divoky, London, Penguin, 1981), which is a warning about what labelling can result in for children. In the USA over a million children are being given drugs to 'treat' behaviour problems. If David was in school there, he would be more likely than in Ireland to be referred to a doctor and put on medication of some sort to slow him down.

The label of 'hyperactive' is abused, overused, there. There are children being treated as medical cases where the problem is really one of management and education. When teachers, faced with major problems of controlling students, start to medicalise them (by using terms like 'hyperactive' that sound medical), the scene is set for the abuse of medication.

Of course there are children who are so restless that they are hard to live with and to teach. You can call them overactive, but that does not mean they have a medical condition, or need a doctor. The cause of their restlessness can be emotional or temperamental or just boredom.

Most parents will recognise the restlessness that comes from boredom. Such children have not enough scope or space to use up their surplus energy, and the remedy is not so much in themselves as in their circumstances. One of the basic needs of children is for new experience, for a chance to move their limbs, explore, and try out new feelings, materials, places, textures and skills. Their curiosity may be hard to live with in the years when they ask questions all day; but it is one of the most precious God-given gifts. Aristotle saw it as the spring-board for all philosophy and science, for all man's searching. If curiosity dies or wilts, or is killed by the put-downs of parents or teachers, nothing, not even the best schooling in the world, can substitute for it.

It is harder to live with the restlessness that is caused by the child's organic disposition, and is there from early infancy. All mothers will recognise how newborn babies differ in their output of energy, and also in their attention-span and distractability. The hyperactive baby needs less sleep, wears out clothes, toys, and later shoes and bikes. He (most of them are boys) is fidgety, cannot keep his hands to himself. His attention span is short, shifting and undirected. He is never still, keeps rising from the table, from his bus seat, his desk in the classroom, his place in the cinema. He is always rushing and impulsive and is more prone to accidents than most children.

Some restlessness is common in children, but hyperactivity springing from temperament is severe, is there from morning to night, is evident from infancy, and is associated with serious defects in attention and concentration. It is quite clear in children by the age of three or four, and already by that age parents will have suffered a great deal. The hyperactive child is seen as a messer by other children, he finds it hard to keep to the rules of a game, so he has few friends. In school the teacher finds him a nuisance, sometimes ascribes the restlessness to naughtiness, and is provoked into anger, which sets up a vicious circle of aggressiveness in the child. But hyperactivity is not necessarily associated with aggressiveness.

At the beginning of this sad story is an organism like an overstrung fiddle. There need be no brain damage nor any physical condition that can be identified as odd. At one stage these children were misleadingly referred to as MBD (Minimal Brain Damage): the current description is ADD (Attention Deficit Disorder). Many brain-damaged children are not hyperactive, and many hyperactive children are not brain-damaged. The two need not go together. But for David's parents and teachers, his condition may pose problems more severe than those of a physically handicapped child.

For those who live with him, the first essential is to recognise where the problem lies: not in the adult (sometimes mothers and teachers blame themselves for not managing well) nor in the naughtiness of the child, but in his body. If the parents start to feel guilty or self-reproachful because David is a nuisance in public places, they will lose their calm, which is indispensable for grown-ups handling very un-calm children. So often the problems of hyperactive children are heightened by the parents' feelings of guilt, anger or helplessness.

They are not helpless. There is a place for medication to slow him down, but the dosage needs to be monitored constantly. There is a price to be paid: you notice a difference in David's reactions when he is on medication, as though he is not quite himself; so there is a case for confining medication to those periods, like school term, when concentration is particularly needed.

There is a place for diet too; I have seen restless children transformed by faithful adherence to a diet that respected their allergies; but identifying these allergies requires medical help.

Apart from medical help, there are immense differences between the Davids who are managed intelligently and calmly, and those who experience a constant diet of irritation and anger from the adults around them. Calm and intelligent handling must start early, with a recognition that David is distractable, impulsive and restless to a degree far beyond the normal. The whole family needs to share this recognition. To give David his best chance, he needs regular daily routines, firm, clear and positive indications on the behaviour expected of him; and in school, short-term, easily attainable targets, constant feedback on his successes, structured learning, and positive focus on good behaviour rather than bad. Easier said than carried through.

Let me quote a useful summary of accepted wisdom:[13]

1.  ADD children make up 3.5% of the population, but many children who have trouble paying attention may have problems other than ADD. A thorough evaluation can help determine whether attentional deficits are due to ADD or to other conditions.

2.  Once identified, ADD children are best treated with a range of approaches. Best results are obtained when

behavioural management programmes, educational interventions, parent training, counselling and medication, when needed, are used together to help the ADD child. Parents of children and adolescents with ADD play the key role of co-ordinating these services.

3.  Each ADD child responds in his or her own unique way to medication, depending upon the child's physical make-up, severity of ADD symptoms and other possible problems accompanying the ADD. Responses to medication need to be monitored and reported to the child's physician.

4.  Teachers play an essential role in helping the ADD child cope with the procedures and demands of the classroom. Sensitivity to self-esteem and frequent parent-teacher contact can help a great deal.

5.  ADD may be a life-long disorder requiring life-long assistance. Families, and the children themselves, need our continued understanding and support.

6.  Successful treatment of the medical aspects of ADD depends on on-going collaboration between the prescribing physician, teacher, therapist and parents.

## To the Mother of Aggressive Michael

Your Michael is always getting into fights, whether with his brothers at home or with boys at school. You seem to be for ever trying to break up fights, and grow weary of it. He is ten now and you wonder will he ever learn to keep the peace.

Is Michael bothered by the problem as much as you are? You must often have heard the protest, when you go to break up a fight 'But we were only playing, it isn't serious'. Michael is your first boy after two daughters, and his boisterousness took you aback after the gentleness of his sisters. Male aggressiveness is not just a matter of how boys are reared. It is in part biological. Boys are generally more physically aggressive than girls, and some boys have much more energy than others.

By the age of sixteen Michael will almost certainly be able to live without fighting, both with brothers and with school companions. He will still feel angry about upsets or injustices, but will have found calmer and more effective ways of responding than just hitting out. Even now you will probably find that while Michael may squabble with his brothers at home, he will stick up for them at school.

Meanwhile you have your problem of whether or when to interfere if you see a fight outside. Sometimes interfering really helps the children. It protects the weak against the strong, and may save Michael from becoming a bully. At other times you are right to let children alone to learn to sort out things for themselves. Michael is always going to meet people in life whom he does not like, and he must, however slowly, learn tolerance and how to control his temper.

You have a number of optional strategies:

(a) *Refuse to get involved:* this throws Michael back on his own resources, but sometimes children are not able to sort things out without adult help.

(b) *Interfere in person, give out to the fighters:* this will protect the small and weak, but may lead to children relying on you for defence.

(c) *Urge retaliation:* this may lead to Michael learning self-defence, but the tit-for-tat method rarely solves anything, just leaves the fighters angrier.

(d) *Urge withdrawal:* this is physically the safest way, but it may not always be possible, and can lead to Michael being walked on or called a coward.

(e) *Try reasoning or diplomacy:* this does help to develop Michael's ideas of right and wrong, but it may be difficult for Michael to accept, and sometimes his idea of what is fair will differ from yours.

There are advantages and disadvantages in all these strategies. You know your Michael better than anyone, and have probably tried different approaches. Be clear about one thing: is it your problem or Michael's? Which of you is more upset by the fighting? I have known some parents successfully set up a fighting hour, at a time to suit the parents, during which all the quarrels of the day are sorted out. All squabbles have to be saved for this special hour. In many cases the quarrels will have evaporated by then, and children find it hard to fight to order. But Michael may simply not have the level of self-control needed for that remedy.

If you decide that you have to intervene in a fight or quarrel, one general strategy is useful: *Impose a truce, and help the children to work out a treaty.* Your size enables you to put an end to the physical and verbal abuse of the quarrel. Then get the fighters to agree on what was the cause of the row. If this is achieved, then get them to suggest positive solutions to the problem — they can be both inventive and fair if given a chance to be heard. In this way they escape the notion that somebody always wins and somebody always loses, because the solution is usually a compromise. The emphasis is not on punishment but on everyone giving a little. The quarrellers are given the job of sorting out their own problems. You are simply imposing a framework of peace in which they can learn to find their answers. You do not have to be judge and jury, so it is easier for you to keep your cool.

Since Cain killed Abel, men have tried to solve problems by striking the other down rather than talking and listening. Our own country has its share of the curse: adults who are emotionally infants, who imagine that problems can be solved only by winning or losing, with the fist or bullet. As parents and teachers we can rear a wiser generation by interfering in fights when children need us; and then by imposing a peace and letting them work out the treaty.

## To the Mother of Bad-tempered Seán

You find your eleven-year-old worse-tempered than other boys of that age. He constantly fights with his older sister and younger brother. Obviously you know children, and can be fairly objective about what you see. Sometimes parents report on their children's aggression in tones of such depressed resentment that you can feel the anger is in the parent more than in the child. Parents who suffer from depression know, or should know, that the world they see is darker than the real world, and charged with threats and aggression which are projected from their own inner misery rather than a reflection of the people around them. But you have watched three children growing up, and find Seán different.

Can you understand his anger? Human aggression is mysterious and deep, much more mysterious than the aggression of other animals. We are the only species which will follow through attacks on our own kind to the death, and that on a massive scale We can find entertainment (watch TV tonight) in the sight of humans maiming and killing each other. In this we have regressed since the beginnings of theatre. Among the Greeks violence was never perpetrated on stage. Bloody deeds were never seen, only reported by a messenger. A Martian visiting our island, and finding humans fighting, even drawing blood, over politics, football matches, or patches of land, would be mystified. *Star Wars* is a human invention, not something we have observed in any other species. It is self-defeating, everybody loses, and it seems to make no sense in human terms.

To move from the cosmos to the little boy, Seán's aggression may stand him in good stead as a footballer or businessman. It probably stems from a high level of energy and assertiveness which you have seen from his infancy. He needed outlets for his energy, and was frustrated by the sort of inactivity that would be bliss for a less energetic child. But in the family his aggression is destructive.

The first and last remedy is to preserve your own calm. He does not like losing control, and if he sees you reacting with hot anger, it makes him panicky. I often wonder how far we have unlearned the old Semitic attitude of 'an eye for an eye and a tooth for a tooth'. Our children's anger provokes our own, and some fathers even feel it is their duty to be visibly furious and violent, to retaliate in kind, as though he and the child were on the same level. Whatever about duty, it just does not work. Do not let his way of treating you determine your way of treating him.

This does not mean there is no place for anger in a parent. Look at Jesus whipping the money-changers from the Temple, and overturning their tables, and you see anger at its most appropriate and effective. It was a human response to an abuse that turned Jesus' stomach. Mothers and fathers are entitled to anger on occasion, when they are dealing with calculated malice and selfishness. Most children's faults are not of this nature, and most parents' anger is in fact more destructive than appropriate, piling guilt onto children who already know how foolishly they have acted.

How often have you been kept waiting for a child — whether eight or eighteen years old — who comes home long after he was due? The dinner is spoiled, your plans are possibly ruined, and your impatience is mixed with panic about what may have happened to him, and anger and resentment at his thoughtlessness.

On these occasions, watch what your *first remark* is, when eventually he shows up. He comes home knowing he is in trouble and at fault. You will be tempted to start off with an outburst about his thoughtlessness and how you have worried, and there is not going to be any more of this nonsense. That will put an end to all real conversation, and lead only to a heightened row. If you want to do him any good (as distinct from venting your own indignation) start with a neutral remark, possibly even a thoughtful and concerned one — 'You look as though you could do with a cup of tea'. Then there is some hope of going on to talk about what kept him late, and reaching the truth.

Apart from keeping calm, remember that anger involves physical changes that require discharge. The angry boy has different brain waves, high blood pressure and peripheral circulation, a faster pulse, an outpouring of blood sugar, more rapid breathing, less sensitivity to fatigue and pain. Also he is less sensitive to arguments. When Seán comes home in a bad temper, you may be weary yourself, and annoyed that he brings only grumpiness into the house, but there is no point in saying that for the moment.

First accept him as he is, show that you know what he feels like — he does not enjoy being grumpy — and then you have some chance of being heard by him. You can accept angry *feelings.* Feelings are innocent, they come unbidden, and our children have to learn the difference between the involuntary feelings, and wilful acting on them by being nasty, in word or deed, to others, especially brothers and sisters. 'You can't help feeling angry, but that gives you no right to abuse Mary, or to hit her.'

Because anger affects the body, it is usually wise to look for some constructive way of using up the physical energy other than in fighting. Football or running or working in the house or garden, or riding a bike — all these can be precious outlets in a moment of temper. It may not give you any moral satisfaction. You have not pinned the blame on Seán or received an apology. You have simply diverted the energy that might otherwise have gone into a fight. And you have kept yourself calm and out of the centre of the hurricane.

If there were easy ways of soothing human anger, the world would long ago have become a better place. It is a lifelong struggle to learn not to meet violence with violence — always the weak response in fact — but with adult calm. Children are mimics, and they copy the response of their parents to stress and conflict, whether that be an intolerant fury like the baby screaming because he is hungry, or the calm thoughtfulness of a mother who sees the storm signals in Seán's face as he comes in the door, anticipates the sort of situations that may trigger an outburst, and instead steers him towards an activity that will use his energy and help him feel better about himself. When we think about children's anger, we are always pushed back to thinking about our own anger and our own capacity for calm. 'Lord, make me an instrument of your peace.'

## LEVELS OF OBEDIENCE

### (i) To the Mother of Four-year-old Simon

He is your first child. Your husband is strict, with high moral standards, and he thinks you spoil Simon. You wonder when will he develop a conscience, and understand the meaning of obedience.

Are we agreed that Simon was born without a conscience? Some adults seem to think that there is a little voice inside a baby and toddler, programmed by God, which will tell it what to do and what not to do. Nonsense. That little voice develops gradually, and it is programmed by the parents. God gave us a capacity for developing a conscience. Notions of right and wrong are to be found in every human culture. The shape, content and severity of that conscience came from our upbringing, not from some God-given programme. Many adults reach a stage when they are wise and free enough to look hard at the 'Do's' and 'Dont's' they received from their parents, and criticise them. 'They were too severe about sex and not strong enough about honesty' — or the other way round. But for the first few years, the little amoral creature born to you, a bundle of needs and possibilities, is still learning, and you two are the teachers.

What is Simon learning? What is the aim of your instruction? Not to make him obedient to you, and dependent on you for instructions, but to control himself, to obey his own conscience. He will not know how to behave until he can tell himself. Somebody defined a little child's conscience as 'the still small voice that tells you somebody's looking'. It is a description that would fit the behaviour of many adults in our society, for whom the only real sin is to be caught out. If we want to make a better society, we can start with Simon, as you are doing.

It is easy enough with a baby, because we know he cannot do anything on purpose, he cannot be obedient. His behaviour is made up of involuntary expressions of physical need, and spontaneous reactions to your behaviour. If he cries, you read his need and meet it, with an insight and care for your own baby that nobody else in the world can rival. There is no such thing as spoiling a baby. You do not lecture him, or tell him to wait. At this stage the basis for goodness is built up by your timing and consistency in meeting his needs, so that he develops a trust in the world as a place that is geared to him, and that makes sense.

As Simon grew to be a toddler (and the age for this varies considerably with the child's endowment and rate of development) he became more than a bundle of needs and reactions. He became an active, exploring, often negative and difficult child caught in a real conflict. One part of him hankers for the security of his early paradise when he only had to cry and his needs were met. The other part wants to be separate and increasingly independent, trying out new skills like walking, talking, handling things, opening windows, sticking fingers in plug-points, dipping them into wet paint for its colour and texture, and putting all sorts of objects, of all levels of dirt, into his mouth.

This exposure to the irrational, uncivilised activity of a small child can be unnerving, especially for a parent with a strong conscience and sense of control. The desire to control Simon's activities starts with concern, even with panic, at the possible dangers he will get into. It can move into a sort of moral indignation: 'When is that child going to learn to behave himself?'

What matters is not so much *when* Simon will learn, as *how*. The foundation is his love for you. Other things being equal, he would rather please you than displease you. But a moral approach by a parent, stressing obedience and 'Do it because I tell you to do it', will not work. He builds up a conscience gradually, and a good summary of how to help it comes from Penelope Leach's *The Parents' A to Z*.[14]

(1) *Do as you would be done by.* Simon will not show you more consideration and respect than he receives from you.

(2) *Register and reward good behaviour.* It can be so easy to find yourself rewarding unwanted behaviour, like an ice-cream for the whining child in the supermarket.

(3) *Try to keep your instructions positive.* 'Do' works better than 'Don't', because small children prefer activity to inactivity, and because being forbidden to do things easily arouses rebellion. If your instructions are negative and dictated by your fears, you will put

strong and concrete ideas into children's heads: 'Don't drop that glass now... Don't point that gun at the baby.' Rather than shout 'You can't eat that in the sitting-room', you are more likely to get results with 'Bring your plate and eat here with me'.

(4) *Be clear in your instructions.* Few are less clear than that phrase so beloved of teachers and parents: 'Behave yourself.' It may mean 'Don't do anything I wouldn't like', which leaves a considerable task for the child, to work out what will or will not be acceptable.

(5) *Whenever there is time, tell him your reasons.* You are trying to build up his self-control for the time when you are no longer around, and for this he must be told again and again *why* he should not drink the paint, or walk on the flowers, or poke fingers in the power points. Prohibitions and protections by themselves will not help to build up self-control. He must start to understand.

(6) *Keep a sharp 'No' for emergencies.* If you fill your days with cries of 'No', the word will not pull him up short in the crisis when you want to stop him from stepping onto a busy road.

At Simon's age it is easy to become so involved in everyday rebellions, accidents and bursts of temper that you forget the overall purpose of your journey with him, namely that he learn to manage himself. Some parents are so strong on control and so short on explanation that the child never takes responsibility or learns self-discipline. Other parents are so strong on the moral virtue of obedience that the child, as yet unable to grasp principles, simply feels he is disliked and disapproved of. The parent's art is to gear your teaching to the state of Simon's development, to teach good behaviour positively in terms that he understands, so that he slowly learns about right and wrong in that accepting atmosphere of love which is the basis of all moral development.

## (ii) To the Mother of Ten-year-old Sarah

Sarah is growing up is a scene very different from that of her mother's childhood. We obeyed in a more unquestioning way than today, but also we were protected more totally than we can protect our children now. Unquestioning obedience to grown-ups was inculcated into our grandparents. It would be foolish and dangerous to inculcate it into our children, because they are exposed to so many adults who cannot be trusted: not merely the opinion-makers in the media, but the man who tells a little girl to step into his car, the smooth talker at a party who persuades a boy to try this drink, or that cigarette. We have to teach our children from an early age to be questioning and to discriminate between orders. The old attitude of obedience to adults will not help them.

You are Sarah's mother, with authority over her, and something is going wrong between you. Suppose we forget the word 'obedience' for a moment, and try to understand why she does not co-operate when you ask her.

You tell Sarah to come in for tea, and she wants to finish her game with friends. It would be over-simple to label this as disobedience: she does not want to defy you, or to be guilty of a moral fault; but she is caught in a *conflict of desires,* between obeying you and finishing her game. It may be that you can compromise, and give her ten minutes more play without spoiling the meal.

You told Sarah not to go out, and ten minutes later you see her in the garden. If you give her time to explain, it turns out that she thought you were banning her from the street, not from the garden. *She did not understand the order.* Again it would not help to label it as naughtiness. Sometimes our orders are not all that clear. I have heard a mother say 'Don't make too much mess' — that sort of vagueness invites trouble.

You told Sarah to buy butter on the way home from school, and she arrives without it. This may be tiresome and careless; but *forgetting* is a different thing from disobedience

You tell Sarah to keep away from Jean, because you have reason to think that Jean is bad for Sarah. Next day you see the two of them coming out of school together. Again it does not help greatly to see it simply as disobedience. Friends are terribly important to a ten-year-old, and Sarah is caught in a conflict of loyalties, which she certainly would not wish on herself. You may well be right about Jean, but you have to spend more time explaining your worries to Sarah. To write her off as a disobedient child is to ignore the real dilemma she faces. At the moment *what you ask seems to her impossibly difficult and unreasonable.*

You tell Sarah to tidy her room, and an hour later you go up to find her stretched on the bed, listening to music, with chaos around her. Here at last you have disobedience: she is out to defy and annoy you. Does she succeed? You certainly won't solve problems by fuming and invoking the fourth commandment. Keep your cool and avoid a fight: 'Fancy you acting like this. You must be in a silly mood.' She is out to provoke you, and you refuse to be drawn. You still have to work out what is making her like this.

Families cannot survive without obedience. But when there are problems, it is often better to seek the reasons why our children do not co-operate, than simply to quote the fourth commandment at them.

### (iii) To the Mother of Unmanageable Gerry

Your Gerry will only do what he wants; he gets harder to live with every year. After nine years you accept that something has gone very wrong with the rearing of Gerry: he is unbiddable, still as self-willed as a three-year-old.

You have taken me through the origins of this when you talked about Gerry as a toddler. The marriage was rocky then, you felt unloved, and found it hard to say no to the cries of little Gerry. In that second year of life, when he should have been learning that his needs are not the centre of the universe, and that there were other people in your life, things went wrong. He should have learned the limits to the illusion of omnipotence — 'cry, and what you want will be done' — that helped him through the first precarious year of life.

The trouble with Gerry and thousands like him is that they never learned that lesson. He continues to think that his wanting something means that it will be provided. In some families, by shouting, and manipulating adults, the child manages to remain the almighty boss, the way the baby was. He still lives with a fantasy of omnipotence, because his parents have been unable to confront him with their authority. They need to set limits, gently and firmly, to encroach on the power of the boss.

Gerry is nine, and still thinks he is in charge. If he retains that illusion as he goes into his teens, you are likely to face still more behaviour problems, possibly leading to delinquency; and anger will be added to his defiance. You have a battle to win, harder and longer at nine years than at two years of age. You will not win it by anger or violence. If you are to win you must plan the campaign.

I wonder is your husband with you on this. Without him it will be twice as hard. You have something precious to give Gerry, self-control, worth more than all the toys in the world, and only you two can do it. I must first ask: Are you in control of yourselves? Can you manage your own temper? Or are you sometimes so exasperated by Gerry that you lash out at him? Battered children have parents who are unsure of their own self-control, and feel doubly threatened when their children are hard to control. They lash out, with fist or foot, and children are seen in hospital or school with the tell-tale bruises (there is always a made-up story about accidental falls) that the hospitals know as NAI (Non-Accidental Injury). If you feel that danger, then the first task is to assure control of yourself. Learn how to walk away quickly if you feel yourself in danger of being violent or losing your temper.

The next stage is to improve the relationship with Gerry before you tackle the real problem. How? By overlooking a lot of misbehaviour and focussing only on the behaviour in him that you can praise. It sounds simple, but is fearfully difficult, especially if things are as sticky with him as they sound. Both sides are hard, turning a blind eye to boldness, and finding things to praise in a child who aggravates you. It is a crucial step, and I have known households turn themselves completely around by working simply at this. Until you have eased the tension between you and Gerry, it will be almost impossible to move to the real problem.

That consists in tackling non-compliance, and consistently establishing yourself and your husband as the ones in charge. The full programme calls for calm parents, clear, positive and limited targets (doing what you are told first time), rewards for compliance, maybe a chart to graph Gerry's improvement, set sanctions for disobedience, and consistency and persistence in the programme. When applied with constancy and courage, it works. Before that you must ensure control of yourself, and improve relationships with Gerry.

## To the Mother of Foul-mouthed Tom

Your ten-year-old Tom is not unduly aggressive, but he is foul-mouthed. You know where it comes from, the gang of friends at school, whose swearing goes beyond anything you hear among adults. Is there anything we can do to clean up his speech?

It should be easy, but it isn't. It jars on me when I hear 'F... off' floating up to my window from the children (aged six to twelve) playing outside. It is all round us, in a way that it was not twenty years ago. Girls as much as boys, mothers as much as fathers, are using unthinkingly what was once called soldiers' language. Not as a matter of emphasis, not as an expression of anger, just a habit. If I pick them up on it, they are often unaware of what they have said. It can be good-humoured: 'It was f..... great in school today.' The adjective adds nothing to the message. He does not know he has used it.

In one way it is simply a sign of stupidity. Swearing is the refuge of the inarticulate. If you can't think of the right word, you throw in the soldier's word. It does not make people sit up; it is just boring but also offensive. It is possible to make an impression with simple language. What we hear now is not just the soldier's word, but every variety of 'strong language' which has now lost its strength. Really strong language is achieved when you say exactly what you want to say, with the right words. When people (and the example comes largely from films and TV) do not know enough to find the right word, they throw in an oath, so that what was once strong language becomes weak and cheap.

A mother is annoyed with her five-year-old: 'If you do that again, I'll break every bone in your body.' The boy is bright enough to know that she cannot carry out that threat, so he is relatively safe. If she had said what she meant, he might have heeded her. This kind of language shows a law of diminishing returns. When you want to impress, shock or chide your child, you cannot, because he has heard it all and worse, from you or others before.

Apart from debasing language, is there anything wrong with swearing? Most oaths are either sexual in origin, and refer to sex in a debasing way; or blasphemous, and refer to things or people which through the centuries have been revered as holy. I must add that among children, the word that currently seems to be the ultimate insult, 'knacker', is neither sexual nor religious, but an expression of class distinction, or snobbery. Does that say something about them?

Those who know the Ten Commandments may be moved by the command to keep God's name holy, not to take it in vain. Those who do not know the second commandment should still take account of the feelings of others, and the possibility that they may be deeply offended.

What to do with Tom?

First, lay down the law in your own home. What is acceptable and used in other homes will not wash with you. Standards vary greatly from home to home. Have the courage and persistence to stick to your standards. If you feel strongly enough, and have the energy to carry through the system (obviously father and mother must be in agreement on this) open a Swear Box, to hold the fines (perhaps 5p for children, 10p for adults) for swearing in the house, the proceeds to go to charity.

Secondly, accept that most children use swear words at some time or another. Words like bum, bottom, knickers, have a fascination for children of a certain age, and cause great giggles, because they are 'naughty words' — but they lose their interest and become an accepted part of ordinary vocabulary. Make clear to your children the difference between words like these, and swear words, which are sexually or religiously offensive.

Thirdly, it is important not to over-react to bad language. If you show too much disgust or horror, the child will have succeeded in provoking you. Better be bored than shocked, but insist, with a minimum of fuss, 'Not that word in front of me, please'.

Fourthly, set a good example. Say what you mean without overstating, and avoid the sort of overstatement that leads to swearing in children. There is something to be said for substitute swear words when you are really worked up. They can express your strong emotion, without offending others' sensibilities.

As with every other aspect of child-rearing, children learn more from modelling than preaching. Teenagers may swear to look big. Children may swear because they cannot control their temper. They find it hard to be calm, and resort to foul language to give vent to their emotions. Don't let their way of treating you determine your way of treating them. Remain unimpressed and calm, but insistent: 'I don't want you to use that word.' As with Jesus' words, which were mild but unforgettable, it is not so much what you say, as the way you say it that counts.

## To the Mother of Centre-stage Sally

Ever since you fostered Sally at the age of six (she is eight now), you have marvelled at her sense of drama, she is such a little actress. You wonder should you let her grow up with this insatiable desire to be centre-stage in every company.

It is a dangerous thing to associate occupations with personality types, but it is done all the time: librarians supposed to be withdrawn types, accountants obsessional, clergymen exhibitionistic, referees authoritarian, and so on. Like so much in journalism, it conceals a small half-truth in a generalisation that does not stand up. We would not spend so much time watching films and plays if everyone who acts had the same personality type. All the same, there is something in what you say, and in the name you gave to Sally.

She does tend to take centre stage. She loves to be on show, and in many ways she fits the description of the hysterical personality: 'dominated by the urgent need to please others in order to master the fear of being unable to do so. This results in restless activity, dramatisation and exaggeration, seductiveness, either social or overtly sexual in manner (often creating disappointment in the other person), and immature and unrealistic dependence upon others.'

I have read what her teacher said about Sally, in a perceptive report: 'She day-dreams quite a bit and has not separated reality and fantasy sufficiently. She combines naivety with egocentricity and a lack of self-confidence. She craves attention *all* the time, and needs to monopolise the attention of adults and children. This leads her into trouble with both her peers and her teachers. On the other hand she is attractive, kind and compassionate, and really talented.'

In fact, despite acting the princess, Sally is a defeated person, who considers herself incapable of competing with others on equal terms. More especially she feels herself to be disregarded. If a child finds that grown-ups do not appreciate her needs, or try to meet them when they are made manifest, she becomes demanding and attention-seeking, exaggerates her needs dramatically, or adopts tricks to get what she wants indirectly. The deafer parents are, the more the child has to shout to gain their attention. Sometimes (it happened more often a hundred years ago) hysterics develop symptoms to gain by sickness what they cannot gain by request.

Since hysterics feel unlovable as well as ineffective, they often try to make themselves appear sexually irresistible, by dress and make-up. This is not a sign of vanity, but of neglect. It is those who have never received enough attention who lavish attention on themselves.

It is not true that most actresses are hysterical, but it seems true that many hysterics are drawn to the stage. Why? First, it offers an opportunity for the display of emotion, something at which hysterical personalities are often expert.

Secondly, actresses, if at all successful, are approved and applauded by the crowd, and this collective adoration is important to someone who has not felt appreciated by her own family and who consequently has no inner conviction of being personally acceptable. Even though the rewards of the stage are superficial and the audience is fickle and unfaithful, it thrills Sally to be a public figure.

Thirdly, actresses are by definition playing parts, pretending to be someone other than themselves. Sally has failed to gain what she wants by being herself, and so is prone to adopt all kinds of masks and roles which she hopes will be more acceptable to those around her. In doing this she loses touch with any sense of continuity in her own personality, any sense of the inner core which constitutes the real 'I'. Sally comes alive, feels more real when acting a part than when confronted with her own inner emptiness.

There is no sudden insight that will make Sally more at peace with herself, although as an intelligent girl she should, with time, gain more sense of her own style and personality, so that she can manage social encounters better. When she is in good form, or when she is wounded by being rejected by her peers, help her to see her own desire to be centre-stage, to hold teachers' or other adults' attention, and her difficulty in being just one of a group and accepting low-key existence and drudgery; and how this can contribute to her difficulty in making or keeping friends or getting a good report in class.

More important than insight is trust. Sally is passionately anxious to find someone who understands and cares for her, and at the same time has almost given up hope of ever finding such a person. She is apt to behave badly in order to find out whether you will be able to tolerate her, whether she has to earn her place in the family by good behaviour.

From your own account, Sally is suffering the effects of maternal neglect throughout her early childhood, before you fostered her. In her attachment to you, she may repeat over and over again the disappointments of her childhood, because she makes impossible demands upon you and then becomes furiously disappointed when those demands are not met. She is apt to be impressionable, and easily influenced by others or by fads. She is apt to be overly trusting of others, suggestible, and showing an initially positive response to any strong authority figure, who she thinks can provide a magical solution for her problems. Though she adopts convictions strongly and readily, her judgment is not firmly rooted, and she often plays hunches.

In the management of Sally, whether at home or in class, the traditional wisdom is relevant: ignore what is merely attention-seeking behaviour, but reward her with care and affection when she is operating well as one of a group or of the family, and when she is accepting low-key, off-centre existence.

Like many foster-mothers, you are called on to be more than a mother: to be in part a therapist as well, compensating for wounds in the past, and offering this promising girl the experience of unearned love, the sort that is not won by histrionics.


## To the Mother of Shy Garret

Your thirteen-year-old is so shy, he is afraid of the sound of his own voice. He hates to be the centre of attention, is frightened of parties, and all he seems to like is computer games and watching TV.

You feel it is a problem. Does Garret? Is he miserable on his own? There are differences of temperament between normal children. Introverted children, who are happy with just one or two friends, and can play by themselves quite contentedly, are just as normal as the extroverts and hearties who like to be the life and soul of the party.

Sometimes a boy who is really lonely and miserable can put on a good front in school. When he finds he is not part of any group, he spends his break with a book or a solitary game, and persuades himself that he is so busy with it that he does not need friends. In fact he may rebuff other children who approach with the hope of playing with him. You, his mother, will know whether he is miserable or not, and whether he is able to join in with others when he wants to. In the early years of secondary school it is particularly painful to be excluded from a group. I doubt if there is anything that causes boys and girls more pain than that sense of exclusion, often so painful that they cannot admit it to themselves.

What you see in Garret seems to be a general shyness which afflicts him even at home. Were you like that at his age? There is something inherited about shyness, and within the same family one child may show the strain where his brother is outgoing and loves company. Shyness is also affected by the circumstances we grow in: being overshadowed by a bright sister or brother, or an acute experience of failure without much support to help us through it, or — I remember it vividly myself — the insecurity that comes from being moved from school to school repeatedly, having to get used to different customs and styles, and feeling an outsider, nervous that your voice, or the language you use, or your clothes, may mark you as different.

Whatever the cause of it, you are living with a painfully shy Garret, and he is probably suffering as well. One thing obviously you should *not* do, and that is to talk about his shyness. He must not be ridiculed or scolded for his shyness. It is stupid to tell him not to be shy; he cannot help it, and ridicule can do nothing but harm. If you focus on a pothole when you are driving, you are likely to go into it. If you focus on fear and shyness, you will find it hard to escape from them. The remedy must be indirect: to build up his confidence by enhancing his skills; and to make him happier in his own skin by reaffirming, again and again, how dear he is to you.

Do you make it easy for him to have friends into the house? Can he present them to you without fearing a critical or unwelcoming eye?

You say that Garret is shy of the sound of his own voice; and he may well find it hard to make his voice heard at a chatty family table. It is doubly important for you parents to ensure him an appreciative hearing when he does say something, so that he feels that he has something worthwhile to say.

Outside home, he is probably easily embarrassed about clothes, and it is important to let him wear what will not make him look conspicuous or odd; remember, in some circumstances, formal clothes look quite odd to a teenager.

Use your own inventiveness on how to build up his confidence. He is almost sure to have some interest that could put him in touch with other boys of his age. Has he enough music to join a band or a group or a choir? Many a shy person has crept into society behind a musical instrument, and through it made friends and gained self-confidence. Even solitary pursuits like computer games can link a few introverted boys together.

For a boy who fears the uncertainties of group conversation, an easy way in can be by giving him clear roles to play, at home and at school. Has Garret some standing for jobs he does in the house, that no one else does, such as cooking a meal one day a week, managing part of the garden, or looking after particular messages? In the same way, many a teacher has helped shy children into the group by giving them a clear and public responsibility that does not involve speaking in public but that gives them some status with their peers.

In general, respect his temperament; do not be intrusive or do violence to his shyness. He may be the sort of introvert who can live happily and productively with just one or two good friends, and feels no need of parties or large social gatherings. He does need to be able to use his own voice, to speak with confidence, and the indirect way to that will be by building on his competence in whatever area God has best gifted him, and making that a springboard for contact with his peers.

## To the Mother of Fearful Bernie

Your six-year-old Bernie, now in her second year at school, has become anxious. Her teacher has not noticed any change, but at home she is clingy, and developing little complaints on school mornings. How hard should you push her?

You have picked up Bernie's fears with your sharp eye, and you will be the best doctor for those fears. They can be well disguised. No wonder the teacher has not noticed them. Bernie feels insecure and extra-dependent on you and on the teacher who takes your place, so she tries extra hard to behave as you would like her to behave. She is more in touch with your 'do's' and 'don'ts' than with her own sense of play and fun and the invitations of her friends.

What other signs of anxiety have you picked up? Bernie is extra clingy at home, and prefers always to be with you than to play on her own or with friends. She is nervous of exploring new places or people because she dare not leave you. Going to sleep has become an ordeal. She sings to herself as she goes up to bed, clearly warding off her anxieties. She keeps adding to the teddies and other toys she wants to take into bed with her, and keeps inventing more excuses to have you stay with her to tuck her up and kiss her goodnight yet again.

On the occasions when you have to go away for a day, you can see how hard Bernie finds it to cope without you. She greets you as though you had come back from the wars. In her mind, that is obviously where you have been, exposed to all the mugging and murder that fills her imagination, so that she wondered, minute by minute, would she ever see you again.

You find that she picks her friends from children who are shy, anxious to please and not very popular. Perhaps she is 'playing safe', avoiding the risk of friendship with children who might reject her. If you watch the days on which she develops 'schoolitis' — little complaints that with luck may get her off school for the day — you find that it happens on days when there is physical education. This can mean a shyness about changing clothes for gym, or a feeling of being clumsy, awkward in doing exercises that the others seem to manage easily.

So you have picked up the signs of anxiety. Nobody, not even your husband, knows Bernie as you do. It can still be difficult to know when to come down hard on this six-year-old girl. Her big brother had no problems at that age, but your children are all different. Bernie had a good deal of sickness as a baby. A week in hospital at the age of two, even though you stayed with her, left you anxious about her. She has internalised some of that anxiety. You wondered would she cope. So does Bernie. She has survived well, but at six she is looking forward and back.

At six, she is moving from one model of happiness to another. Up to now, happiness has meant being looked after by mother, as a baby at the breast, or as a toddler whose needs are anticipated by you. At six, another notion of happiness is taking shape: the joy of being competent, of managing on her own, of being able to cope with friends and learning exciting skills, of being able to swim, ride a bicycle, read and write. Some blessed children move forward into competence almost without a backward glance. Most will have periods of hesitation when they ache for the security of being looked after, and hanker for the indulgences of babyhood.

What has triggered these backward glances in Bernie's case? Maybe a shout from teacher, which terrified Bernie though other pupils hardly noticed it. Maybe one of her class called her a name when she was changing for gym — I remember a girl who took an emotional nose-dive after she was called 'Fatso' by a classmate.

Whatever the reason, you will not cure her by impatience. The fact that Bernie's anxieties are a phase of growing up, does not mean that she will weather them without your help. Your first job is to help her put words on what causes her fears: something to do with teacher, or classmates, or a particular class, or the playground, or a fear that you will die on her.

All through her life you have helped her by knowing about her fears, putting words on them, and making them bearable for her by the fact that you can live with them. That is still true today. What matters is not so much reassurance or saying her fears are nonsense. After all, mothers *can* die young, and children can face particular problems in learning, or in getting on with others.

You cannot save Bernie from the uncertainties of life or from tasks that she finds difficult. But you more than anyone can give her a sense that mistakes are good events, steps to learning, that success is what we do with our failures; that it is nice if everybody likes you and teacher approves of you; but if they do not, it is not the end of the world.

When she is suffering as at present, she needs your company and attention more, but she will not be helped by running away from the anxieties of school. The more she stays away from it, the more fearful it becomes. You and teacher need to pinpoint the causes of fear and engineer ways of increasing her competence. Feeling competent will help, feeling helpless will increase her anxiety. Lots of praise for things she does well will help her to feel she is on top of life.

See this as a hiccup in the forward move towards a new sort of happiness. You too may be sad at seeing the end of her dependence on you, and children notice quickly if mother really wants them at home, and connives with their fear of growing up. What Bernie needs from you is your patient and perceptive eye for the causes of her fears, your ability to absorb and carry those fears, and your confidence that she will cope, and grow towards competence rather than slip back towards dependence.

## To the Mother of Lazy Emma

Emma is eleven, and one after another her teachers have called her lazy, capable of far better work than she produces. How do you get movement out of a lazy child?

'Lazy' implies a moral fault, the last of the seven deadly sins, less targetted in preaching than some of the others, perhaps because at times we all, including preachers, feel open to the charge of laziness. It is a lazy word, and does not explain much. Until you explain Emma's idleness, you will not get much change out of her.

You may wonder what is there to explain? Was Dr Johnson right when he remarked: 'We would all be idle if we could?' It is not really true of a girl of eleven in a good school. Emma is not choosing the easy path. She is under constant pressure from you and from her teacher. She is missing break and her friends when she is kept in to complete the homework she neglected last night. She does not enjoy the 'lazybones' reputation she is getting among her friends and classmates. She is missing the joy of using her undoubted talents, and of pleasing you, her parents.

What keeps children active is not pressure from parents or teachers, but the natural dynamism that is in every human being, wanting to explore the world and use their mind and limbs and skills. If instead she is dreaming away her time, with no energy for anything, there may be other explanations besides the seventh deadly sin.

First, look at her body, diet and sleep. A permanently tired girl is not healthy. Nobody will know better than you if there is something ailing Emma. Some children come into school with baggy eyes, a sign either of late-night viewing or listening; or else of not being able to sleep for other reasons, fears or worries.

Secondly, she may be unable to cope with classwork, but unwilling to admit it. Children will often prefer to seem lazy than stupid. I have seen girls with a limited but crucial problem, perhaps in reading or writing or basic Maths, which has not been identified by the school, nor by themselves. They only know that all homework is an unspeakable burden, shy away from it and give up trying altogether. Talk this over with the teacher; the next step may be a careful assessment of Emma's attainments and abilities, so that you both know what can be expected of her, and if any remedial work is needed. You have to make the first move: you see Emma closely, but for the teacher she is one of thirty-five. She becomes a more interesting pupil when you help the teacher to focus time and energy on her.

There is of course another possibility, but from your question I am pretty sure it is not the case with Emma. I know children whose parents are so preoccupied with their own careers that they hardly know what class their daughter is in, or who is the teacher. They move away from the home with an eye on their own projects and promotions, and expect the children to be equally ambitious in their school work. That may work for over-sixteens, who are beginning to see the link between their schoolwork and their future career. At Emma's age, however, the main reason for doing Maths and Irish is to please mother and father. I have known the child of two career-minded parents to feel: Mum and Dad are not worried about my work, so why should I be?

You know the vicious cycle in children's motivation. Idleness breeds bad work, and bad work breeds discouragement and loss of joy in the work. So many children feel they are good for nothing, and unable to please either parents or teachers. A boy put it this way in a letter to his headmaster, after a row at school:

'You probably think of me as a waster, who doesn't give a damn about my family. My parents are the best parents a boy could ask for, and I'm the son that no parents want. That's the way I feel, and since I have no talents to make them proud, I can do nothing but waste my time here.'

It is quite true that he had been called a lazy waster by his teacher, who never dreamed how closely she was reflecting the boy's view of himself. All she saw was a disruptive pupil who did no work. The devastating self-image shown in this letter came as a shock to her and led to a turnabout both in their relationship and in his work.

Do you know how Emma views herself? She may have learned to defend herself against your prodding, and to appear bored by the notion of work, while underneath she longs for a way out of her misery.

A key question is 'Where are her joys?' What turns her on, engages her energy? What does she gravitate towards when there is no pressure on her? You may find that she has no concentration in Maths but can work for hours at music or dancing or skate-boarding.

The strongest motivator of all is the experience of success, in anything at all. Build on her strengths, and try to bolster up any weaknesses. Look for her areas of special interest and encourage her to join a club, read, go for visits, do those things which will develop her special interest. One area of competence, a skill acquired, a hobby encouraged, is worth a thousand words of advice.

Of course there are really lazy children, and some have much less energy than others. But it would be lazy of us adults to accept that as the final verdict without first exploring what makes Emma tick.


## Maurice is Too Tidy

You worry about your nine-year-old who is *too* careful. He has fixed ways of undressing and getting to bed, of eating his dinner; he is always counting things and worrying about unlocked doors. He is hard to live with.

Obsessionals *are* hard to live with, and Maurice seems to fit that description. I have been obsessional myself at times. Many people are: fussy about rituals, about set ways of doing things; upset if things are not put back in the right place. Such people worry a lot, and keep their anxiety at bay by having routines, sticking to what is predictable. They tend to be particular about cleanliness and punctuality, they are orderly but indecisive, they slow up and worry about small things, they love counting and collecting. They are born to be bursars or accountants, but only in safe and steady jobs, if there are any such jobs left.

We talk about 'having obsessions' about things, and we meet such people all the time: housewives who are always emptying ashtrays and dusting away imaginary dirt; footballers who are worried sick if they can't put their togs and boots on in a certain way. Generally we can live with such obsessions. Children go through periods when they won't step on a crack in the pavement, or grow worried about germs on their hands, and wash repeatedly. It makes sense to have some order in the way we do things. A habitual way of dressing saves us making decisions every morning. A set place at the table saves quarrels about who will sit next to Daddy. It is normal for a teenager in a large family to be fussy about her personal things, and to be angry if someone has messed with her hairbrush or radio.

I'd be concerned if obsessions start to interfere with Maurice's happiness, his friendships and his work. If you find him so caught up in bedtime rituals (laying out his clothes a certain way, or repeated visits to the bathroom) that it is taking chunks out of his sleep; if he checks repeatedly that the front door is locked and the radio switched off, then he has lost too much of his inner freedom, and needs help.

Inside he is anxious and rigid: 'I must do it this way or something terrible will happen.' How do you meet that? Obviously not by being anxious and rigid yourself. To handle it inside the family, *keep your sense of humour and stay flexible.* Obsessional children often have perfectionist parents, who themselves want everything under control, including their children's behaviour. Help has to start with the adults, with us. Obsessional people, small or big, need a lot of *play,* where you are relaxed and involved and where things are naturally unpredictable.

Maurice may well try to involve you in his rituals, persuade you to check doors and windows, to become part of his anxieties, on the grounds that he will be even more worried if you do not go along with him. Draw the line here. The house is secure, we have done our checking. I am going to bed. After all, what he is learning is how to live with the sort of insecurity that is part of human existence. None of us can be sure that a meteorite will not fall out of the sky, or lightning hit the house. We are taking reasonable risks all day long, and rather than assuage Maurice's irrational worries, your job is to model the courage that is able to take reasonable risks.

To show that Maurice's worries are groundless, you may go some distance with facts and explanations. You will go further by taking time off with him, relaxing in his company, in a game or an outing to town or to the country. In this as in every other area, if Maurice is to get home help with his worries, he finds it rather by absorbing the calm and good humour of his parents than by hearing their explanations. If home help is not enough, if you find him still unhappy, and his work and friendships impaired, then it is time to seek help from your GP or a Child Guidance Clinic.

## To the Mother of Paul: You are Missing Money

You have been missing it for some time, and feel sure that Paul, your ten-year-old, has been taking it, though he denies any knowledge of it. You are terribly upset and worried, and hate to have the role of detective thrust upon you.

It happens all the time. Mothers have to know what is happening in the house, without ceasing to be mothers. If Paul has been stealing, then almost certainly he will lie about it. The two forms of dishonesty are almost inseparable. Children who have stolen can look you unblinkingly in the face, invite you to search them or their room, offer explanations as to how the money disappeared. It is generally a mistake to start a lengthy and painful questioning of the suspect. Better to look for evidence to satisfy yourself, and when it points clearly towards Paul's guilt, confront him; ask if he has spent all the money, and on what. It is upsetting enough to have to face his stealing. Do not make it more painful by an inquisition which will probably lead to his lying as well. Instead look for evidence elsewhere.

The rationalisations and excuses will come in plenty. 'I borrowed it, I was going to give it back.' Some parents are so reluctant to accept that their children steal, that they let themselves be persuaded by those excuses and stories. That is always a mistake. You are allying yourself with the dishonest, excuse-making part of Paul, and deep down he knows it. He needs to be blamed, confronted with his guilt, and be obliged to pay back what he has stolen. He knows clearly enough what he would demand if somebody stole money off him. He would be upset and concerned too, and would demand the money back. It is a mistake to be too bland, calm or controlled in the face of stealing. There is every reason to be upset, and show concern, but with some cautions.

Many parents in this situation respond by giving 'a good scolding' or 'a good thrashing', and hope the lesson has been learned. This may ease your feelings of indignation, but produce nothing more than a lonelier thief or a cleverer liar. It is right to show indignation and impose a just punishment.

157

It is wrong to make prophecies of delinquency and involvement with the Gardai.

A parent's prophecies have a terrible power. They draw children towards fulfilling the prediction, or imagining that they do. I remember one lovable but hyperactive boy whose mother, in a moment of weariness, groaned 'You'll be the death of me, John'. When he was ten, she dropped dead, leaving him with a burden of guilt which took years to lift.

Threats are generally a sign of weakness. It is enough that children know it is wrong to steal, and why. You do not need to warn Paul in advance that you may bring him down to the Gardai, or face-to-face with the shop-owner he has robbed. It may be a good move when the time comes. It is nearly always a mistake to rehearse it in advance by threats.

When you ask Paul why did he steal, he will say he does not know; he does not understand his action. So it is up to the parent to seek an understanding, a harder task than showing indignation and imposing punishment.

Two key questions are: Who did Paul steal from? How did he spend the money?

If it was your money that he consistently robbed, it is worth looking hard at that relationship. Does he feel let down by you, ousted by another child, pressed too hard, blamed too much, stroked too seldom? Can you read his feelings and surmise the answer? It is surprising how often stealing goes back to a feeling of not being understood by parents — see the letters below.

I remember one boy whose shoplifting led to a major row with his father, the best thing that ever happened between them. The boy felt his father had been pushing him too hard, asking for standards he could not reach. He knew stealing was wrong, but the pressures in his life, and the absence of affection, made him feel sullen and cheated. He felt deprived of the only currency that matters, parental love, so made up for it by taking cheaper goods.

The other question is also revealing. How did he spend the money? Younger children sometimes want to buy friends with sweets or other gifts — then the problem is social, not financial. Others feel they get too little pocket-money compared with their companions: no easy answer here, but you may be able to help them earn a bit more with jobs. Others are simply greedy, self-indulgent, compulsive eaters. Others have fallen into bad company, in which conscience is blunted and robbing is condoned.

Understanding why Paul stole does not solve the problem, but it is the only key to a permanent solution. Take time with him, get him to imagine being the victim. You want to make wrong-doing unattractive for him, but you do not want to make him pay so hard that he does more naughty things just to spite you. And of course if he sees dishonesty in his parents, then the problem lies not in him but in you.

In case some of this seems like soft psychologising, let me add two letters, the first from a Scottish woman in middle age.

'I often used to wonder why out of a big family of God-fearing honest children, I was a thief and a liar — the two go hand in hand. I remember stealing a small thing from school when I was only five years of age — I think I was caught when it dropped out of my clothes. At an early age stealing was for my own gratification, but then I started to take money in order to gain loyalty from pals. I thought I could buy friends. At times I was absolutely petrified of my mother's anger and ashamed of my father's disapproval. The punishment I received only alienated me and filled me with guilt, and I became even more deceitful, even in confession.

Although I in no way blame my mother, who was the very soul of honesty, I do think that if I had been blessed with children of my own and was faced with this problem I would immediately single out the child for extra love and try to get a close loving relationship going. I am deeply convinced that I would have been spared years of misery — of my own making, it is true. Happiness is a good conscience, and children have different needs of affection, even in one family.

I am telling my case to let mothers know how much children need warm love in their young lives — some more than others — and they won't have the need for wrong-doing. Even today, with wives out working, lots of them buy expensive clothes and things for the kids, but it won't make up for time given to the children along with patience to attend to their emotional needs.'

The other letter, from an eleven-year-old boy who had been caught in petty stealing from his mother, was written in crude lettering on a big sheet of paper, and left for her to find in his bedroom.

'Dear Mum, I have got a bad feeling that you have had enough of me Mummy. Do you think I will go to court Mummy, will you care if I go to jail? I have got a very good feeling you won't care if I go to jail, and Mum do care for me and forgive me because if you don't I have got a feeling you don't care for me and Mum I do care about you. Love, Stephen.'

In Ireland, especially in clerical circles, we reach too early for a moralistic approach to all questions. These two letters, one written in the calm reflection of middle age, the other in the fierce agony of feeling rejected, make us pause and think hard about our own children, who are unlike any others. If they steal, they are often using a language. It may be saying not just 'I am evil and greedy', but 'I feel cheated, hard done by, in the most precious currency of all, and I am looking for a poor substitute in hard cash, and if all goes well, in my mother's attention.'

## NOTES

13.  Parker & Storm: 'Medical management of children with ADD', in *Chadder*, Winter 1991

14.  Leach, op. cit. p. 249

# School

## A WELL-SCHOOLED GENERATION

There are few greater achievements of the last thirty years than our educational revolution. We have reared a clever and well-schooled generation. It is awesome to watch the energy and poise with which they use their opportunities. Seventy years ago only 4% of fifteen-year-olds could stay in school long enough even to sit the Intermediate Certificate. Today about three quarters of our children go all the way through to the end of the senior cycle, and we rank high in the international league table of educated young people.

There are some factors in the present setting that will make such change harder in future. All attempts to improve the system will be complicated by the fact of a declining pupil population, and a static, aging teacher population, with dwindling energies and a firm hold on the status quo. The panel system operates at both primary and secondary level to close teaching jobs to merit and youthful energy, and guarantee them to those already in the system. The Posts of Responsibility system at second level makes it virtually impossible for secondary teachers to move from school to school without substantial loss of income.

However seen from the outside, our educational system has shown a dynamism and capacity for change that has few parallels in Europe. It says something for our capacity for self-reproach, that we do not feel particularly successful, either as a society or as individuals.

Some years ago the brightest graduates of Northern Ireland Grammar Schools were surveyed, the girls and boys who had gone through the system up to A Levels. They were asked one question: Were you a success at school? By objective standards these were the most successful young people in the community, bright to begin with, and blessed with every educational advantage. You know how many answered a simple 'Yes' to that question? *Just 3%!* The others, despite all their prizes, had failed to develop the confidence in their own abilities and goodness that education should give, the feeling that 'I'm OK'. That confidence comes, of course, from the very start of our children's education, which is years before they set foot in school.

## WHEN DOES EDUCATION START?

You wonder about when to start teaching your children. Jenny is a happy four-year-old, who could play on her own or with other children all day long. You have been hearing about the importance of the early years, and seeing suggestions about teaching toddlers to read in these receptive years, and you wonder should you be using these years more constructively.

I hear in you a struggle between your instinctive enjoyment of Jenny at play, and an anxiety generated by neighbours or advertisements that you should be 'working on her' from an early age. For goodness' sake, trust your instincts. Let us think for a moment about how she is learning.

Her personality and intelligence grow not by being acted upon but by acting, by doing things to you and to the world. From the moment of birth you and she were almost a unit. You talked to her long before she could understand language, yet in your talking she was learning not merely the sound of language, but all the love and other emotions that break through the human voice. You have been teaching her since you first held her and looked at her.

Then she started not merely to look back at you, but to reach for you, to call for you, to babble at you, and, marvel of marvels, to smile at you. The biggest leap in learning comes when she finds that she can make things happen. She cries and you come. She smiles and you smile back. She babbles and you talk back. There is the first experience in a dangerous world that activity is safe, that the world — meaning just you at that stage — makes sense, is a responsive place that she can influence. That is the moment of fastest learning, more crucial than any doctorate she may achieve in the future. Your teaching is instinctive, and it consists less in talking than in responding, in an understanding way, to the child you know better than anyone.

So when you wonder 'How soon should I start teaching Jenny?' you are talking about something that has happened since the first day of her life, and that sprang from your own instincts. None of the teaching that you attempt consciously in later years, whether of reading or of cycling or whatever, will be as effective as that, because the best teaching is a one-to-one response to the desires and curiosity of the child.

What about these long hours of play that Jenny enjoys? It is difficult for an adult to adjust to a four-year-old's rate of learning, and to the sort of questions that are important to him. We take for granted the feel of things like clay and metal, and their temperature and hardness, and whether they can float, and how they smell. *Everything* that Jenny sees and feels, starting with her own body and its products, is a brave new world for her, to be looked at and smelled and felt and often put into her mouth. All marvellous and intriguing, and all a matter of learning. It is not just the names of things that she learns, but their colour, feel, coldness, softness, smell, taste, heaviness. We would find it hard to stay with her as she explores one thing after another; but if we interrupt her, and try to accelerate her learning, or make short-cuts, we are interrupting something precious, the natural desire of the human child to experiment and understand. That is a rose, you tell Jenny, as she toddles round the garden. She knows more. She has smelt it, felt the thorns and the soft blossom, the contrast between stem, flower, leaves and rooting earth, the taste and texture of the petals. Weighed against all that richness, what's in a name?

At the age of four she has moved further, and some of her play will be with other children. It is still valuable for her learning and growth, probably more useful than anything she would be doing at school, because in play we are going at our own tempo, solving our own problems, experimenting with our own questions, learning how to get on with other children, feeling the limits to our fantasies. Games with other children gradually show the need for some other rules than the ones we invent for ourselves in our fantasy games. Above all, in a game with other children, we learn that the world does not come to an end if we lose.

Outside my window, in the garden of St Declan's school, is a spreading cypress, and underneath it is a collection of stones and sticks and bits of boxes which a gardener might easily sweep away as rubbish. When the children go out for a break, a few of the youngest girls and boys get down on their knees for the latest episode in a story about houses, cars, accidents, hospitals, and a thousand incidents of bull-dozing, renting, sharing, building extensions, and all the big things they have heard parents talk about.

Some of these children have been described as having poor concentration. Watch them when the latest instalment is in full swing, and you find a concentration that Einstein would envy, listening to one another, thinking ahead, guarding their corner, so intent on the story that they *really* do not hear the teacher calling them back to class. When they are called, they pour out to her what has happened in the last ten minutes, more real than anything they see on TV or hear in class.

In class we are teaching them to concentrate, but in fantasy they are learning precisely that, and spontaneously. In class we want them to learn self-awareness and self-control. Out at play they are demonstrating that, in their imaginary victories and defeats.

We invent lessons to help them better appreciate how others feel, and why they do things; none of our lessons are as effective as their games in achieving just that.

We talk about teaching them to co-operate, but they teach themselves when they are caught up in a game, and they seldom need to call in an adult umpire to settle disputes.

Some of these children have been given expensive toys for Christmas, but these will not have given anything like the pleasure that their twigs and boxes and stones afford under the tree. Expensive toys often require learning, and trammel the imagination. The joy of the tree is that it leaves them free to invent.

Above all, in their make-believe play they are working out problems, defeats, frustrations, and in their own unplanned way releasing all sorts of tensions. They learn so much from it, I often wonder should we bring them into class at all; but part of its pleasure is that it is a break from the drudgery we impose on them. Children can put up with an awful lot of boredom and misery if there are a few bright spots in their week.

As adults we tend to think of play as something competitive, like the sports we watch on television. Such sports, or the Olympic Games, are different in nature from the play of children. They are closer to the world of entertainment and business than that of play. In young children's play the rules are made and changed by the children, the nature of the games can be changed at will, and the game itself is fun. The result does not matter. I remember a four-year-old like Jenny asking me, when a certain game was suggested: 'Is this a fun game or a winning game?' Winning or losing adds a new tension to something that otherwise would be simple enjoyment.

It is tragic to see adults — fathers are worse than mothers here — intruding on children's games with a stress on winning rather than the enjoyment of playing, working out their own dreams through their son's occupation, until the son starts to feel it is not his game any more but his father's. This can happen with toys. Dad starts to show the happy, experimenting child some new or 'proper' way of using the toy. It can so easily lead the boy into feeling inadequate and learning to dislike the toy which he is not allowed to play with in the way that his own fantasy leads him.

You sometimes worry that Jenny may lose touch with reality, she so loves to enter the world inside her own head where she can try out different roles and enter different situations. Is this fantasy too close to madness, where an adult lives in his own world of hallucinations and illusions?

A healthy child will know when she is fantasising. She will not argue if you respond to her stories with 'That is the way you'd like it to be, wouldn't you?' Most imaginative children will not need to be brought down to earth like this; they recognise what is real. If they do not, and cling to their tall stories, or if they consistently, over a long period, neglect the ordinary demands of family and school to escape into a fantasy world, then imagination no longer serves them well, and it is important to find out why they cannot face reality.

As to your Jenny, bubbling with the poetry of life, I would be in no hurry to drag her into the often dull prose of adult existence.

Children at play, with space and time to do their own thing, are learning faster than we could ever teach them: reliving and coping with painful experiences (playing school with a cross teacher), practising future roles (girls with baby dolls), overcoming their own sense of helplessness (little boys with guns). Child's play has its own purpose and meaning, and because it is personal and active (TV is the enemy of this sort of play) it can teach deeper lessons, in a more lasting way, than any classroom teacher.

## To the Mother of Ronan, Starting School

The fourth of your five children had been looking forward to school for months, and started just after his fourth birthday. Now, after a few weeks there, he has gone right in on himself, and cannot tell you why.

You know he could wait two more years before enrolling. The state expects children to start school at six, though it allows them to go before that. Nobody can tell you when is the right time to start, because nobody knows your son like you and your husband. You two know better than anybody else when Ronan is ready. Many children do start too early, and in the first months at school go backwards rather than forwards. I have known tragic cases of conscientious parents who pushed immature four-year-olds into crowded classes, and spent years trying to remedy the damage done. Even after six, some parents give their children a better education than they could ever receive at school. Maire Mullarney is the Irish apostle of this approach, with her book, *Anything school can do, you can do better.* It means hard work for the parents, especially to ensure companionship for your children; but it can be done, and within the law.

Ronan has passed one of the great watersheds of human existence — breaking away from mother — and it was harder than he expected. He had visited the school for an open day, and admired the shining, smiling uniformed girls and boys, the best of their paintings and writings and projects up on the walls. School seemed a place where you could do wonderful things, had new skills, and adults were pleased with you.

His first day as a pupil was so different. The walls were bare. There were gangs of rowdy and somehow menacing older boys racing around the corridors and playground. The toilet was smelly, unlike anything he had known before. Everything was so large, so strange, he clung to the overcoat in which you had wrapped him even though he was not cold, because he needed to have an extra layer, something to remind him of you.

Teacher was so busy meeting new pupils and parents, looking after books and counting heads, that she did not seem to know him. In fact on one occasion she called him Ross, which upset him. Ross is his little brother of whom he is quite jealous. Later in the morning she grew annoyed when some boys started to wander round the classroom, and shouted at them. You have never had to shout at Ronan, and he was surprised and upset to see an adult who could not stay calm.

Young children invest so much expectation in the teacher, as the centre of power and authority and comforting, as knowing the answers, and being able to maintain order and calm when children are high and excited. She has to do with a big crowd what you do with your five: absorb the animal spirits, the excitement and anger and jealousies and panic and rioting, and contain the emotions so that they do not become too threatening for small children. If they see the teacher losing control, fear of breakdown seizes many little ones in the guts. When you collect Ronan, you can see he is upset, but all he can say is 'The teacher was shouting'.

There was another disillusionment when the class began work. Ronan is able to read quite well. Like many good readers, he learned first from his parents and big sister reading stories to him, and then sharing the reading with him. Teacher told the class to look at the alphabet, and when Ronan told her he knew it, she did not hear him. A few days later the teacher sorted out the different groups in the class, putting the good readers together with work that extended them. But the flavour of bafflement from the first day carried over in Ronan's feelings about school. He had somehow expected that once in the classroom, he would be able to produce the pictures and projects he had seen on the walls at open day. Instead of these instant skills and achievements, there was the drudgery of wading through dull work with a big group, many of them much slower than himself.

There were so many children in the class! Ronan had not reckoned that teacher would hardly have time to talk to him. All the grown-ups he had ever known had had time for him, but now he felt lost. He felt teacher did not even know his name, nor have a space for him in her mind. As in the family, he wanted to be the best, but feared he might be the worst.

So he came home in a turmoil of emotion, so overflowing with feeling that he could not remember anything the teacher had said. He was ashamed of not liking school. It seemed babyish to find so much that he could not cope with. He whispered his misery into the ear of his cat, but could not talk to the family about it.

No use asking Ronan what is wrong or why he dislikes school. The 'Why' question on mother's lips always sounds like an accusation. You have to read his feelings first, guess from his face just what emotions are filling him, and lead gently from the feelings, especially the shame at being unhappy, on to the other details, the strangenesses that make the start of school so hard for him

It may be a case of supporting him through the early weeks until he is sure the teacher knows him, and until he has made some friends and become used to the routines of the day, and learned his way round the, to him, vast spaces of the school.

Or it may be a case of saying: 'I was wrong. He is too young for school. It can wait another year or two.' Age is a poor guide in this decision. When is Ronan ready for school? When he can mix with other children as possible helpmates, not just as moving objects; when he has moved from aggressive or destructive play (throwing, messing, hoarding, taking things apart) to more constructive play, which is the next stage to work; when he can stay in one place long enough that the classroom chair will not be a prison.

There are many other issues, mostly in the home, that affect the decision to send Ronan to school, but *his* readiness must be a prime factor. When he does go, make sure that you are in touch with how he is feeling when he crosses this enormous threshold.

## To the Mother of Eight-year-old Grainne, who is Refusing School

Last week she refused school every morning, saying she was sick. No problems on Saturday or Sunday. You worry about school phobia.

The hardest things in childhood, for children and parents, are the separations; and going to school can be one of the most painful. What Grainne is going through is far from rare. It is vital to understand just what has gone wrong.

It may be that the moment of separation from mother is fraught with pain or panic. Sometimes mother herself is the cause of this, if, for instance, she always hated primary school, and has passed on some of that attitude, quite unconsciously, to Grainne. I have known mothers who were clinging to their children just as much as the children were clinging to them. The problem disappeared when Daddy started taking the child to school.

Grainne may worry deeply that something will happen to you or her Daddy during the day, and that distressing anxiety, often tinged with guilt, is harder to deal with. Usually there is something in the recent past that triggered the anxiety: a row with you that left her fuming, and then afraid that her anger might damage you if she leaves you out of her sight; a row between you parents, or the sickness of one of you, a mother's bout of depression or feeling trapped. Where mother feels cooped up within the four walls of her house, it is easy for Grainne to pick up her feelings of loneliness. The problem, and the solution, lie with mother. Re-plan your life to reduce those trapped feelings. Children go to school happier if they know that mother is busy and active, not too miserable or lonely.

Grainne may be run-down or tired, especially if the weather has been harsh, or it is towards the end of a long term. She needs to ease up. School has just got too much for her. Of course there are parents who are too easy on their children, yield to every sigh or headache, and are manipulated up to the hilt. Teachers easily distinguish these children from those who are stressed or run-down. If there is real communication between home and school, this sort of truth can be conveyed.

Or Grainne may be reacting to something in school that she deeply dislikes or fears: a new teacher who seems menacing, or older children who bully, or the realisation that she cannot keep up with the class or cope with the work, or the repeated experience of failure. She may not be able to explain exactly what makes school so disagreeable. Whatever it is, the essential step is to talk to the class teacher. The solution of this problem is important for both of you.

There is another sort of school refusal, close to panic, which is harder to explain because Grainne is so frightened that she cannot talk about it: wetting or soiling in class, or fear of dirty lavatories, or some sort of sex play that terrified her, or being told off severely for something she had done wrong. Again, contact with teacher is essential, and a determined, calm effort to discover exactly what frightened Grainne. It is also very important to get her into school, with the necessary safeguards. Anxiety grows on absence, and the longer she stays out of school, the more she will fear it.

So Grainne's complaints need to be taken seriously. It does not help to ignore the problem, or think it will go away, or let her stay at home whenever she wants. It does not help to invent sick notes when the reality — which affects the school as much as the home — is that Grainne is upset. It does not help to make unreal threats, about sending her away, or fetching the Gardai. These will only frighten her further.

Mothers can generally discern true illness, by watching appetite and signs of interest in life. Few would be taken in by the sort of pains that improve miraculously by 10 a.m., just in time to enjoy a day of home entertainment. Most mothers will use the wise precaution of taking Grainne's temperature, and offering to keep her at home in bed all day, in a darkened room with no TV. If she is not sick, then you must tackle whatever frightens her, and for that you need a working relationship with her teacher.

## To the Mother of Dyslexic Gavin

You always knew he found school hard, but teachers thought he was simply slow. The fact is, he's good at Maths, brilliant at music and computers, and obviously bright in many ways. Now they tell you he has a specific reading difficulty and they have no specialist on the staff. What hope has he?

So far, Gavin fits the description of a dyslexic child, clever in non-verbal ways but weak in what concerns written language. The relatively new term *dyslexia* is often used loosely, sometimes by parents of children who are simply slow, in reading, spelling and everything else. Gavin on the contrary must know he is quick at picking up information in other ways than the printed word, and he is frustrated that this particular channel of learning — reading and writing — dominates nearly everything he does in school.

These are the signs normally taken to identify the dyslexic child:

(1) *Intelligence is average or above average.* If Gavin is slow all round, then it would be wrong to treat him as having a specific reading difficulty.

(2) *His hearing and vision are normal:* If either of these are impaired, then see your doctor about remedies for the physical defect. It is obvious that a boy who has problems with hearing or seeing is going to find reading more than ordinarily difficult.

(3) *There is no evidence of damage to the brain or nervous system.*

(4) *He has had the normal opportunities for schooling up to now.* You say he has had several changes of teachers, and that is regrettable. Has he survived these changes worse than the rest of the class? The biggest leap forward in reading tends to come before the age of seven, and I gather that in those years Gavin had a stable schooling.

(5) *He had no marked emotional upset that pre-dated his reading difficulty.* Most children with reading problems are upset on account of them, grow angry with demands that they cannot meet, or discouraged and depressed. However your question is whether Gavin was an upset child before he ever looked at a book, and whether that trouble interfered with his early learning.

If he has survived unnoticed this far, his condition must not be too extreme. I have known clever ten-year-olds to write a page which could be read only by putting it to a mirror. They did not realise they were writing backwards. They found it unbelievably hard to recognise and remember the shape of simple words like 'home, she, walk'. They looked with awe and gratitude at the great dyslexics like actress Susan Hampshire, who achieved success against similar odds.

All the time researchers are uncovering more about dyslexia: that it is commoner among boys than girls (in nearly every measurable way you are the superior sex!). It seems to be carried in families — chromosome 15 is suspected of carrying the weakness, which is transmitted easier by mothers than fathers. There may be links with concentrations of cells in the area of the brain associated with language processing; and with whether children are consistently right-sided (hand, foot, eye) or left-sided. Much of this is speculative, and not useful to Gavin at this stage. One feature you can perhaps link with his history: dyslexics often come to notice during the 'leap at Fifth Class level', when normal readers become fluent and hungry for books.

Dyslexics are children with normal intelligence, hearing and eyesight, with no brain damage, who seem emotionally stable, and have received an appropriate education, but cannot read even the simplest new word, nor use individual letters as the building blocks of words, whether in reading or in spelling. They are often confused about right and left, and therefore also about telling the time, tying bows, and the placing of digits in arithmetic.

You are wise not to label Gavin as dyslexic too quickly. There are many milder reading problems which can be overcome with skilled tuition. But let's suppose he is found to be truly dyslexic, then some long-term strategies are needed. He cannot improve his reading and writing by phonic methods. Instead he has to learn by boring rote and prodigious feats of memory.

His handwriting is almost certainly chaotic, and will always be a huge labour for him. So if you or the school can afford it, teach him to master the keyboard of a word-processor, and to use the spelling check on most programmes, so that when something needs to be presented well, he can print it. Gavin could probably develop a strength in computers, both for presentation of written material and because children whose language skills are below average can still be highly competent in learning the *operational* sequences needed for computers.

If you are within reach of BBC TV programmes, Gavin's learning might be helped by the use of educational TV, which presents material visually, and in story form, with ingenuity and thoroughness. Look for details from BBC Education Information, London, W5 2PA.

You will know better than anyone how to avoid situations where Gavin's problem can make him look stupid. If eating out, read the menu to him without comment. Avoid writing messages to him; many families have tape recorders, and

Gavin should quickly learn to use one for passing on messages, planning stories and essays, and possibly even doing exams in school.

Gavin's basic learning cannot be a pleasure to him. You can anticipate unusual levels of frustration, and you need to work to support his motivation all the way through school. Build up the areas (you mention music and computers) where he can show his gifts.

Severe dyslexia remains a problem even after school, so Gavin may have to be steered towards schooling and work that uses his strengths and does not require a lot of reading. The Leaving Certificate examiners may make allowance for dyslexia, and this should be planned in good time through the school. Do not use the Leaving Certificate, won with such labour, to get Gavin into a job where he will still depend to any great extent on writing and reading.

Over the last few years, the Association for Children and Adults with Learning Difficulties (ACALD), has developed many resources to help the likes of Gavin, and it can be contacted at 1, Suffolk Street, Dublin 2, Tel. (01) 6790276.

## Declan is Being Bullied

Your ten-year-old tries to dodge going out at break time, and will make any excuse to avoid going to school He is not a strong child, and you are keenly aware of his misery. You want to help, maybe with memories of having suffered yourself at school, memories of a bullyboy or girl that still make you burn with anger. I have those memories too, and often wondered what made children into bullies, always trying to take advantage of someone's weakness, knowing when others are upset or afraid, and using it against them.

Wasn't there an old Irish curse on three wretches: a young man mocking an old man; a rich man mocking a poor man; and a strong man mocking a weak man — or woman, as the case may be. There are bullies among girls too, more likely to use verbal and psychological tactics, but often enough being physical too.

Bullies are not just one sort of person. Sometimes it is a boy who finds it hard to make friends, and finds that frightening another child is less lonely than having contact with nobody. Such bullies need a victim because they have not learned to make a friend. Or sometimes a bully is a girl who has been put down at home, and takes out her unhappiness on others at school. Usually bullies are miserable people inside, and often they feel inferior. Nearly always they are cowards who will run scared from somebody stronger.

There seem to be natural victims too among children, and bullies gravitate towards them: children who have not learned to defend themselves, or who, like the bully, have not learned to make friends, and unconsciously encourage the bullying as preferable to getting no attention at all. Sometimes it is an accident that makes them victims: arriving at school at a different time from everyone else, or looking, dressing or acting differently, in a way that draws mockery.

Among boys one natural victim is the Mamma's boy, dependent, over-protected, able to manipulate his mother and get her to fight his battles for him. He may have a history of delicate health, so that it was necessary to take great care of him. When his health improves, and he is fit to stand on his own feet, he does not particularly want to forgo the emotional rewards of being delicate, and tries to prolong his dependence.

Your Declan is suffering, and you feel you have to do something. First, make sure of the facts, from Declan himself. It is important to listen in a calm, matter-of-fact way, trying to grasp the story clearly, not rushing to take sides. Declan may be so frightened that he will not even name his persecutor to you, lest you go rushing off and he falls into a deeper mess. So keep it calm, and listen carefully. I have known children come home with an angry story about being bullied that day; and once they had a good audience from an attentive mother, they recovered quickly and forgot the incident within the hour.

However Declan is beyond that stage, and you will need to check with his teacher to see if the school has noticed the bullying. It may be necessary to chat with whoever looks after the children at playtime to see the full picture. If it becomes clear that one child is making life a hell for others, then make sure that the responsible people in the school, the principal and Declan's teacher, know all the facts, and that they will move against the bullying

Declan himself can learn from the experience. His best protection is to have a group of friends and stay with them. He may need to stay within sight of whoever supervises the playground. He will defend himself better if his confidence is built up by success in some area; not necessarily Karate or Judo, though these can be a real solution. Even a taste of success in swimming or football can raise his courage to the point where he will not be easily victimised.

Suppose all this has been tried and failed, and a big boy called George is still making Declan's life a misery, what about tackling George's parents? I have known this sort of thing to work, but only with adults who could avoid entanglement with the other parents, and instead were able to keep it calm and discreet. The aim is to indicate clearly to George that you all know what is going on, and are determined to put a stop to it. Obviously George needs help as well. That is another day's work.

## Kevin Hates Homework

Aged nine, he does not mind school. He likes his teacher and enjoys his friends, but he loathes homework, dodges it when he can, has to be press-ganged into starting it, says he has forgotten his notebook, spends hours more than he needs, and in the end the results are poor. Kevin's homework is a plague for all the household.

You are not alone, nor is Kevin. You may find young children who are delighted to have homework because it makes them feel grown-up, gives a purpose to their drawing and writing, and the prospect of an attentive adult audience. That stage passes. For many children and young people, homework appears a grinding and often futile burden of additional work when they feel the day's work should be over. It becomes a focus for rebellion by children, resentment by parents, and exasperation by teachers.

Yet right answers are hard to come by. There are as many parents who criticise teachers for not setting, examining or correcting homework, as parents who grumble at the amount of homework that is set. Many teachers say they could cheerfully and competently teach using very little homework, but that there is a constant pressure from parents asking that it be set.

It is not only households that are disrupted by homework. It adds enormously to the work of schools: dividing out exercises for different subjects over different nights; spending much of the class first examining last night's lessons, then collecting exercises, setting tonight's homework, thinking up schemes to mark and keep records of homework done, maintaining the ritual of the homework notebook, checking to see that children write in the work to be done; parents and teachers trying to communicate through messages in the notebook without hurting the other's feelings; parents pressuring teachers to correct homework carefully, teachers pressuring parents to supervise the work done at home. In the centre of it all is Kevin, for whose benefit homework is supposed to exist, who generally loathes it, and tries to keep parents and teacher at a distance from one another.

Kevin is at primary school, with just one teacher. *Keep in touch with her.* Let her know that you are interested and involved, but are not going to do Kevin's work for him. Father and mother have their work to do, and homework is Kevin's, nobody else's. If he once manipulates a parent into sitting beside him and prodding him towards the right answers, then there is trouble ahead. The whole point of homework is to train in independent work, and if he leans on others to get it done, the teacher is misled, Kevin loses its value, and the rest of the family are persecuted to lend a hand. Far better let him get into trouble than do it for him. At least the teacher will see what Kevin is able for. If he is left on his own, he will find he is able for far more than appeared at first.

There will be huge differences between children. Where parents of the same class meet, some will grumble that homework takes over two hours, others that it is done

177

National College of Art and Design
LIBRARY

comfortably in twenty minutes. Same teacher, same work, but the capacity of children for dispatching the work varies enormously.

What sort of routine have you for homework? Nearly all children need a set time and place to reduce the agony of deciding to get down to it. When Kevin comes home tired from school (tiredness often showing itself in nervous energy and restlessness), he needs a break, needs mother there to listen while he lets off steam about the frustrations and pleasures of the day at school, needs a snack to push up the blood sugar level, and probably, especially in the summer, needs a chance to run around, at least for half an hour.

The difficult moment is at the end of the break. It is worth anything to establish a routine by which Kevin settles down to his work without prompting. It may be useful to set up a reward system: Kevin will get something extra — TV, something tasty, extra pocket-money — if over the course of a week he sets himself down to homework on time without prompting. At first you may need a day-by-day reward to move him out of a bad habit. This is different from bribery, which means giving payment for doing something dishonourable. Here you are simply training by rewards in an important area, and doing it systematically.

You may need the reward system also for training him to work through the homework fast. A nine-year-old should not be spending more than an hour at homework, and you may need teacher's agreement that he pack it in after an hour. Children have to learn to use the hour well, not answering the telephone or the door, keeping eyes and mind off the TV, avoiding conversation or movement or any of the stratagems we all use for distracting us from things we dislike.

Children are born with diverse capacities for this sort of concentration, and it may take Kevin years to learn to manage himself in this way. Learn he will, if the targets and the incentives are clear. It is a crucially important training in self-management, and it becomes more and more important as he moves into the bigger burdens of secondary school. Your art as parent is to stand back from Kevin's work, set up routines and rewards that help him to manage, and keep in regular touch with the teacher so that you can judge your success.

## Why Does Peter Work? Why Does he Idle?

Ten-year-old Peter is in Fourth Class. During school terms you can see he is not working, and his parents are the target of regular warnings from his teacher. How can he be motivated?

It is the commonest question about school children: how can I get him to work? Why are some of them idle and some of them industrious? When Pope John XXIII was showing visitors round the Vatican, and was asked 'How many people work here?' he answered 'About half of them.' As Dr Johnson remarked, 'We would all be idle if we could'. The children who work are more remarkable than the idle ones, but it is the idle ones you worry about.

Peter's teacher has commented: 'He seems to have poor concentration.' This is only partly true. His mind wanders when faced with a page of sums or Irish grammar, but he can scan the football results and TV programmes like lightning, or spend half an hour practising bunny-hops or wheelies on his BMX bike with no sign of distraction. If he can do that, he has excellent powers of concentration, provided he is interested. There are unfortunate children who cannot keep their minds on one thing for thirty seconds, no matter how much they like it. They are the hyperactive, with an overstretched nervous system, and no span of attention. They have major problems in learning anything. It is an unusual condition, and is seldom the explanation for the poor motivation that worries parents (see pp. 127-30).

Usually there is no cause to blame either parents or teachers, if Peter seems distractable. Children's span of attention varies from the day they are born. Even from infancy some are much better able than others to focus on one object (it may be a ball they are following round the floor) and stay focussed on it. Intelligence tests measure this capacity for attention, and the range is enormous, from the hopelessly distractable to the intensely concentrated.

If you could tailor your teaching specially for each child, the distractable and slow learners should have structured teaching, with plenty of drilled learning, associative learning and guidance, and short tasks with frequent encouragement

179

through feedback on their progress. Because they see such a short way ahead, they need their learning broken up into short morsels, and much reinforcement through knowledge of results. Children with a longer span of attention are better able to motivate themselves, and better subjects for learning through discovery.

There is no greater joy for parents and teachers than to have a child with a *need for achievement,* who enjoys a deep satisfaction from doing something well and registering his success. He likes to have his homework looked at and marked. He is rewarded simply by knowing that he has done a good job and been recognised.

That need is not inborn, but comes from a particular form of upbringing, especially in the first few years of life. His parents will have been warmly and intensely interested in all he does, but in a non-intrusive way. Anything he can do for himself, they let him do. They show an encouraging but not uncritical interest in the results. They would rather see him try something alone and make mistakes from which he can learn, than do it perfectly with their help. Homework is his job, a way of learning how to work independently; and from the beginning his parents will stand back from the tackling of homework, though keeping a keen eye on the results.

Back to Peter now. Could the reason for his not working be physical? Not enough sleep, or food, or the wrong sort of food, or an undiagnosed condition of the glands, or eyes, or ears, or digestion (usually mother is the first to notice such conditions). Or it could be the aftermath of sickness. Children who have recovered from a delicate phase often find it hard to adjust to the demands of everyday work, after being accustomed to the cottonwool existence and emotional rewards of being delicate. It is like a second weaning.

Or the reason for Peter's idleness could be simply *inability to cope* with the work of the class. He may be genuinely too slow for a normal class, or have lacked the foundations in one or more subjects, or have a specific difficulty with reading or spelling. Then the remedy must be special teaching, if it is available. If he is genuinely unable to cope with the work, he will probably react to it either by depressed withdrawal into himself, or by acting up in class and disturbing everyone.

Quite often the reason for idleness at school turns out to be *upset at home.* Peter has overheard a shouting match between his parents, or resents a new baby, or feels in the shadow of a bright big brother; and there is too much emotional turmoil under the surface of his mind for him to focus on classwork. Perceptive parents can usually pick out what the trouble is, and either talk it through, or support their son through a bad time.

Up to the end of primary school, children's main reason for work is to please their parents, and the teacher who stands in parents' place. Towards the end of secondary school, they are motivated, some of them, by the prospect of a job or third-level college. They appreciate the link between a good Leaving Certificate and a good placement, whether in work or further education. In between, that is in the early years of secondary school, is the bad time for motivation, and it coincides with the early teens when bodies are changing and social life is in turmoil. An external target like the Junior Certificate can be a useful carrot to motivate them to schoolwork which is becoming increasingly abstract and difficult. It is the valley period for motivation. Those with an internal incentive, like the need to achieve, will go on studying.

For the others, the nearest approach to a formula for motivation seems obvious but is often forgotten: give them *some experience of success*. If they start to do well in some area, like sport or music, they will learn how effort leads to reward, and there is usually a spin-off in their schoolwork. Children learn very little from failure; but their noses are sometimes rubbed in it by parents who are more in touch with their own anxieties than their children's needs. Contrive some way in which Peter will feel himself moving forwards rather than backwards. It is not new wisdom. '*Mol an óige...*'

## School Reports: Should Anthony Repeat a Year?

You have had reports on him every term, but were surprised when, out of the blue, his Principal suggested that he repeat Fifth Class next year. Have you any comeback?

You are wondering if there is really a partnership between you and the school in the education of your son. If the Principal's suggestion takes you by surprise, then you must ask about the meaning of the term reports, of which the purpose is to keep you in touch with what is happening, and what is likely to happen, between Anthony and his teachers.

Writing reports is hard work. It has to be done at the end of term, when a teacher is probably tired, possibly downhearted. It is not easy to find something constructive and accurate to say about each of thirty-five pupils. As a teacher I always try to work out who will read the report, and what use they will make of it. Some parents would immediately put it into Anthony's hands. Others would guard it like a top secret document, or read selectively from it. Others would flaunt it before grandparents and relations without consulting Anthony. Others would use it as a weapon to beat him with, or read it in black-and-white terms as simply good or simply bad — and any worthwhile report is a mixture of the two. There may even be parents who would take it personally, and feel any criticism of Anthony's performance reflects on them.

A report is a telegraphic message, telling only a fraction of what has to be said. In a good school, it is an invitation to further discussion between parents and teacher. Without that, a report tends to be uninformative, misleading, and sometimes rude.

There are some phrases that crop up so regularly that they can be discounted. They mean virtually nothing without further explanation. For instance, 'Anthony could/should try harder. Anthony will need to make a greater effort'. So should we all, pupils, teachers and parents. Who can say just how hard I am trying? When you read 'Anthony tries hard', what does that mean? An unspoken 'God help the poor child', that he is a hopeless case and for all his efforts cannot keep up with the class? Make an appointment and ask the teacher directly.

What do you want to know from a report?

(1)  How Anthony is managing his work, whether he is keeping up with the class, or showing particular strengths or weaknesses; whether (as in your case) he is in line for promotion next year, or so weak that he will have to lose a year to catch up.

(2) Whether the teacher is satisfied with the way Anthony does his homework. The teacher of course also needs to know if you are satisfied with the way she/he examines and marks the homework.

(3) Whether the teacher is managing Anthony the right way, with a proper mixture of challenge, encouragement, control and praise. There are real personality clashes in school classes, and if parents and teacher are working on the same side, those clashes can be avoided or ended. If you know that Anthony, for instance, feels the teacher has nothing for him but criticism, and you know that like most children he needs a measure of encouragement, then meet teacher and say so, in a way that she can listen to.

(4) How Anthony is behaving in class with the teacher and other pupils. Language like 'lazy', or 'lacks concentration' may point to a bad relationship developing with teacher. The stronger word 'disruptive' is a warning signal that you cannot miss.

(5) What teacher would like you to do at home to back up the school's efforts.

Treat the school report as only one part of the communication between you and the teacher, to be followed up with a meeting of the 'partnership'. Some parents, and some teachers, are hard to partner, hard to talk to; but it is rare that you cannot improve things by making a serious approach which respects the role of the other partner.

You are both vulnerable, and privy to one another's weaknesses. When you approach teacher, you will be conscious of times when your care of Anthony and his work was sloppy; and she will remember times when she was unfair or careless in managing your son. So the meeting has to start from that shared awareness of your inadequacies. From Anthony's point of view, you are both unsackable: maybe not the best parents or teachers, but the only ones he has.

What about his repeating a year? The Principal is not likely to recommend it unless it is necessary. Keeping a child back can upset the numbers, make one class too big, another too small. So the suggestion is unlikely to be made lightly. If Anthony is not coping, it may be because of real inability, a pace of learning that is significantly slower than that of his age-group. Or it may because he has idled — so tackle his motivation.

If he was my child, I would not agree until I had had a hard look at the *teacher* he will have next year. Going over the same ground with an uncongenial teacher would be a poor use of a year. If it offers him a chance of a remedial year with a good teacher, who has an eye to the individual and can bring him on, then it can turn a corner in his school career.

He will not like it: losing friends, falling back among younger children, perhaps being pointed at as slow. The worst of the year is the first week in the new class. Anthony will need much calm and reassuring support until he has made friends and got used to the new setting. Make it a positive decision, a move to bring him on faster. It must not be seen as a punishment for failing to cope — that will only lead to him failing again.

Remember, the Principal's letter is only the start of the discussion. Anthony is your child. Go and talk to the Principal as your *partner*.

## The Final Hurdle for Jim

Your Jim is coming up to his Leaving Certificate in June, and you are worried sick about him. His work has been up and down, and he is so moody, it is hard to live with him without explosions. You dread the next month.

If it is hard for you, it is harder for Jim. What you say to him matters less than what you model. He has probably heard again and again what you have to say, and could give you your *spiel* word-perfect before you open your mouth. Save your breath, and concentrate instead on being all the things you would want him to be.

You want him to be regular in his habits, sleeping and eating in a normal, regular way while coming up to this big test, which makes physical demands as well as mental. Then be regular yourself. Make better meals than usual, with dishes to tempt his appetite. If Jim won't eat, do not fuss him. He will not die of malnutrition, and you would do more damage by nagging or force-feeding than by letting him go hungry. You will certainly help him by keeping a solid background of routine in the household, avoiding any appearance of panic. Make sure you eat and sleep and exercise regularly yourself, so that you remain buoyant through these weeks.

You suffer from Jim's emotional ups and downs. Then do not reflect them, but work on your own equanimity. You do not have to do the exam, and it will not help Jim to feel he is throwing the whole family into a state of nervous excitement. The calm and balance has to come from the grown-ups. In general, keep the emotional temperature as low as you can. Be ready to absorb his impatience and anger, without retaliation or lecturing. At this stage, modelling good manners is more effective than lecturing.

Be there when Jim is, ready to listen if he wants to unload, but not intruding or questioning. He may treat the house as though it were just for lodging. For these weeks, excuse him the regular chores he may have in the household, put up with his inconsiderateness, and make yourself into a cheerful and calm presence, standing on the bank of the river in which Jim is struggling. He may not take any notice of you, but he would certainly miss you if you were not there.

You know Jim better than anyone, and you know what helps him. His father needs to follow the same line. This is a time when both parents have to keep their own emotional life secondary to the needs of the household. Sometimes Dad feels overcome by the need to do something about his son, who he feels is not working as hard as he should (anyway who ever works as hard as they should?) He decides to give him a talking-to, man-to-man. It may give the father emotional relief. He feels he has done something. But if it is badly timed, it may undo all the patience and tact shown by his wife over months. You both know what works with Jim. Be guided by that, not by your own desire to *do* something.

You may have to lay down the law about one or two things. See that Jim has a decent night's sleep, and gets out of bed in the morning. Do not let him waste a lot of time watching TV. Study done against a background of music is not as efficient as study done in silence, no matter what Jim may think.

Many schools tend to leave students free to come and go in the weeks before the Leaving, and end classes long before they need to. I know how hard it is to manage young people when they are edgy before the exam. I know how some of them agitate to be left free to stay out of school; and a small minority of students will use the time well if they are left at home. The majority will not. They grow more restless, do not organise their time well, and irritate the family. Even if they are mitching on some days, it is better for them to have access to their teachers up to the time of the exam than to be left to fend for themselves. In my book, it is a better service to students to expect them to come to school than to leave them at home. Parents can have an influential voice here.

In your own mind, take the mystique out of the Leaving. It is a job, like building a wall. The more time Jim spends at it, in study and revision, the better he will do. Worrying about revision is more painful than settling down and actually doing some. It can only be done a bit at a time. The danger is that when he starts into a subject, such as history, he is overwhelmed by all the courses he thinks he knows nothing about, and cannot bring his mind to focus on the bit for tonight. The only way to climb a mountain is by putting one foot in front of the other till you reach the top. Every foot of work that Jim does will bring him further up; but to look at the whole mountain is discouraging rather than helpful.

This is a hard time for the perfectionists, who feel 'I must not make errors, and if I do it's terrible. People and events (the shape of the exam paper) must always be as I want them to be, and if not, life will be unbearable.'

You may have to remind Jim that, on the contrary, doing things well is satisfying, but it is human to make mistakes. You can concede a goal in the first question, or first paper, and still win the match. Success is what we do with our failures. You know far more than you imagine. Use everything you have in your head, whether learned from radio, or friends, or other questions on the paper. The Leaving is a marathon rather than a sprint, and you can improve performance with every paper you do. Stay to the end of the paper, re-read your answers. You can always improve on them, given time. If you are feeling mad with the system that puts you under such stress, don't get mad, get even, put your energies into beating the system.

No need to remind you to pray for Jim, that he will do justice to himself. And pray for yourselves, that you, his parents may stay calm, regular, cheerful, and keep this exam in perspective.

# Living with the Teens

## THE TASKS OF ADOLESCENCE

One fact gives demographic shape to the teenage population of Ireland: our birth rate peaked in June 1980, just nine months after the Pope's visit to Ireland, and has been declining ever since. That bulging age-cohort, nearly 75,000 strong, turned ten in 1990, and will be in their teens until the turn of the century: the most numerous teenage population we have had in a hundred years, healthy, clever, well-schooled and generous, but different in ways that often baffle and alarm their elders.

Any attempt to make sense of the teens, to understand adolescents, will be vigorously and understandably resisted by the target group. It was bad enough as a teenager to have one's waking hours filled with the work imposed by adults, dull subjects made duller by the teachers who presented them. It would add further insult for them to control one's whole existence by assigning life-tasks and life-skills which would account for what was left of one's life. Adolescents do not want to be understood, because they would see that as a move towards manipulation, imposing adult solutions on one's life. If there are to be patterns and solutions, if there are to be mistakes, they want them to be their own.

Let us take another approach: this chapter attempts what Aristotle saw as the function of the mind: to put form on raw matter, to shape crude experience into concepts that do justice to it. We have all lived through the teen years, and watched many friends live through them, although our teens differed enormously from today's experience. How do you map them? Apart from 'surviving to man's estate', as my mother used anxiously say, what must the young girl or boy do?

The question has bothered observers for a long time, but has not always engaged their energies. Shakespeare did not want to know about it. 'I would there were no age between sixteen and three-and-twenty, or that youth would sleep out the rest; for there is nothing in the between but getting wenches with child, wronging the ancientry, stealing, fighting.' (*A Winter's Tale*, Act 3, Scene 3)

## WATERSHED OR NO-MAN'S-LAND

The tasks of adolescence must obviously vary with the culture. We know the teens as a no-man's-land between childhood and adulthood, lasting several years. Many cultures eliminated it, by focussing it on a single initiation ceremony, which one entered as a child, and emerged from as an adult. The granting of the *toga virilis* to the Roman boy, the Bar Mitzvah to the Jewish boy, a period in the huts with her elders for the Zambian girl, all marked a watershed between childhood and adulthood.

One might hope to achieve something like this today by a careful preparation for the sacrament of Confirmation, ritually marking the end of childhood and the assuming of adult responsibilities. Our culture makes that difficult. In fact the nearest approach one sees here to a rite of passage is the ritual drunkenness with which Leaving Certificate results are greeted.

The law itself sees adolescence not as a watershed but a protracted period, with milestones marking the advance to maturity. From fourteen on one is assumed to be capable of crime. Up to sixteen one is bound to stay in school and can claim shelter and care from parents. From sixteen on one is allowed to marry without special permission, to drive a motor-bike, or, from seventeen, a car. From eighteen one may vote in national elections, purchase alcohol, sign contracts, allow medical examinations or operations on oneself. Other regulations take age into account when admitting to classified films or granting half-price in transport.

## WHEN TEENAGERS WERE INVENTED

The invention of adolescence as we know it dates from the 1950s, when the business opportunists of the Western world discovered that a large population of teenage boys and girls, still living at home, were earning money in part or full-time jobs, with few commitments and much disposable income. A huge market was created and served, with blue denim, T-shirts and tops, constantly changing styles of hair, boots and runners, with magazines, and above all with music, first in records, then tapes and compact discs, music in a thousand distinctive styles, but all *young* music. Put together, it amounted to a separate culture, which at its loudest conveyed values hostile to those of most adults, and shouted sex, drugs and rock and roll.

The sociologists define adolescence in terms of *socialisation*: absorbing the values, standards and beliefs current in society, and *role changing* — learning new roles, moving from the dependent student to the young worker, from the dutiful daughter to the girlfriend, etc.

The psychoanalysts date adolescence from the upsurge of instincts which follows puberty. This leads the youngster to look outside the family for appropriate love objects. Anna Freud described the teen years as 'the slow, painful end of one's first love affair — daughter with father, son with mother'.

The manuals on adolescence offer more concrete summaries of what teenagers have to achieve: to come to terms with a new body, managing one's diet, sleep and appearance, and learning how to care for one's own health, a job hitherto managed by mother; to stretch an intelligence that is reaching the height of its powers; to live with a turmoil of moods and emotions; to learn how to manage one's peer group, to get on with the opposite sex, to accept one's own burgeoning sexuality so that it may become a mode of love;

to achieve independence of parents and a style and identity of one's own; to find a place in society by choosing and preparing for a career; and finally and slowly, to move towards a sense of what life is about.

## BIGGER YOUNGER

The first task of adolescence is implicit in the word *adolescere,* meaning to grow up. Thanks to better nourishment and control of disease in infancy, physical growth is happening earlier than ever in Ireland. Though we have better research data on other western countries than on our own, it is clear that our children reflect the secular trend evident in all developed countries over the last century, the trend towards an earlier puberty. The beginning of physical puberty, marked by the first period in girls, the first emission of seed in boys, is coming earlier by about four months every decade.

Now growth itself is simply a happening, determined by nourishment, health and genetic factors. The *task* lies in coming to terms with that new body, and with the fact that the timing and pace of growth vary so hugely. The growth spurt can happen in normal children anywhere between ten and seventeen, so that a class of fourteen-year-olds seems to include everything from boys barely out of short pants to well-formed young ladies. Those who are well ahead of, or well behind the posse, can still be counted normal, but they do not feel it.

Lewis Carroll depicted the alarm of Alice when her body started to shoot up after she drank from the magic bottle. Most children pass through an awkward, coltish period of perhaps two years when their limbs have stretched beyond their strength; when (in males) the voice is unstable, neither boy's nor man's; when the body image is so fluid that they are unsure where their arms and legs end, so tend to knock things over, or trip on a pattern in the carpet; when their figure has lost the trimness of late childhood and shows puppy fat or gangly limbs; when their smooth face grows rough and pimpled, and the mirror both draws and repels them.

## To the Mother of Under-sized Mark

He is a small fourteen-year-old, the shortest in his class, and he hates it. In the last few months he has given up football and swimming, and his work has become slovenly. You are afraid he is in a downhill slide towards a poor Leaving Certificate.

Overall, children are growing bigger, and developing sexually, at an earlier date. Presumably the trend will level out with time. The first careful Irish research into the matter (1986) found the average menarche of Irish girls to be thirteen-and-a-half. Girls from higher socio-economic groups and urban areas tend to mature earlier, while those with poor nutrition, chronic illness, psychological problems or excessive exercise have a late menarche.

Where does that leave you with Mark? The sequence of growth in boys obviously differs from that in girls. In girls the growth spurt — putting on four inches a year instead of the two and a half that has been the average through childhood — precedes the other signs of puberty. In boys the growth spurt usually comes later, after the changes in the genitals, the appearance of pubic and facial hair, and the first emission of seed.

As in so many other matters, we know more about other countries than about our own. There are no clear figures for Irish boys. In Britain the sharp spurt in growth comes generally after the fourteenth birthday. But that is only an average. Normal children (statistically normal, that is) may enter puberty at any time from ten to seventeen. They do not feel normal, any more than Mark does. He feels the odd man out, with a high-pitched voice compared with the deepening and breaking sounds of his classmates; with a child's hairless body that may draw comments in the changing rooms from his hairier, more developed peers.

I can remember another Mark whom I taught, a bright, quiet boy, always reserved rather than outgoing; as clever as they come, a hard and ambitious worker, and a good swimmer and footballer up to the age of twelve. Like your Mark, he was late in the growth spurt. Around fourteen, he became so conscious of his smallness that he gave up

192

swimming and football rather than stand the comparisons and comments of the changing-room. His handwriting became small and crabby, he became visibly despondent, and his work gradually deteriorated to the point where teachers were saying he would have to repeat a year.

He was a healthy boy, he was eating well, and his parents were both reasonably tall; there was no physical reason for him to be small. Doctors could do nothing. Parents were understanding and concerned. Nobody was to blame, and it was no use moralising or exhorting Mark; that only made him feel worse. He knew how badly he was doing on all fronts, but he felt inadequate every time he looked in the mirror, or spoke aloud in class. As with most teenage problems, the solution was to be found not in intervention but in the passing of time.

He made it in time. By the beginning of Fifth Year he had put on several inches, was shaving and deep-voiced, developed a bolder, more confident handwriting, and his work took off to the point where he was able to opt for medical school after a good Leaving Certificate.

There is no denying that early developers have an advantage. Generally they do better both in sports and social relationships, and even academically, probably all stemming from the self-confidence that bodily maturing can bring with it. There are bonuses for the late developers too. Their personalities are more formed, their intelligence more alert, by the time they face the excitements and anxieties that sexual maturity brings with it. Even their small stature can help. We have seen superb sportsmen who in their teens were small but nippy and agile, and able to run rings round their lumbering peers with long, coltish, badly-controlled limbs.

Whether they develop early or late, those years of physical change are uncomfortable to live through. Mark will lose a sense of the continuity of his body, will not know how he appears to the world, as his limbs stretch, his face grows spotty, and he loses control over his voice. Most teenagers are sensitive to their changing body, and critical of it. One way or another, it is important to them, and it is little use our telling them it will soon change. If we wait patiently, pray steadily, and make sure they know they enjoy our blessing and approval, we will be delighted with what the years effect.

## TAKING CONTROL OF THE BODY

This new body has not merely to be lived in, but to be managed: teenagers are gradually taking over control of the body from mother. By twenty they should know how to choose, buy and cook healthy food; how to get themselves into and out of bed in a way that gives them enough sleep (it is extraordinary how many twenty-year-olds still see going to bed and getting up as an arbitrary demand forced on them by parents); how to plan their clothes and style and put a personal signature on their appearance. There is usually a period of unassumed responsibility, when the young person feels free to take risks with a healthy body that feels immortal, but if things go wrong, somehow expects mother to make it better. This is the time when they tell her that risks with their body and their health are theirs to take: with motor-bikes, hazardous hobbies, and drugs, especially alcohol and nicotine. By twenty the business of taking risks should be worked through.

There is more to cope with: the awareness of sexual drives, of being looked at with interest by the other sex, and of seeing them with new eyes. Time was when children discovered this gradually, in one another's company. Now sexual awareness is thrust on them by the visual media long before it has a meaning in their inner experience.

## SELF TO OTHERS: PART TO PERSON

For Irish children there is a special conflict, in that so much TV and film material reflects one eccentric culture in North America, with a lifestyle based on what is, by global standards, quite freakish wealth, and lacking the roots and values we could take for granted until recently. The task for our children is still the same, though harder than ever to achieve: to grow from a self-regarding and self-indulgent sexuality, to finding in their new body a way of loving someone else; to move from the fascination with part-objects (the hair, breasts, lips, skin, clothes of the girl or boy they like) to a sense of the whole person.

To say that the teens are years of sexual experimentation makes them sound too exciting. For some, sexual uncertainty and self-questioning take the joy out of discovery. The questions are often unformulated, and the worries, about whether one's sexual preferences are normal or not, burrow away in secret (see Chapter Four).

## To the Shocked Mother of Aoife

Quite by accident you heard your fifteen-year-old tell a friend how she had been in bed with a boy. It is hard to handle your feelings about it, much less know how to deal with the situation.

What are all the feelings? Fury at the boy, who you feel seduced Aoife, and who was committing a crime? Panic that Aoife may be pregnant? Fear for what she may do next, now that she has started? Disgust that all your efforts to rear her have come to this? Anguish as to whether you should get her onto the pill? Bewilderment that she should have gone this way? Grief that she is now hiding so much of her life from you that you never suspected what was happening? Hopelessness in face of the tidal wave of sex that sweeps our children? Fear that when your husband hears of it, he may turn violent against either Aoife or the boy?

A combination of all these feelings are present, and when such a rush of emotion is on you, reason goes out the window. This discovery, in a daughter who has seemed a child up to now, has parallels in many encounters with your teenage children, when as parents you are so overwhelmed with anxiety or anger that you tend to burst out with a rush of words, and say things you regret later. You may feel you have to moralise, and stand up for the Christian viewpoint. For a close look at this viewpoint, let me point you to its origins.

In St John's Gospel we read how a ring of slavering, vindictive Pharisees surround a woman taken in the act of adultery. They are hungry for her blood, but want at the same time to trap Jesus by putting him in a dilemma: between the demands of the Mosaic law on the one side, sentencing such a woman to death by stoning, and the call for forgiveness and mercy on the other side.

The emotion is running high, and any words will be seized on and turned into a raging quarrel. Jesus stoops and writes in the sand. Nobody knows what he wrote.

The effect was to leave the truth some space to surface. Jesus had time to find his own answer; 'Let the one among you who is sinless be the first to throw a stone at her.' There is help there for you in your dilemma: be slow to judge. How you wish you could find a curtain-line like Jesus does: 'Go away and from this moment sin no more.'

The first remark is crucial. In your anger you want to punish, to impose a final solution. You are inclined to say: 'That's it. You're grounded for a month', or 'I never liked those friends anyway. And I suspect you have been drinking' or something of that sort. Your strong feelings threaten to swamp you, so you cut off conversation, impose your decision, and discourage Aoife from explaining herself or sorting out where she is.

When she was seven you knew what Aoife was feeling, and could read her face and her body. Now at fifteen you find yourself afraid of what she is feeling, and you do not want to listen in case it confirms your fears.

As a mother you can still be useful here. Aoife had probably been drinking, had been under pressure from the boy, had listened to the group's talk about 'going the whole way'. Now that she has gone the whole way she too is overwhelmed by feelings she cannot sort out: shame at her behaviour, disgust at giving into pressure, fears for her future relationship with the boy in question, and with other boys, and perhaps an underlying hunger to try it again.

Some mothers in this dilemma invade their daughter's room and rummage in her private diary, rather than listen to what the girl may tell them. This is the end of honesty. You cannot expect her to be honest with you if you pry behind her back like that.

You will help Aoife and keep the love flowing only if she knows that you are on her side. For that you must be able to listen to her. No listening will take place unless your first remark is one that keeps communication open. Jesus did it by saying nothing, doodling in the sand. Whatever words you use when tackling this charged encounter, they must mean: 'I am interested, I love you, and I am ready to listen if you want to talk.'

This leaves many issues to be tackled, about drinking, going with the gang, what you think of her friends, sexual behaviour, and the like. You will not tackle any of them unless conversation takes place. It is small comfort to exchange high sentiments with your husband if Aoife is not in touch with either of you. After a discovery such as this the first exchange can easily be an explosion, in which you vent your own feelings and fears, but leave no space for Aoife's.

The other way grows out of quiet prayer, and considers these priorities. What is Aoife feeling? What are your own feelings and worries? How can you help Aoife? By information, practical and emotional support, discussing values and setting limits. A conversation that *begins* with you setting limits and passing judgment, is likely to leave both sides fuming and all communication pushed underground.

Remember Jesus in that highly charged scene, faced with accusing men and a sinful woman. He does nothing to aggravate the situation or cut off communication, but helps the truth to surface.

## INDEPENDENCE AND IDENTITY: RELUCTANT CHICKENS

With the rise of unemployment, the achieving of independence from parents is harder than ever. Ireland is overstocked with nests full of reluctant chickens, fledglings who want to fly but cannot find the wherewithal. At the turn of the century the average child moved into the world of work (often on the land) before she turned thirteen, years before sexual maturity, which arrived about four years later then than it does now. Today's teenagers see themselves as physically mature, able to pass for over-eighteen when they want to, but facing an indefinite moratorium on the essential badge of adulthood, namely earning their own living.

197

Having a job constitutes so much of our identity that its absence often leads to aberrant developments. Some go for a pre-packaged identity, in totalitarian bodies like fundamentalist cults or the Provisional IRA, which offer the still unformed youngster a set of attitudes, morals, companions, and style, and save him from making any choices other than to obey. Others seek their true selves in premature intimacy with a lover: two bodies coming together before either knows either him/herself or the partner. Others again find a negative identity in rejecting everything that smacks of security or establishment, a rejection that can find musical echoes in the angrier music of Punk and Heavy Metal. These and other forms of foreclosure are ways of avoiding the tentative and uncomfortable process of working towards a personal identity.

## The Change in Timothy

He is your eldest, a tall thirteen-year-old, and has always been a joy to you. Since he started secondary school he seems to be changing. He questions what you say, thinks he is old enough to do everything adults do, and seems to be different from the child you have known. What is wrong?

He is the first child you have seen saying goodbye to childhood, and it is a difficult and sad experience, for you as well as for him. The Jews marked, and still mark that watershed with a single celebration, the Bar Mitzvah. The fourteen-year-old boy (it happens to girls in the Bar Mitzvah also, but not in Jesus' time) who celebrates this feast with his family and relations, is accepted as a 'Son of the Commandment', which is what Bar Mitzvah means. He answers God's law personally, no longer simply through his parents. In one bound he moves from childhood to adulthood.

We have nothing like it in the Church. In Ireland at least, the Sacrament of Confirmation comes too early to mark this watershed. It does mark a time when children begin to feel that childhood is over, and when attitudes to parents change in a subtle and secret way. Younger children idealise their parents, see Daddy as the strongest and wisest of men, and mother as the best mother in the world. They may kick against parents, but still see them as larger than life, and basically invulnerable.

Timothy is coming to the end of that secure period when all his emotional nourishment came from you two, and all his attitudes and opinions were a reflection of yours. Like a rowing boat pushing out from a large and stable pier, he needs you to push against while he floats out over deeper waters, on his own. He will show that dizzying in-between state. One day he seems independent, competent, able to manage public transport, computers, machines in the house, and, if you let him, even the family car or tractor. The next day he is furious because you have not put out a clean shirt for him or you expect him to cut his own bread, or he wants to weep on your shoulder over something that happened at school.

You are caught like Britain in the 1940s and 1950s, anxious to give independence to her colonies and empire, but uncertain of the timing. If you move to stand back from him too fast, he will blame you for lack of support. If you move too slowly, he will blame you for keeping him in nappies.

You cannot be right. Family life is changing, and has to change. If the family is a success, Timothy will be able to manage without it in a few years. The in-between stage is difficult to negotiate with any feeling of success. You are dealing with a moving target. If you keep him too tight, or are intrusive, wanting to know everything about his developing life, you may feel more secure yourself but you may stunt his growth to maturity. If you bow out, and act as though he was already grown-up, you will terrify him, because he knows that he still needs you to place limits, no matter how much he may resist them.

With your first adolescent, you are learning at the same time as he is. His teen years are different from your teens, and it will keep you young if you learn with and through him what it is like to be thirteen today. It is a sign of your success that Timothy is secure enough to feel a child no longer.

199

## Is it Harder With a Daughter?

In the last year things have become awful between you and thirteen-year-old Margaret. She follows you around the house asking for what she knows you won't allow, and abusing you if you say no. Do things have to be that bad between a mother and her teenage daughter?

There is a pain about the separation of a mother and daughter, especially if they have been very close through childhood. Boys do it earlier: between the ages of two and six a little boy comes to realise that in one important way he is different from the mother on whom he has totally depended, and models himself on his father, or any big male in sight. His separation comes early. For girls, issues of feminine identity do not depend on separation from mother. When the separation comes, in the early teens, it is not, as for the little boy, male differentiating himself from female, but young woman establishing her independence from older woman.

In order to become a separate person, Margaret will challenge the values and opinions she has taken from you through the years of childhood. She may well — probably will — come back to them, but first she has to scrutinise them and make them her own. More than that, she has to take you off your pedestal in her mind.

With puberty she has rapidly grown to your height, and with her first period has a sense that she can reproduce children. She has the body of a woman. With this can come a mood of manic grandiosity, a feeling 'I am as big as they are'. It is manic because it is unrealistic. Margaret could not manage on her own, she could not be a proper mother. She denies her fears of incompetence, helplessness and the loss of mother, and claims arrogantly that she does not need parents any more. There is often a period of denigration, of actively putting down parents. It is one painful way of growing out of the childhood idealisation of them, and childish expectations of support from them. So Margaret follows you round the house, pushes you to say things and make decisions, and then uses all her energies to showing how silly they are.

It is not a happy time for either of you. For Margaret, the manic self-assertion alternates with moods of depression, with realising how truly dependent she is and will remain for some time to come. At times she mourns the end of childhood, when you were the emotional anchor of her life. She has moved into an emotional vacuum, and looks for any sort of excitement and thrill to fill the vacuum, to release her from the silent void. She will tend to act big and independent in noisy and visible acts of self-assertion: slamming doors, leaving home, impressing others by making a lot of noise, dressing to be seen a mile away. It is not rational behaviour, though it may be vehemently defended in arguments. She is acting up under the impulse of primitive processes that have taken over from reflective and mature ones.

Maturity has to come from you. But how? Face your own feelings first. You can be lonely for the child who, having been your faithful companion for years, would suddenly rather be with anyone but you. Hurt adult feelings can easily lead you into cycles of nagging and unnecessary, wounding remarks, for instance about Margaret's 'unsuitable' friends. As a mother you find it hard to stay friendly when Margaret rejects your carefully considered and mature advice, and looks instead to a clueless youngster of her own age.

This impossible situation will not last for ever, if you weather it patiently without becoming vindictive or being drawn into a cycle of retaliation and punishment. The most successful parents seem to be those who go through a sort of mini-adolescence themselves, talking and listening to their children as intelligent human beings, while going over their own beliefs and conduct to find a new firmness for themselves. At the same time they lay down clear and positive limits on the big issues in which they have to control Margaret's life and protect her. In that way teenagers teach us to be parents, a painful and humbling process for us as for them, fraught with uncertainties, but rewarded at the end with greater maturity for both adults and children.

## Matthew in the Doldrums

Matthew is sixteen and in Fifth Year. He earned a couple of honours in his Junior Certificate, but he has not studied since, and nothing you do seems to motivate him. He is a nice boy, easy to live with, but idle and letting the precious months slip away.

For Matthew, I imagine, the importance of the Leaving Certificate, and its value as a job currency at home and in Europe, is just so much adult talk, with no real bite. He is in the doldrums, a boy of average ability who is faced with the sudden added difficulties which the Leaving Certificate course brings. He finds the new courses much longer and more complex. He notices how much more quickly other students master the work than he does. He realises now that the Junior Certificate was a relatively unimportant dry run for the big exam — and a fairly easy dry run, giving little idea of the complexities ahead.

He is having a first introduction to some new subjects like Accountancy, with a strange vocabulary and a new way of thinking about money. Try a few lessons yourself in some new subject, say Russian or Japanese, and you will taste the sense of barely subdued despair Matthew may feel: a sense that it is all too much, that he will never get on top of all this strangeness; that the teacher is moving too fast, and he has not yet mastered what she covered last week.

On top of that, Matthew is trying to discover what he wants to be, not just in terms of a job but also in his lifestyle, clothes, taste in music, and philosophy of life. In six years' time you will see a young adult who knows who he is, what he wants and what he likes. He cannot jump into that finished state. It comes by experiment, and that can seem a threatening process. Some will opt to be clones of their parents, prolonging childhood and taking their tastes and opinions from their elders. Some will do just the opposite, and reject everything represented by their parents, but be unsure what they want themselves: a negative identity.

It sounds as if Matthew is neither of these. You still matter to him, yet he knows he is not a child any more, knows also that his choices are going to differentiate him from you in a way that never happened in childhood. It is no good trying to impose solutions on him. Whatever he works out has to be his own. At this stage he has made the important decision about Leaving Certificate subjects. The next urgency will arise when he has to make choices about courses after school, and that is some distance away. Meanwhile he feels in the doldrums, seldom coming to life. He is made constantly aware of the targets proposed for him by the adult world. What are the targets which, consciously or not, he would set for himself?

The first is *to avoid false solutions,* the sort of compromises with society's demands where the price seems to be one's deepest dreams and integrity.

Secondly, in the doldrums of the teens it seems important to *feel real,* with all the intensity of which a healthy young body is capable. The occasions for this may be rare, such as good concerts and parties, when young music, and the heightened emotion it generates, make you want it to last for ever. If you cannot feel real, then many opt to feel nothing at all, and the easiest way to do this is to stay in bed or watch television. One could form a populous club in Dublin of oldish teenagers who live at home, stay in bed all day, and at night watch TV or talk to their friends: an unnerving sight for parents, who fear depression or psychotic breakdown, sometimes with reason.

The third target is *to prod society* repeatedly so that society's antagonism is made manifest, and can be met with antagonism. Secondary teachers will remember the barely concealed delight of older students when they have wrong-footed a teacher or Principal into a display of injustice or temper, which then legitimises their protests and indignation.

The final target is *to defy* in a setting in which dependence is met and can be relied on to be met. Nothing makes more demands on parents than this: to hold the limits within a family, to face unreasoned anger and ingratitude, and meet it with firmness but no retaliation, no vindictiveness. Nothing tests the vocation of a father more than this: to experience the limits of his control over his children, to run out of punishments and rewards, but not out of love. Nothing teaches the single mother more painfully her need for a partner than to face this unsupported.

Even as this is written, it seems bland and complacent. The agony of a parent is not just about the immediate crisis — will Matthew come home before morning? How to answer the headmaster when he tackles me yet again about his behaviour? Some crises reflect more than a passing phase.

Parents' deeper concern touches the long-term effects on their children's lives. There are sixteen-year-old alcoholics, whose planning and pleasures all revolve round the availability of drink There are teenage mothers whose unplanned pregnancy will affect their emotional life for years, and, if they keep the baby, will radically affect their career. Those who idle before the Leaving Certificate will pay for the idleness in having few doors open to them after school. Those who fall into delinquency will find that the possession of a police record dogs their movements and opportunities for years. Where adolescent defiance leads to drug-dependency, unwanted pregnancy, delinquency or academic failure, then it is more than a passing phase: the inevitable consequences are not transitory. Yet it remains true that the great majority of what adults see as teenage problems, are cured not by intervention, but by the passing of time.

That wise observer of adolescents and children, Dr D.W. Winnicott, put it pithily in *The Family and Individual Development* (London, Tavistock, 1965, p. 87):

'The big challenge from the adolescent is to the bit of ourselves that has not really had its adolescence. This bit of ourselves makes us resent these people being able to have their phase of the doldrums, and makes us want *to find a solution for them.* There are hundreds of false solutions. Anything we say or do is wrong. We give support and we are wrong. We withdraw support and that is wrong too. We dare not be "understanding". But in the course of time we find that this adolescent boy and this adolescent girl have come out of the doldrums phase and are now able to begin identifying with society, with parents, and with all sorts of wider groups, without feeling threatened with personal extinction.'

In the course of time, writes Winnicott. Is that all that a parent or concerned adult can do, wait? There is scant comfort for them in the gnomic wisdom of Shaw: 'If youth is a sickness, it's soon cured.' What will you do meanwhile about the warning notes from school, the money wasted on alcohol or other drugs, the furniture or walls damaged in youthful rage, all the other signs of the doldrums phase? Matthew will find a solution to his doldrums in the passing of time, not in what other people do to him. Meanwhile, what can *you* do?

First of all, believe in Matthew. Keep the conviction alive in yourself that he will find what he wants. Secondly avoid the tempting solution of treating him as a child, supervising his homework to the point where he may feel it is your job rather than his. Avoid the other extreme of going along with the unrealistic proposals Matthew may make: of blaming the school and looking for a change, or pinning his hopes on a breakthrough into the pop music scene where nobody requires a Leaving Certificate. Do not imagine that putting him into a boarding school with supervised study will produce working habits. Some of the most idle sixteen-year-olds I know spend three or four hours a day in supervised study, in a sort of trance in which they barely get through their homework, much less tackle revision.

It is an age at which an encouraging and well-liked teacher can make a greater impact than you. The particular skills and training of a Guidance Counsellor can be at their most useful here, in helping Matthew to see where his strengths of personality and ability might lead.

Do not think that by removing all his pleasures you will wean him to work. He needs some point of joy in the week to sustain him through the drudgery of school. I have known parents who in a moment of pique banned their son from the one bright spot of his week, and saw things go from bad to worse.

You and your husband are in the best position to fathom why Matthew is not working. Remember yourselves when you were sixteen. You pass on more than you intend to your children, and more than they intend to learn from you. You may say that life was different then, the world a harder place, and opportunities fewer. It was indeed different, but families have a way of reproducing patterns, especially of how teenagers relate to their parents. You may learn much from your memories of how you viewed schoolwork and parental pressure when you were Matthew's age.

Let me suggest a few possible reasons for idleness, from sixteen-year-olds with fictitious names.

*Maurice* had been puny, weak and the target of bullying. With puberty he put on several inches, developed muscle, and for a while his only thought was to avenge himself on boys and adults for the misery he had gone through. He became a reckless, self-destructive rebel, always in trouble at school. His parents stayed close to him, would not be provoked into retaliation, and their understanding of what was moving him gradually seeped through to Maurice, who calmed down just in time to work for his Leaving Certificate.

*Jack* was equally rebellious, equally self-destructive, but in a bizarre way. After long agonising his parents brought him to a psychiatrist, who saw the beginnings of a psychotic breakdown, helped him back to managing his life calmly, and helped his parents and teachers to live with him without panicking.

*Siobhan* was big and beautiful, but so angry that she had no energy left for work. Her anger had not started inside her. It was her mother who was the really angry one, furious and resentful at loss of communication with a husband who was faithful and kind, but could not pick up feelings. Mother targetted big, idle Siobhan for her fury, a sort of scapegoat for her frustration over the disappointments of marriage. When she understood what was happening, the fury of both of them eased and work began again.

After that series of happy endings, what about Matthew? I can picture him, well-grown and handsome. He looks eighteen and makes friends mainly with older boys. He is passionate about computers and guitar — not so good at the latter, but full of fantasies about making it in the pop scene. He is a boy of his generation, accustomed, through TV and computers, to stimulation that keeps pace with the quickness of his own brain. At sixteen his intelligence is at its fastest, and the desires of his body at their keenest. In an earlier age he would now be part of the adult world. He is at a good school, but bored out of his mind by classwork, by the routines of book-keeping and French grammar and the predictable oddities of teachers. Boredom is not so much the absence of feeling, as the frustration of unexpressed desire, and it is not easy, when your powers are at their height, to submit to the drudgeries of preparing for exams.

However the prizes are there, if he is ready to work for them, boring though that work is. His generation will have opportunities in Ireland or abroad, provided they finish school and seek some further training. The three groups who will have little access to those opportunities are the drop-outs from school, the frequent job-changers, and the single mothers.

What about you? With a boy like Matthew coercion does not work, but negotiation does. He may be rather full of himself, and hard to live with, but part of that is unspoken envy at your security, while he has all the crises in front of him. Recognise the points of pleasure in his week, which make the drudgery more bearable, and keep the real opportunities in front of him.

The prizes within his grasp are more exciting than anything that I faced. I never experienced the entertaining and attractive adults on TV, and the fascinating responsiveness of computers, to throw the boredom of classwork and teachers into stark relief. My generation was inured to boredom, and found it easier to tolerate its frustrations.

It would be easy to envy Matthew his opportunities, but that would spoil your dealings with him. Instead, help him towards self-control by your own self-control, and keep the realities of his future calmly and repeatedly before him.

Today's forty-year-olds may have acquired knowledge and some wisdom about the ways of the world; but they have never experienced the life of today's teenagers They have not lived with the dominance of computer games and the built-in categories of thinking they impose; or the accessibility of sexual experience together with the new hazards of AIDS; or the fierce academic competition with little prospect of employment at the end; or the shadows of a drug culture which has to be faced in one's peers; or the political disalignment of the globe, with the uncertainty about what is next. This is a different world, and young people sense the falseness of formulas for living which do not take account of these pressures.

There *are* abiding values. Teenage children rely on their parents to draw limits and to challenge — even though the limits are constantly broken and the challenges ignored. Parents will not communicate those values by quotations from a book, but by listening and talking to their children as intelligent and good humans; with a readiness to go over their own beliefs and conduct to find a new firmness for themselves; with a determination to survive as a couple by mutual support in face of pressures; and with passionate resort to the Lord, often with the desperation of King David in the darkest psalms, hanging in there while the floods seem to be rising.

## To the Mother of Moody Ciara

Ciara is fifteen and has become awfully moody. You know about moods — you are up and down yourself, going through the menopause — but she is often hard to take, going from crazy levels of noise and activity to deep melancholy when life seems pointless. You wonder is she going mad.

Ciara — I've met her — is late coming to puberty, still expecting her first period, for which she has been prepared since twelve. You remember Hilaire Belloc's couplet:

'Kings live in palaces, and pigs in sties,
But youth in expectation. Youth is wise.'

Living in Ciara's sort of expectation is not easy. Her body is now beginning to prepare for the first period, so there is much hormonal turmoil, the first experience of premenstrual tension, and like all first experiences, unnerving to live through because you do not know when or how it will end. Boys and girls can do nothing but wait for the changes of puberty, which will come, but at different ages. Waiting puts a considerable strain on all, but especially on the late developers. So the late ones like Ciara can be found imitating her classmates who have developed earlier, and this leads away from a natural tempo of development to a false sort of maturity. She acts older than she is or looks.

Once she is twenty she will never again have to face the ambiguities of this age. She feels she belongs in the adult world. She is clever and quick-witted, can pick up plots and allusions on TV faster than her parents. But she is still so small that she could claim half-fare on buses, and be refused entrance to an over-15 film, when many of her friends could get in without a second glance, and could order alcohol in a bar without being questioned.

There is nothing you can do to help her grow. She eats well enough and her body is simply waiting for internal signals to develop. For Ciara it adds one exasperation to the irks she already suffers. Though she works well enough, she is bored by school, is not motivated to study when there is no public exam to put pressure on the class. She feels the daily drudgery of class and homework as a burden imposed on her, not as a means towards realising her ambitions; and the easiest culprits to blame for imposing the burden are parents and teachers.

She is becoming aware of the cruelty and suffering in the world, of the killing that TV shows. It is a measure of her own good childhood that she is horrified by this, and cannot yet accept the capacity for hate and anger that is part of herself. It will be years before she has accepted the shadow side of herself. Meanwhile the miseries and conflicts which she views and reads about touch an uneasy chord of anger and guilt in her. Her reaction is to throw all the blame on the adults who have made such a mess of the world.

Evil remains a mystery, but all young people, at some level, whether emotional or intellectual, try to make sense of what life is about, try to face the questions of God, of life and death and life after death, and moral values. That development continues through life. One aspect of it impinges sharply on the teenage girl or boy, namely coping with evil, taking on the responsibility for suffering and cruelty in the world; and learning that the guilt we feel over that suffering can be assuaged by work and dependability in a job.

In *A Wreath for the Enemy* (London, Signet Books, 1964, p. 135) Pamela Frankau wrote:

'When children emerge from the kindly-seeming prisons of schools, they meet the world of true dimensions and true values. These are unexpectedly painful and irregular. Reality is always irregular and generally painful. To be unprepared for its shocks and to receive the shocks upon a foundation of innocence is the process of growing up.'

Ciara is unaware of much of this, and you will not get far by suggesting these ideas to her. So much of living with teenagers demands being able to be quiet and dependable, being able to absorb anger without taking it personally. There is an even more basic conflict that Ciara faces, of which she cannot be aware. Growing up means taking the parent's place. In the unconscious fantasy it is inherently an aggressive act. Ciara is caught between her love for her parents and her sense of having to displace them. It takes a wise parent to face the unexplained anger of a teenager and not retaliate.

Do you feel at times that Ciara is shouting at an imaginary parent, not at the real you who loves her? She cannot accept her own anger so she projects it onto you, and acts as though you are persecuting her, rather than the other way round. It would tempt you to be vindictive, to return angry word for angry word. Never let her way of treating you determine your way of treating her. The first response asked of a grown-up is calm.

Ciara can make you feel useless. At times she is clearly in distress, unable to cope with social life or her own emotions, so miserable that she almost forces you to intrude; but then makes you feel you are interfering and anyway have nothing to offer. She burdens you with a sense of her own depression, and frustrates your attempts to help her. She ends a conversation with 'Ah, what's the use?' — which by making you feel useless only reflects her own feeling of uselessness.

Can you sometimes pick this up, say 'You feel hopeless at the moment?' It will help more than any attempted solution. You are taking in her misery, containing it, changing it into something she can bear. When Ciara leaves you after a conversation, ask yourself how you feel. Without trying, she can make you feel as she does: exhilarated or useless, controlled or chaotic, depressed or determined, looking to the past or the future, the bright or the gloomy. The feelings you pick up in yourself when Ciara walks out of the room are often feelings that she has dumped on you.

The art of living with Ciara, as you know better than I do, is of being able to absorb anger without retaliating; being able to set limits that are wise and helpful, without being vindictive or using limits simply to punish. It means being able to listen to her complaints about her less-than-perfect parents and teachers without internalising the blame and feeling guilty. Above all it means being able to *survive* as a reliable buffer she can kick against, somebody whose moods will not go up and down as her own do. In the middle of your own menopause that is a pretty heroic task.

## Is Fiona Depressed?

At fourteen she is cranky and broody. She always has a long face and does not want to go out, and you wonder is she really depressed.

By 'depressed' you do not mean downhearted in a normal way, but clinically, psychiatrically sick. It may not be easy to tell the difference, but it is important. If she is clinically depressed, you will need the help of a psychiatrist. Otherwise you should be able to manage within the family.

When did you first become worried about Fiona's moods? She may be reacting to the sort of blows that can upset a fourteen-year-old: being ditched by a friend, failing an exam, shifting to a different class, having to wear a brace on her teeth, moving out of a familiar house or neighbourhood, getting a hard time from a teacher, or worse still, sensing serious tension between her parents. Normal enough blows, such as we have all survived, but while we survived them, the world felt bleak.

Supposing Fiona is upset in this way just at a time when her resistance is low: when she is tired, or physically out of sorts, or suffering from menstrual problems; then the blow will hit her more than twice as hard, and her recovery will be slower. She will need the sort of support that parents give best, not trying to moralise or jolly Fiona out of it — that is futile — but ensuring rest and physical recovery, an easing of pressure, and tender, loving care.

It is more worrying if you cannot put your finger on any cause for Fiona's broodiness. That still does not mean that you call for a doctor. From infancy on, some children are sunny and some seem gloomy. Temperaments vary. Even a healthy child may be more inclined to frown than to smile.

There are signs that suggest a more serious upset. A girl who is clinically depressed will usually show some though not all of them:

(1) There is a mood of *hopeless sadness,* not warranted by what Fiona has actually experienced. It is just there, and she does not try to justify it. She feels tired, lethargic, with no heart to tackle anything.

(2) She has *lost the capacity for enjoyment.* The savour has vanished even from activities that normally give her pleasure.

(3) She *feels worthless,* unimportant, and deserving of all the misery that afflicts her. She dismisses her real achievements, expects to fail and to lose her friends, and sees no reason why people should like or respect her.

(4) A sense of *guilt* may complicate this: guilt for upsetting her family, for doing badly at school, or a vague unspecified guilt for some larger crime that seems to cloud her conscience.

(5) *Anxiety* may show itself in restlessness, inability to sit still or settle down to anything.

(6) There may be *disturbances of sleep* (slow to drop off, early to wake) of appetite and normal bodily well-being, in the shape of aches, constipation or menstrual disturbances.

(7) Fiona may seem preoccupied with thoughts of *death* or injury, and raise the fear of suicide by remarks, threats or carelessness about her life. These have to be taken seriously.

A list like this is alarming, but difficult to use. It takes the informed and practised eye of a doctor to diagnose clinical depression with any assurance. The only point of diagnosis is to lead towards appropriate treatment and help, which is far more available and effective today than thirty years ago.

We are often too quick to give children labels like hyperactive, handicapped, depressed, in a way that is simply destructive. Once we have pigeon-holed Fiona, we may see her simply as a problem, no longer as a young girl with all her hidden desires and richness. Even if there is a medical problem, and a medical treatment, she remains someone unique and special, with a life and treatment that go far beyond a label like depressed. Throughout her treatment she will continue to need you, her parents, family and friends more than ever before.

## WHAT DO THEY EXPECT OF US?

There has been such a change in our children's lives and values, you are sometimes puzzled as to what they think or expect of you. Especially in the teens, they depend so much on what their friends say, you wonder do parents matter at all.

You still know your own better than anyone else, even their best friend. It is still useful to look around for evidence of what groups of young people think. Opinion surveys rely on small samples, and sometimes the questions are set in a way that expects one answer. When you put the better ones together, they can give us some insights, not all of them expected.

Not long ago a sample of Dublin girls and boys in Fourth and Fifth Year of secondary school were asked about television as it was used in their families. It was surprising to find that

95% of them *expected* their parents to control TV for them. They doubted their own will-power to set limits for themselves, and would prefer to grumble against the restrictions imposed by parents, while secretly welcoming the wisdom of them.

However they did not all see their parents as models of wisdom or fairness. 'They send us up to study for the Leaving in a cold room, while they sit at a warm fire watching TV. They impose that sacrifice on us, but will not make it for themselves, and it is very hard to concentrate on dull study in the cold while the sounds of some good film or programme are coming from downstairs.' Boys were particularly critical of their mothers who put television soap operas before house-work.

One boy commented: 'I haven't spoken to my father for eighteen months, except to say hello. He is a TV addict, and if I want to talk about something I want, or that is bad news for him, he always pushes me off because of some programme that he *has* to watch. The best night for years was when an ESB strike led to a power cut and we had neither light nor TV. The whole family was forced to sit round the fire by candlelight and *talk*. It was marvellous, the first real communication for years.'

It was curious to see the envy of some young people for the opportunities their parents had. 'They talk to us about the "home games" they played in the family when they were young — sounds as if it was great. But they have never taught us any of those games to play with us. They seem to think television makes them impossible. So they had the best of both worlds, family games when they were young, and TV now. I feel cheated.'

It is not surprising to find them critical of their parents' self-indulgence if the same parents are urging restraint on their children. A girl was hammered for smoking by her mother, who went through fifty cigarettes a day. A boy had logged his father's drinking over a four-month period, in helpless anger at the family money feeding an insatiable thirst. 'How can he talk to me when he is going on like that?'

Another boy was sent to bed early, before he could finish his homework, because 'Me ould fella's on night shift and me ould one is courting another fella, so she wanted me out of the way.'

Coming through all the comments is the sharp eye of teenage children. They start with high expectations of their parents, and it does not matter greatly whether Dad or Mum makes appropriate speeches about good behaviour. It *does* matter how they behave. Parents are offering a model of behaviour all day long, and that makes a much deeper impression than what they say about it. They want their elders to act like adults, with some consistency between what they preach to children and what they do.

Lest the picture seem to be one of inevitable conflict, one should note a recent, careful survey of parent-adolescent relationships in the western world.[15] Strife is the exception. Four out of five families survive the teens with relatively little serious conflict. They work through these years in harmony, with perhaps two or three arguments a week, but arguments that do not stop the love flowing.

The notion of adolescence as a period of unavoidable warfare and strife, does not square with experience, and is probably an artifact of clinicians who are confronted by the casualties rather than the normals. Only 20% have serious disputes of any substance, and less than 10% show a dramatic deterioration in parent-child relationships during adolescence. Sometimes these parents are conscientious and hard-working, utterly devoted to their children, yet constantly at war with them.

This can happen if the parents' fears for their children have banished all enjoyment of them. When Sinéad meets her mother, she runs into a sense of anxiety and foreboding, about friends, dress, discos, study, behaviour at school, smoking. Every conversation is overshadowed by mother's *fears* for her, leaving no room for pleasure in her company.

Children know when we have delight in their company, a delight that is clear-sighted, not blind to faults, but powerful. Children are nourished above all by our unselfish enjoyment of them. The two-way love between parents and children can survive an awareness of the other's human weaknesses.

## Fergal Thinks he Smells

Your fifteen-year-old is just coming into the growth spurt, a handsome boy; but he hates how he looks and smells, and his misery affects his daily existence to an extent you cannot ignore.

Obviously there are some features that you are given at birth. Over two thousand years ago Aristotle pointed out that you can do nothing about the bone structure and basic shape of your face, but you form the expression on it with your moods and personality.

You can see in some faces that the muscles have become so used to frowning that they can hardly muster a smile without what looks like pain. Other faces reflect peace and good humour in the lines of the mouth and the eyes. I am not thinking here of the teeth-flashing smile you see in glossy magazines, but something more stable, deep and attractive. Faces show cruelty, contentment, pride, tenderness, anger. To an extent they are the mirror of the soul. The face you have at forty is the face that you deserve.

Fergal's face — I know him — has promise of good looks, but he cannot see the promise. He has lost the fresh, winsome rounded look he had at twelve. There is down on the lower face and a few spots on the skin.

It is neither a man's face nor a boy's. It changes from month to month, and he hates the uncertainty, the discontinuity of it. He sees the spots as developing acne. He would rather have a boy's clear skin or a man's moustache than the unshaven down on his lip.

He agonises in front of mirrors, drawn to them by anxiety and longing, but disliking what he sees. To him, his nose seems enormous, and he cannot forget the occasion when a boy in school called him Beaky. Fortunately the name did not stick, except in his self-consciousness. Also lodged there is the slagging he got at scout camp for smelly feet.

You and I can be pretty sure that time is on his side, and will be kind to him. In five years he will be able to look in the mirror without anxiety. But you have picked up how much he suffers from his appearance and smell.

You know what can be done with acne. The glands secreting oily sebum are more active in puberty. That can often result merely in oily skin. However in many teenagers the sebum does not flow freely but concentrates in the hair follicles. There it thickens and produces blackheads and whiteheads. Blackheads are caused not by dirt but by skin pigments caught in the thickened sebum. Whiteheads are caused by the thickened sebum itself.

So anything that helps to keep the hair follicles clear will lessen the chances of acne. Washing with ordinary soap can help. So can the sun's ultra-violet rays, as long as over-exposure is avoided. Hair should be kept free of grease by shampooing, since greasy fringes can positively encourage acne on the forehead.

Fergal, like many teenage boys, has been made aware of smelly feet. They smell because bacteria colonise the sweat on his feet, and are trapped for hours in synthetic-fibre socks and plastic shoes. If he washes often, uses clean socks of cotton or wool, wears shoes of canvas or leather, and airs the shoes at night, he will suffer less. You can help here.

His nose you cannot change. How real is his worry? Fergal may be focussing all the worry about his changing body (especially the fastest-developing but most private area) on the part he cannot change. The size of his nose, ears, lips, or chin, as well as features such as puffy cheeks or high cheek-bones, can be picked out by classmates in a way that devastates a fifteen-year-old. It may be months or years before Fergal comes to accept and even like the new body he is growing into.

If he shows misery about his nose or about the slagging he suffers, you can help by countering: 'It looks OK to me. What's supposed to be wrong with it?' Given time and patience, Fergal will probably leave behind him the discontent about his body that bothers him at the moment. He will then be in a position to discover that true beauty grows, not from conformity to whatever model is fashionable at the moment, but from within himself, from inner contentment.

## Aidan Embarrasses you with his Appearance

You hate the look of your fourteen-year-old. He wants to get his ears pierced, his hair dyed, and to wear screamingly loud colours.

It is difficult to survive Aidan's teens without some battles, and it is important to choose your battlefield, and not be exhausted in an endless series of skirmishes. You could spend all your energy and time arguing about clothes. It would be worth your while to pause first and examine what bothers you.

It is obvious not only that styles have changed and go on changing, but also that the promoters of clothes, hairstyles and jewellery tend to call the tune, and to keep changing the tune so that today's buy will be unavailable in a few weeks.

On a Friday evening you see young girls galloping home to get out of their school uniforms, and an hour later appearing on the streets in clothes that are so similar to those of their friends that they might well be thought a new uniform.

You may well feel sore that so much expense is going on clothes that will be obsolete so quickly. If your children are to learn the value of money, you must work out a way of budgeting for clothes, while allowing your children space to develop their own taste and style. I know a man in his thirties who still relies on his mother to choose his shirts and ties for him — and she still enjoys his dependence. It is little compliment to her that after thirty years of rearing he still cannot choose for himself.

Aidan sounds quite the opposite. It is not that he has discovered what his style is, but rather that he is at the experimental stage of trying out everything, even the most far-out, to see 'What is me?' Much of the teenage behaviour that catches our attention is that sort of try-out behaviour, testing a variety of scripts to see which one will suit your part in life.

One thing is sure, and you may be glad of it: he wants to 'look good', whatever that may mean in his mind. You may remember a time when you could not persuade him to care how he looked, clean or dirty, tidy or ragged. Your problems then were quite different. Now he wants to look *good,* and a large part of looking good is looking *right* — in the group and setting where he finds himself.

What looks right in a disco looks wrong at Sunday Mass or on a sunny beach. At fourteen you want your clothes to convey the message 'I belong here' or if you are press-ganged into an outing against your will, you may want your clothes to proclaim — 'I'm only here under pressure, I belong somewhere else'.

Sometimes a defiant message like that is what sparks off disquiet. Before you as a parent move in for confrontation with Aidan over his clothes, prepare yourself.

First, try to remember remarks made to you as a teenager about your clothes, by parents or others you thought much of: both the compliments — 'Red really looks good on you' — and the negative remarks or silences, which are often interpreted by teenage children as disapproval. Remember how much such remarks counted with you, whether to please or infuriate. Then weigh well what you are going to say to Aidan.

Work out how you feel about his clothes, and why — the real reasons are often not on the surface. Try completing this sentence: I feel..(angry, ashamed, proud)... when Aidan wears (describe the clothes and the situation, Mass, shopping or whatever) because... (describe why you feel that way).

Then decide if it is worth making an issue of this. You may feel he is giving a bad example to his young brother, or he will displease a potential employer. On the other hand a confrontation may well lead to a big row in the family; is it worth that? In any case he must learn how to choose his own clothes, and live with his choices.

It is possible that Aidan thinks your style of dressing is fuddy-duddy or pompous. He may be as embarrassed by your appearance at school functions as you are by him on the street. Has he even said as much? Aidan's style may look far-out to you but entirely appropriate and right for him.

Almost certainly he will have changed his style in a few months, and may then be embarrassed by photographs of what he likes now.

Obviously clothes are meant to be noticed, and Aidan will remember your comments. Christ had little to say about clothes: just that the body counts for more than the raiment, and we are unlikely ever to rival the lilies of the field in our adornment. If you think it is an issue worth raising seriously with Aidan, prepare well by clarifying how you feel, and be prepared to listen to what he feels about your style.

## Kevin Came Home Drunk

He had been at a football celebration for an Under-15s cup win, and he was carried home footless. You worry that you have an alcoholic on your hands, and feel helpless against the teenage plague of drinking.

He is one of the majority. Most Irish boys have tasted alcohol by the time they are fifteen. Most do not become alcoholics. But any alert adult will have seen alcohol ruin so many marriages and families and individuals, and fill the hospital wards with casualties, that it is easy to be alarmed. A shock reaction will hand Kevin a weapon in any rebellion that is coming. Here as elsewhere panic is a bad guide. It leads to hasty reactions, such as an explosive telling-off and forbidding Kevin ever to touch drink, or removing all alcoholic drink from the home, or making him drunk again 'to teach him a lesson'. Teaching is essential here, but it has to be done thoughtfully.

Kevin's only hope is to develop his own moral stance, which in all likelihood will involve some experimenting with drink. This does not mean that you are helpless. There is a plague of teenage drinking in Ireland, and more could be done to protect teenagers on a public scale, by enforcement of laws about under-age drinking. They will only forge identity cards if we introduce them, the pessimists say. Experience in the USA has shown that they can be an effective means of lessening teenage alcoholism, when the laws are enforced. In Ireland we have too many laws and not enough enforcement. Even when they are not strictly observed, the laws are useful. They make it more risky for under-age drinkers to order in a pub, for fear they will be embarrassed by questioning about their age.

The law is not your only way of protecting Kevin. Before you barge in with a heavy hand, think about where you stand — and *you* means both of you, parents of and models for Kevin. If you are going to sit down with him, choose your time well. When confronted by two parents Kevin will easily become defiant, angry and cornered, so do not tackle him unless relations are relaxed enough for a real discussion.

Keep an open mind before you talk to him. The celebration that left him drunk may have been his first and only taste of drink. If so, it may have done a useful job in warning him of what alcohol can do. In any case you need to be clear about the size of the problem. One drunken evening does not make an alcoholic. Was it part of a pattern or a unique occasion?

The discussion will only have been real if Kevin has voiced his own concerns. It is not real if it consists of parents delivering a lecture. High among Kevin's concerns is almost certain to be his standing with his friends. His drinking was social. He was with his friends, and teenagers tend to see drinking as tough and sociable. Try not to force your child to choose between you and his peer group. He may need help in keeping his end up in the group without relying on alcohol. If you stay on his side and accept how important his friends are to him, you have a better chance of being a moderating influence. If you are against him and them, he will find it hard to accept your help.

What are your real concerns here? You may be aware of an alcoholic streak in one or other side of the family, which could reappear in Kevin. You may worry about him breaking the law by taking drink in a pub. You are concerned about the sort of people he may meet there. You worry that he may be so drunk as to be unable to come home, or that he might accept a lift from someone who had been drinking.

These are genuine concerns, and can be shared with Kevin. Do you also accept that risk-taking is part of adolescence, even if it worries or frightens you at times? If

221

you are to live with it, instead of driving it underground, try to agree what Kevin can do to make the risk-taking safer.

In this as elsewhere, our children force us to look at ourselves, at the way we use alcohol or tobacco or pills, our reliability in coming home when we promise, our consideration for the family's needs. Do we model the sort of behaviour we are asking of them?

What do you ask of Kevin? To keep you in touch with the realities of his life, so that you know if he drinks, and why. If it is because the pub is the only place to meet his friends, then perhaps you can make the home more available. You may have advice to offer on how to refuse a drink, or a lift home from a drinker; or offer to share the price of a taxi if that is the only other way he can come home. Heavy teenage drinkers tend to come either from emotionally anti-drink families, or from families in which there is heavy drinking. Parents who treat drinking as ordinary, moderate behaviour, are more likely to have teenagers who do the same.

Kevin has given you a fright and a worry, which must be taken seriously. In tackling it, remember that your aim is not just your own peace of mind, but for Kevin to learn to manage his own life and health.

## Clare was Sniffing

She has always, all her fourteen years, been a lively, often headstrong girl. Last week you found her sniffing solvents, and are terrified that she is on her way to becoming an addict, but puzzled how to approach it.

There *are* guidelines (see below) because thanks to the best of Irish surveys,[16] we know more about the effect of drugs, and about their use among our young and old addicts. Among teenagers, two drugs stand out as much more dangerous than the rest, alcohol and nicotine. Two-thirds of our teenagers have used each of these at some time, compared with around 13% who have used cannabis; 13% sniffed solvents (responsible for about ten Irish deaths a year); 6% have abused tablets of various sorts, and 1-2% have abused cocaine or heroin, which are responsible for about twenty to thirty deaths a year.

The propaganda and changed attitudes towards smoking have made some impact on the young, and saved them from a habit which would claim a heavy portion of their earnings or pocket-money, and give, with time, less pleasure and more likelihood of serious sickness.

Public propaganda about alcohol is mostly for rather than against. Many interviewers in the public media imply that 'celebrating' means, not singing or dancing or praying, but drinking to the point of collapse. The advertising focusses successfully on the young and attractive, but not when they are, as at some music 'festivals', snoring in the gutter in their own dirt and vomit. According to the survey quoted above, nearly a quarter of Irish teenagers have been drunk six or more times (the proportion is higher in the seventeen to eighteen-year-olds). By any standards these youngsters are well on their way to abusing alcohol and being at risk of addiction. Like nicotine, alcohol abuse kills (responsible for over 2,000 Irish deaths in 1988, usually by accidents when control is lowered); and in addition it clearly corrupts the quality of life in many families. The Dublin Coroner, Dr Bartley Sheehan, commented, after a series of inquests, that if alcohol were synthesised and put on the market today for the first time, it would be available only on prescription, so dire are its consequences in addiction and related disasters.

Young people who declared their intention of not using alcohol as teenagers generally carried out their intention. There is a lot to be said in practice for the sort of firm purpose embodied in Confirmation or Pioneer pledges. In addition to their spiritual value, they greatly reduce the danger of addiction.

There are parts of the country where cannabis is easily available, and is pressed on the young as non-addictive. Warnings are in place here too. In a recent IMS survey (*Young Ireland,* Dublin, October 1992) on abuse of soft and hard drugs, half the young adult Dubliners had been offered drugs, but less than one-fifth in Connaught and Ulster. Those away from home were more likely to have had an offer than those living at home. One curious figure here is the difference between Munster and Connaught/Ulster. There are parts of the south-west where drugs are in free circulation. Unlike alcohol and nicotine, cannabis does not kill, but it does scramble the learning processes, disrupts learning pathways, affects short-term memory, turns the bright student into an average one, and the average one to dull. It lingers in the fatty tissue for up to three weeks after a 'joint', and recently some sinister links between cannabis and cancer have been discovered.

Here age makes one wiser and sadder. When you have seen a bright boy from a sound family go down the path of cannabis (psychologically though not chemically addictive) to harder drugs, and from them to suicide; or when you have seen a group of well-endowed youngsters drift through their teens on a cloud of hash, and realise at twenty-five that the world has left them behind; then the notion that it's cool and everybody's doing it, sounds not like children's talk, but evil. It is a relief to see that two-thirds of the young people surveyed have never been offered these drugs. Let's try to improve on that.

It is easy to preach about the danger of drugs, but what about Clare? Your first job is to *understand why* she is sniffing. Most teenagers take drugs through an urge to experiment and see how far they can go with taking risks. Most will learn from this to set their own limits.

Temporarily the drug may fulfil a need. It may give relief from anxiety. It may calm an angry mood. It may make Clare feel acceptable to her peers. It may remove her shyness. It may just be fun.

As she grows into a greater confidence as to who she is, she will find the drug an unsatisfactory solution, and will find other ways to deal with anger.

A few teenagers use drugs as a solution to depression or to severe disturbance, and you will see yourself whether this is the case with Clare. It does not sound like it.

To help Clare you do not need to be an expert on drugs; do not assert more than you know. An educational group has suggested five guidelines under the acronym TEACH:

T is for *Talking,* which includes knowing something about drugs, listening to your children, keeping communication open through all the disagreements of the teens, being open about your own beliefs and values, and not letting disagreement be seen as rejection.

E is for *Example.* Children who see their parents cope with stress or bad moods without chemical help are more likely to manage themselves. Some parents, when tired or stressed, groan 'I really need a drink [or valium, or whatever]'. They do not *need* it, of course; they just want it. The listening daughter will not make that distinction.

A is for *Alternative* activities. So many go to the pub for lack of alternatives. As soon as our children move abroad to a less pub-centred culture, they discover a wealth of more active and fulfilling ways of spending the evenings. Working on a variety of leisure occupations and experiences is a positive way of preventing addiction.

C is for *Confidence.* Many young people tank up in order to gain Dutch courage to ask a partner to dance or date. Genuine confidence grows over the years from the attitudes of parents. Not 'You are bold', but 'You're OK, Clare'. Not putting down, but blessing, stroking, and forgiving or seeking forgiveness after every row.

H is for *How:* how to say *No* to drugs, whether sniffing, smoking or drinking; how to walk silently away from a stranger who solicits; how to persist in saying *No* to a persistent friend, without being more offensive than is needed.

Now that you have found Clare sniffing, involve all the significant people who may help, yet with a respect for Clare's reputation. These significant people may include a guidance counsellor or principal at school, and possibly a friend or two. Do not be trapped into promising 'confidentiality' in a way that would tie your hands. Drugs can lead to far more serious losses than just of reputation, and you need to be hard-headed.

In talking with Clare, focus on behaviour which you can verify, not on addiction or generalised drug-use, which is unverifiable. Do not make threats or promises unless you will certainly follow them up, and know how to carry them out. Express *your* beliefs and convictions rather than trying to get

Clare to admit something. Avoid being drawn into 'proving' statements. Get Clare to reflect on whether her life is getting better or worse. Express *your* belief or suspicion about the role of drug abuse, and clearly state what you will do if she repeats the sniffing. Encourage her to take responsibility for her life, but repeat what you will do if she sniffs again. If you have to seek outside help, it improves the prospect if you do it with Clare's agreement, and do not let her see it as punishment, but as help.

## Cian between Mother and Gang

Cian, aged thirteen, is your one and only. No man in the house, and no other children. It is hard to be both mother and father to him, and you seem to be having repeated rows over his friends. You don't want to rear him on the street, and that is where he seems to be spending his time.

There is no such thing as a one-parent family. The absent parent, usually the father, even if he was never around, is always present in Cian's fantasy. He must also be present in your fantasy at times, maybe with indignation that he is not there, maybe with longing that you had somebody to back you up.

A boy in Cian's situation said to me lately: 'The trouble is, Mum and I are head to head all the time. We love one another, but if we argue about something I want and she doesn't, like going out with my friends, there is no appeal. We're just locked in there.'

All the studies of single-parent families point to the difficulties the single mother has when the children turn into their teens. It is not that fathers in two-parent families always do a lot with their teenage children. But they are a resource for mother, someone to lean on, and someone the children can ultimately appeal to in a disagreement with mother.

So as a single mother, you need to plan how to meet this inevitable difficulty. Not all single mothers are in the same boat. Some are close to their own parents, or to brothers and sisters. There is a larger group for both mother and child to refer to. Mothers, and especially single mothers, need so much moral support in the endless decisions they have to make in child-rearing. No judge on his bench works as hard as you do in handing down justice, deciding what is right, not just for the household but for the development of this dear son of yours. What you need is not so much the right answer in every conflict with Cian, as a sense that you are not alone.

When Claudius was asked what it felt like being lord of the Roman Empire, he replied: *Lupum auribus teneo:* 'I'm holding the wolf by the ears.' Is it sometimes like that with Cian? You are utterly intent on keeping control and feel that if you relax for a second you will be in dire trouble. You cannot enjoy your son; and that in itself is a deprivation for him. There is nothing so good for his growth as the knowledge that you enjoy him, that he is bringing you happiness, that he is contributing to you, not just wearing you out. He is not a husband, not an equal. Ultimately you have to answer for the household, to draw the limits on behaviour and spending. To have strength for that, you need help. You need to pray like the psalmist, complaining and crying out to God, pouring out your heart to him, bemoaning your failures, asking him to keep the love flowing between you and Cian.

You also need help from friends or relations, provided they are not flooding you with unwanted advice, or moralising about what Cian should be like, but simply listening to you, and sharing their own difficulties with you. There can be enormous help in a support group of parents — maybe other single mothers — who trust one another, and meet regularly, not for expert advice, but just to renew their sense that they are not alone, and what they are going through is temporary.

It *is* temporary. Like you, Cian needs a group of friends with whom he can discover who is the real Cian, a base where he can find stability and security and discover what young people of his age are thinking and learning. He has to choose those friends himself. They may look wrong to you, noisy, strangely dressed, badly spoken. The less critical you can be of them, the better. They need each other, and if Cian knows that you can be tolerant even of the unexpected ones, there is a fair hope that you will remain in touch with what is happening in his life.

You do not want to rear him 'on the street'. Then may he bring his friends into the house, and have privacy there? Can you stand the noise, and the endless demands on biscuits and coffee? Not that you will be sitting there with them. But you will be able to meet them, and gradually get to know them. You cannot judge from appearances, and sometimes the ones that frighten you by their appearance may be the kindest or funniest or most helpful to Cian. Can Cian introduce them to you without fearing a critical or unwelcoming eye? They are his friends, not yours, and it may be quite an achievement in his life to invite them back to his house.

It is better for him to make and break relationships himself during these years when he is learning the art of friendship. Only forbid a friendship if it is absolutely necessary, such as if the chosen friend is anti-social, aggressive, a thief, or a drug-taker. Cian will know what you think of them by watching you, and your opinion will almost certainly weigh with him. It may be that he is less than enthusiastic about some of your friends.

What you are watching, with some sadness, is the process of Cian and you becoming separate persons, learning to live together with different personalities, different circles of friends, and each of you with some secrets. There is no going back to the relationship you two had when he was a child. His new confidants and friends are a sign of his growth. The new bond you have with him will be based on your acceptance of him as a separate but loved son, with his own personality and style, which in all likelihood will emerge, after these confused years, as like your own.

## Music has Taken Over Niamh

'I'm worried about my sixteen-year-old Niamh and her music. She and her young brothers get completely lost in pop music. She can't go anywhere without her Walkman — though she's sensible enough about safety, and would never wear it while cycling. I don't understand the music, but it seems wild and unsuitable.'

You do not understand it, but it is important to listen to it. Otherwise what can you object to? Parents can easily panic about teenagers' music when they hear lyrics that seem blasphemous, or drug-promoting, or sexually abusive. That is like panicking about the air we breathe. Pop music is not just the staple pap on the FM radio stations, and many of the medium wave stations as well. Nearly every shop, restaurant, public place has the air filled with it. Sometimes it is soft, shapeless, wallpaper music, the sort Richard Clayderman used to produce in quantities, background music, not to be focussed on. More often it is current top-of-the-charts pop.

Moreover, Irish young people are more music-minded than those of other countries. It is in our blood, from the extraordinarily rich tradition of our own songs and melodies. When Irish people fill out questionnaires about interests which have been created in the USA or elsewhere, we tend to score high on Music Performer, and Music Teacher. Irish youngsters who play no instrument and do not consider themselves in any way musical, will still score high on these measures.

We have produced more than our share of outstanding singers and musicians, despite the poor place that music has in our primary and secondary schools, especially those for boys. Has anybody counted the number of 'groups' that operate in Irish schools, mostly two guitars, a drummer, maybe a keyboard and a singer? There must be thousands of them. While some of them would see it just as a hobby which fills their leisure hours constructively and socially, many of them are hoping to find a place in the sun, and negotiate to play gigs in pubs and dances, for a pittance, in the hope that they will become the next Hothouse Flowers or Frank and Walters.

In 1992, I listened to a talented girl present an overview of current music to an audience of 250 parents. She was in her early twenties, and combined a fresh memory of being a teenager with developed skills of communication and mastery of technical aids. She illustrated her session with seven short video excerpts made by currently popular groups. They were a completely different group from those popular twelve months before, though one of them, ABBA, was popular twenty years ago and illustrates the revival of classical pop groups — Genesis is another obvious example — in reaction against synthetic, computer-produced, Rave music.

Two things struck me as I listened and watched. First, that nothing is more transitory than this music: what is popular today will be forgotten in a year, just as most of last year's top singers are almost forgotten despite their efforts to keep an audience as sex objects (Madonna) or *enfants terribles* (Sinéad O'Connor).

Secondly, these middle-aged parents, once they listened to the music, enjoyed most of it. They also enjoyed perceiving the differences between groups, and deciding which flavours they liked, which they found unpleasant. They loved a melodious song by Simply Red, and disliked the brutal, macho symbolism of The House of Pain.

They laughed at the anti-establishment (that means musical establishment) song of Cork's Frank and Walters, and found their feet tapping to the dancey hotch-potch of old melodies in The Spin's Techno-rave. Does this rave music 'erase your social and cultural programming' as its gurus claim? It seems to me to do just the opposite, i.e. it tries some 'social and cultural programming' of its own, hypnotising the dancers by its beat and loudness. Some of its groups, like The Smart Es, are interested in Ecstasy drugs, but most of those who dance to it may be barely conscious of the Ecstasy message embedded in Es. It is worth stressing that in Ireland Ecstasy is a tiny threat compared with the damage inflicted on old and young by the two most used drugs, nicotine and alcohol.

Many teenage boys love Heavy Metal music, which comes in a range of styles, but is all aggressive and can be anti-woman, or anti-community, in a horrible way. Yet many of these young people love their mothers and family, and use the music to vent some of the frustration they experience from school, exams, and other pressures. Similarly some of the sexy videos from groups like Junior could be seen as a safe way of exploring sexual encounters without getting into them.

So if you think it important to know about Niamh's programmes in Maths, Geography and other school subjects, it is no harm to learn about the different sorts of music that pass through her head for longer hours than her schoolwork.

Remember, more important for Niamh than the beat or lyrics of these songs is the fact that they are the music of her group, her generation. When she watches MTV or listens to her Walkman, she is out of reach of school, homework, teachers, and all the other pressures, some of them from home, that make her feel guilty and inadequate. She is in her own space, with her friends, and that is not a bad place for working out how she wants to grow up.

## Has Desmond Gone Mad?

Desmond is sixteen, strong, healthy, bigger than you, and much bigger than your wife. He has you both terrified, with the violence of his language and angry outbursts, which have left their mark on windows, doors, walls and crockery. With three younger children, you are finding it hard to survive.

It sounds improbable, but this story of the violence of teenage children against parents is not rare. Many a household can show the scars of temper tantrums, which are really terrifying when coming from a strong and intelligent adolescent.

The father's story is of course only one version of events. Desmond would tell a different story, and it must be heard. It may be like the demand of the Prodigal Son: 'Give me my share of the inheritance and I'll be off.' When you are big and bright enough to pass for a grown-up outside, it is easy to lose patience at being still a child in the house, under orders at home and at school, still sitting in school-desks, wearing a uniform, doing homework, with your future prospects controlled by adults through the pressure of the Leaving Certificate.

Younger children do not expect to affect the world. It is only when they emerge from the cocoon of childhood that they sense their aloneness, smallness and impotence in face of society; then they sometimes feel it is better to be a vandal, a hooligan or a wild man than to be a nobody.

That occasional exasperation does not justify crazy behaviour, nor breaking up the house. As with all children's behaviour, one tries first to understand it. Some parents are so desperate trying to keep a roof on the house in face of a violent son that they have given up trying to make sense of him. Yet there is a reason for behaviour which seems mad.

It is possible that Desmond is actually 'mad' in the sense of a psychiatric case. Psychotic illness can hit in the late teens, and show itself in irrational anger and violence. In some ways this is an easy way out, a comforting diagnosis, because it medicalises the problem and hands over responsibility to doctors and hospitals.

It is also dreadful, telling your son that his hold on reality and reason is tenuous and will probably remain so for the rest of his life. Some parents have moved towards this explanation too fast, have somehow managed to push their son into the care of a psychiatrist and mental hospital, only to find, after some weeks of observation, that he is judged sane, but conduct-disordered. The boy returns home to the parents who had him committed to hospital, and relations are worse than ever.

The presumption must be that Desmond is sane, but acting crazy and out of control. His aggression may be drug-induced desperation; or the desperation of facing suspicious or unnecessarily authoritarian parents. He may be influenced by a gang of bad friends. He may be feeling a particular stress, such as the loss of a friend, boy or girl, or inability to cope with schoolwork, or realising how much opportunity he has lost in idling. You know your son. Can he tolerate feeling guilty, or does he always throw out the blame onto the world? And you parents are the most convenient part of the world to blame. Part of him knows this, and you have to speak to that part.

With even the wildest boy, there are moments when one or other of you can speak to him. If your wife has a better chance, let her do it. Don't be caught by angry notions that

'He has to learn to obey his father.' At this stage you want first of all the survival of the family, by whatever approach works.

In exceptional crises, parents must stick together, resolve their own differences, listen and compromise. Also it is crucial that they maintain sanity in face of the often insane actions of such teenagers, and keep their own emotions at a cool level, since Desmond's are almost certainly out of hand. He will learn more from parental modelling in keeping cool, than from lectures.

What can you or your wife say that might help? First, that you understand and accept his anger or frustration. Until you do that, genuinely, Desmond will not hear anything else you say.

Secondly, that temper tantrums such as he shows are tolerable in little children but not in a grown boy, and he has to find some other way of letting out his anger, maybe by physical exercise, running or sport or even punching a pillow.

After that, pause. Some men go straight for the bottom line and issue an ultimatum — 'One more outburst and you're out the door'. Can you and should you follow this through? While you have satisfied your legal obligation in housing him till sixteen, you know that Desmond, after using the hospitality of his closest friends for a little while, will be on the streets, with no dole and no hope of work or residence. Showing him the door is the very last resort.

The one factor that can save this situation is the patience of parents, their ability to maintain hope when the son feels desperate and is filling both parents with some of that desperation. I could fill a book with stories of families who seemed at the end of their tether when the son was seventeen, and yet six years later (messy years, full of anguished talk and failed attempts) could relate to their twenty-three-year-old as an adult finding his own way in life. That move from dependence to independence is terribly painful in some good families.

Remember the father of the Prodigal Son, Jesus' closest human image of God the father. He was made a fool of, but left the door open. Meanwhile, do not save Desmond from the consequences of his own actions, even if that means trouble in school or trouble from the law. As long as you offer a safety-net or buffer, he will use it. Do not finance his follies, do not pay money for projects which Desmond may demand but you consider unwise. Keep a hold on the purse-strings, and while you pay for the development of his skills and mind, let him pay for his own pleasures. Do not expect your words or actions to be applauded, but trust that your own moral authority does influence Desmond, even when it is flouted.

## Sinéad Has Run Away

After a series of rows with your husband and yourself, Sinéad, who is sixteen, has just disappeared. She rang home to tell you she is alright, in Dublin, and that she will come back. You don't know where to go next.

No need to detail all the fears you have: that Sinéad is on alcohol or other drugs, or starving, and can be taken advantage of. She is a bright girl and knows your anxieties very well — you have often listed them in your arguments over coming home in time, and choice of companions. She is also a well-developed girl, and could pass for a twenty-year-old. Physically she is at least a year more developed than you were at sixteen. She knows her way round the city and has many good friends, so she will not starve. Girls tend to be sensibly supportive of one another in a situation like Sinéad's, and to offer help without imagining they can stay away from home indefinitely.

The fact that she phoned you so quickly is reassuring. It looks as if she does not want to cut the umbilical cord completely, but rather to win a breathing-space. You know the various meanings that running away can have. It can be a symbolic suicide, a sign of deep depression. Or it can be an emphatic way of saying: 'I'm not a child any more. I can look after myself. You are crowding me, fussing me too much.'

It is usually not thought through rationally. I knew a fourteen-year-old who in foul winter weather, anticipating a bad school report, grabbed his sleeping-bag, computer game, and whatever he could carry from the fridge, and dossed down in a city railway station. He knew that he could not survive there long (he was spotted almost at once), but it was a way of saying that he was desperate.

Sinéad is saying much the same; her running was triggered by the rows with her parents. When she comes home, both you and your husband will have to work on the reasons for her running, more than on your fears for the future. If you settle back into blocking every loophole, and ensuring that she is totally controlled, without understanding what she was saying, you will probably fail to hold her.

The most important thing you say will be the first remark when you meet her again. That will determine whether truth will appear, or the war will continue. I suppose your temptation would be to move in with questions — 'Where have you been? Who were you with? Have you been drinking?' — without giving Sinéad time to explain herself or make suggestions. Or, if your strong feelings of anxiety and anger swamp you, you may try to cut off conversation before it has started: 'This is the last straw. Go straight up to your room, and you're grounded until further notice.'

You need to say something that shows love more than anger or fear, the sort of remark that indicates you are ready to listen: something motherly like 'You look tired. Sit down and have a coffee.' That offers some hope that you will move on to the next stage, of asking her: 'What do you need to sort out?' Clearly a lot has to be sorted out, but you do not do it alone. Sinéad is in a mess, and at sixteen she must have ideas about how to get out of it.

Some of those ideas will be expensive and misguided. She may say she would like to move out to a flat, maybe with a friend. Apart from everything else, that would be prolonging the childish illusion that life is a free ride in which she makes the choices but Daddy pays the bills.

The crisis here is certainly about a longing for independence, and the way forward is by negotiation rather than you calling all the shots. I knew a girl like Sinéad who, faced with an over-anxious and protective mother, and a stressed father, had given up trying to negotiate because both parents simply did not hear her or trust her. So she took to lying about her friends and her movements. When some lies were discovered, the mistrust and rows exploded, and she ran away.

Yet there was ample room for negotiation: in her appearance and choice of clothes, which her mother was still controlling (instead of controlling just the budget for clothes); in diet, exercise, the hours of homework, the time for coming home and endless other details. Her mother could not bear to feel she did not know about and control every part of her daughter's life, with the result that in the end she almost lost everything.

If you look longingly at stable families where the children seem peacefully settled in the home (remember President Bush claiming as his greatest achievement 'that the kids come home at night'), you can console yourself with the knowledge that there are few families which have not known either the threat or the reality of a runaway child.

As adults we have to see beyond our own panic, and distinguish a cry for independence from those dangers which would affect Sinéad for the rest of her life: *addiction* to drugs (especially alcohol or nicotine); delinquency leading to a police record; being caught in a group from which she cannot escape; and of course unwanted pregnancy. Your fears will fix your mind on the dangers. From the sound of it, your greatest need is for calm, to greet her like a mother, and reach a point where you can really hear one another, and together sort out the mess you are both in.

## The Spectre of Suicide

A twenty-year-old neighbour hanged himself last month, and while you were still reeling from the shock and grief of it, you heard your fourteen-year-old Naomi, in a row with her father, threaten to kill herself. You cannot remember hearing of so many suicides in times past, and are terrified that Naomi's threat may be serious.

No, there were not so many suicides in times past. In ten years (1980 to 1990) the suicide rate among young Irish males (aged fifteen to twenty-four) jumped by 78%. Observers speak of an epidemic of young suicides, both in

Ireland and in Europe. Typically those who die are boys —
three times as numerous as girls among 'successful'
suicides. But the pattern of 'unsuccessful' suicide attempts
reverses this: here, girls outnumber boys by three to one. It
may be because girls use less lethal and violent methods
than boys, overdoses rather than hanging or shooting.

It is a hard and hideous topic to think or write about, like
the Crucifixion, only worse. On Calvary, Jesus was able to
show love to the end, and forgive his killers. Suicide , by
contrast, springs not merely from agony but from despair and
often aggression, placing one's own escape above the
indescribable pain, guilt and grief that one leaves behind in
family and friends.

It is true that a suicide note often urges the bereaved not
to blame themselves, and speaks of love for those left
behind. It is also true that those who take their own lives are
sometimes out of their mind, and show a reduced sense of
responsibility. After the event, one cannot assign blame,
even on Judas. To feel you are beyond hope, as Judas did,
is a matter of intense suffering, although the suffering may
not be evident to those around.

Here above all one has to heed Jesus' word: judge not,
that you may not be judged. God is more merciful than man,
and more merciful than some churches in times past, which
banned the body of a suicide from burial in consecrated
ground. The ban grew out of a regard for human life. But the
step was made from saying that it is wrong to take one's own
life, to the judgmental position of punishing the suicide by
excommunication of his body. You remember the agony of
Bull McCabe in the film adaptation of Keane's play *The Field,*
as he visited the grave of his son on a cliff-top beyond the
churchyard. Like many of us in old age, the Church has
learned to soften its attitude and withhold its judgment.

Those bereaved by a suicide are victims themselves,
suffering in countless ways. They grieve, not merely out of
loss, but from the knowledge that their son did not love them
enough to survive. There is guilt too: if I had been more
loving, or helpful, he might still be alive. And there is anger
at being so cruelly deserted, but you cannot allow yourself

to feel angry at one who obviously suffered so much. We have many bereavement counsellors in the country. Nobody needs their ministry more than those bereaved by a suicide.

For you, however, the worry is about Naomi, who is still alive and well, but has made threats. They have to be taken seriously. What can we do? Some things we cannot control. Suicides tend to increase in a recession (observers have identified a 4% rise in suicides for every 1% rise in unemployment), level out in prosperity, and fall in wartime, when aggression can be turned against a common enemy instead of against oneself or one's family.

Some situations are obviously at higher risk: in one Irish prison which holds one hundred men, there were nine attempted hangings in one year, as well as many other serious suicidal attempts. It gives an added urgency to Christ's counsel that we should visit and comfort those in prison, to reduce their sense of isolation and rejection by everybody they ever knew.

Naomi, living in a loving family, is different, but from the study of other cases, we can learn for her. There are patterns. Usually there is a long history of problems, and a period when these problems get worse. Then the young person's way of coping with these problems starts to fail, and isolation sets in. Finally there is a time when all relationships break down and contact is lost with family and friends.

That sense of isolation is the sign we must watch for. If someone talks of preferring death to life, she is suffering. It is up to those around her to see her pain and relieve it.

Admittedly there are attention-seekers — even young children — who will talk about killing themselves as a way of getting under mother's skin. The horror rightly associated with the notion of suicide has been weakened by exposure to TV; and some young people who talk of killing themselves appear only half aware of the finality of death. They use the threat as a dramatic gesture, like a final curtain-line as you slam the door and exit. They do not appreciate, as adults do, that there is no re-entry.

The attention-seekers have to be treated as the rare exceptions. The warning signs of suicide include talking about it, often in the few days before the attempt. Other signs are a persistent deep depression after the break-up of a relationship, the giving away of prized personal possessions, and an earlier suicide attempt.

What can we do in face of such a threat? First, drop everything and attend to her, calmly and receptively, in a quiet place, neither arguing nor advising, but listening in a deep way. Secondly, tune in to your own feelings, which will be a guide to what Naomi is feeling, and try to respond to her at an emotional level — nothing reduces her isolation as effectively as this. Thirdly, spend time with her, do not leave her alone, and make sure that there are others around her. Finally make absolutely clear to her that she deserves to live, that she is precious to you.

There may be occasions when you feel that nobody in the family is sufficiently in tune with her to help, and you look for help outside. Keep your eye on that central danger, isolation. The sort of bullying that isolates the victim in a class at school can be a trigger for despair and suicide, unless the parents or family keep close to him. Judas hanged himself when he had broken with the apostles, and been rejected by those to whom he betrayed his Lord. We owe it to our neighbours above all that they should not feel utterly alone.

## NOTES

15. Hill, op. cit. pp. 69-99

16. Mark Morgan & Joel Grube, *Smoking, drinking and other drug use among Dublin post-primary school pupils*, ESRI, Paper no. 132, Dublin, 1986

# Faith, Values, Morality

## RELIGION AND RESEARCH

In facing this most difficult chapter, I am conscious of two hats: that of the *priest* who is repeatedly asked by practising Catholics: 'How can I pass on to my children the faith which I treasure, and which makes my life worth living?' And that of the *psychologist* who is asked for evidence and the fruits of research.

If one puts the two questions together, and asks: What does research tell us about the passing on of the faith — the answer is simple: nothing. Faith, according to Catholic theology, is a gift. It is given by God, not passed on by parents. They help to form the personality, teach their children how to pray. From the early image of a loving, wise and powerful parent, children form their concept of God. The same parents may have one child who is a devout believer and another who is indifferent to religion. We are in an area which psychology finds hard to scrutinise, intensely interior, dealing with the most central part of the person, and manifesting itself unreliably in behaviour.

What has passed for a psychology of religion has had to rely on shallow manifestations of religious belief, such as stated opinions about God, attendance at religious services, professed habits of prayer. We have only to look into our own souls to see how much deeper faith goes than such behavioural indices. Religious observance can co-exist with a profound alienation from anything spiritual, or from the person of Jesus Christ. An atheistic or agnostic attitude may co-exist with a commitment to something beyond oneself, which in most good theologies would be seen as religious. Nobody I know has explored these anomalies in today's Ireland more profoundly or lucidly than my colleague Michael Paul Gallagher in his book *Help My Unbelief* (Dublin, Veritas, 1983).

There may still be some parents — and teachers — who think of the task of religious upbringing as being to indoctrinate, to brainwash the child into accepting a particular set of beliefs. This would imply total control of children's thinking, which in our age of open media is clearly impossible. Even if it were possible, it would involve a contradiction. Faith is by definition a free act. Anything short of free is that much short of faith.

The aim of a religion teacher is so to present the life of a Christian that when, in their teens, our children choose (often implicitly) a philosophy by which to live, it may be an educated choice, and a free one. Where school and home are at odds on such fundamental questions, the price is paid by the young person in confusion and uncertain identity. A majority of parents want the school to offer their child a reasoned and critical education in their religion, in the creed, moral code and worship which shape one's approach to God.

This is not indoctrination. It simply ensures that one has thought seriously about the larger issues of life, the nature of man, life and death, the problem of evil, the existence of God, and the historical background of Christianity in the Bible, the life of Jesus, and the critical thought that has been given over the centuries to his impact on mankind.

In the USA Andrew Greely[17] found one intriguing link between the religious commitment of the child/adolescent and that of the parent: namely that the father seems to have a stronger influence than the mother. The same has been found in Australian, Belgian and British research, that the child's religious commitment has a stronger correlation with that of the father than of the mother. It seems paradoxical. We think of children learning their prayers at their mother's knee rather than their father's; yet in this area of faith we seem to find the father more influential.

Research offers us correlations but not reasons. These are a matter for speculation, and my own guess is this: that if religion in a young person is associated primarily with prayers-at-mother's-knee and the lessons of early childhood, it is liable to be left behind in the young person's determination to put away the things of a child. But if religious commitment, a sense of prayer and of responsibility to one's maker, is seen in the father who is making his way in a harsh and competitive society (and it is still the case that children are more likely to see their father than their mother as the bread-winner outside the home), then the young person is more likely to see faith as part of the challenge of adult life than as a relic of childhood.

The present generation of parents see an extraordinary change in the religious education of their children. In my Leaving Certificate class, the professed unbeliever was the exception. Now the daily communicant is the exception. Among young adults, especially in the cities, one can meet an astonishing level of ignorance even about feasts like Christmas and Easter which are part of the secular scene. 'Why is the Christmas baby always a boy? Who is the little man on the cross? How do we know that Jesus existed?' Religion has roots in reason and history. Theology, the science of God, has a longer and more critical pedigree than most of the disciplines which are accepted as university faculties. Many young adults who have gone through ten years of education, can think of religion as a matter of eccentric habit, explained by one's emotional needs. It is not that they have moved to other philosophies or religions than the Christian. More generally they have moved to the values of the marketplace and the soap operas of TV, to the sort of consumerism that values people for what they buy and possess. Worst of all, they have moved to the bloody-mindedness that Roddy Doyle portrays brilliantly in *The Snapper*, where any sense of morality or righteous indignation has yielded to a smouldering, unfocussed resentment, unredeemed by any notion of what life is about, except having a laugh. When people stop believing in God, they start believing not in nothing but in anything.

This is an area where parents suffer most from 'Changing Children', and the suffering makes sense, because they are thinking of their deepest beliefs and the child's soul and destiny. Rather than generalise about how children acquire values, and come to live by their faith, this chapter focusses on dilemmas posed by the change in children, dilemmas touching the deepest values — of forgiveness, the sacramental life of Christians, prayer, preparation for marriage, the growth of conscience, and how God touches parents.

## Forgiveness and the Burden of Hate

Ruth was only one year old when Séamus was born. He seemed autistic at birth, and it took all his mother's energy and love to bring him through the first five years. He is fifteen now, and Ruth has always been cold and hostile to him, has never forgiven him for grabbing mother's attention when she was a baby.

Ruth really suffered, and there *is* something to forgive. Through no fault of her mother's, she suffered the greatest wrong a baby can suffer. For a one-year-old girl, the time, attention and love of mother and father are meat and drink, what keep her alive and bring the gleam to her eye and the smile to her lips. She blames the loss of them on this strange, silent young bundle, Séamus, who cast her out in the cold when she was basking warmly in mother's sunshine. She could not understand the claims he made upon mother. All that she knew was a sudden change of life, like a rejection or a bout of malnutrition; and that at an age when she could not talk or put words on things, so it is not even a coherent memory for her.

Her mother has told her again and again how much she loves Ruth, even though she is such a centre of friction in the family. All mother meets is the cold look in her eye and a denial that she has done anything wrong. She finds it hard to forgive either parent. The worse hurt any of us can experience at any age, is the hurt suffered at the hands of someone we love and from whom we expect love. It is hard for mother to accept that she inflicted such pain on her daughter when she was wearing herself out trying to bring

Séamus into the human race. It is hard for Ruth to accept that the cold anger she feels about him goes back to an incident that has a reasonable explanation, that in fact he did her no deliberate wrong, except by being there, with all his clamant needs.

It is no accident that the parables of Christ return again and again to forgiveness. The story that best describes God the Father in human terms is the parable of the Prodigal Son, where the central figure is the father, and a father who has been deeply hurt by someone he loved passionately. The prodigal son had made a fool of him, grabbed his money, squandered it, brought the family into disrepute — you can hear the neighbours saying: 'The old fool, he always spoiled that boy. He was too soft. I could have told him what would happen.'

Down through history there have been countless fathers who responded to such behaviour in an unforgiving way. You have had your chance and wasted it. You will never darken the door of my house again. That is what the older brother, the obedient and conscientious one, felt and advised. Tell the story to children, and they will identify with the older brother, not the father. They feel the anger that anyone could naturally feel against the feckless and wilfully selfish prodigal.

Jesus does not underestimate the difficulty of forgiving; he highlights it. At the end of the story we do not know whether the older brother will remain outside, sulking in unforgiving fury, or whether he will come in and join the party, taste the fatted calf, and lay down the burden of his anger by greeting his brother. What is clear is that the one who suffers from the anger is not the prodigal son but the older brother. He is the one who is still unfree, out in the darkness, his mind and energies consumed in indignation at the sins of his brother. He is still living in the past, and cannot free his energies for his own future as long as he cherishes that passion to get even with the brother who has hurt him and the whole family. The father is free. He does not deny the folly and evil of what his son did; but he no longer holds it against him.

Can Ruth accept what is at the origin of her anger? Can she see that it is she, not Séamus, who is suffering? Those who are injured often feel that by giving up their anger, they will be benefitting the offender in some way. Anger is never given up without reluctance and pain. We are giving up part of

ourselves, something we have cherished. But it is something
that maims us and hampers our freedom.

We can see in Bosnia and Belfast the consequences of the
old Mosaic and Muslim doctrine of 'an eye for an eye and a
tooth for a tooth'. When Jesus took issue with that, and urged
us to forgive our enemies, he was not denying that they are
enemies, that they have wronged us. He was not asking us to
fudge over the past and say that nothing really happened. He
was not suggesting that forgiveness is easy — the older brother
is evidence enough of that.

Christ told us again and again to pardon those who have
injured us, even to the point of putting it into the Lord's
Prayer and making it a condition for offering sacrifice to God:
'If you remember at the altar that your brother has something
against you, go first and be reconciled to your brother, then
come and offer your gift.' There is no human relationship in
which we will not hurt one another at some time; so love
cannot survive unless we are ready to forgive. When we do
forgive, though it feels like losing a limb, we come to realise
that it is not our offender, our enemy, that we are healing, but
ourselves.

## Barry has Given up Confession

The religious sense and character of fifteen-year-old Barry is
admirable. He lives a good life, is generous and considerate
of others, and goes regularly to Mass and Holy Communion,
but hardly ever to confession. He says he doesn't need a priest
to tell God he is sorry.

Communions up, confessions down, is the pattern across
the Catholic world since the Second Vatican Council. Only
God could tell us if sin is up or down. Christ warned us that
we should not judge, but leave that to the Lord. Still parents
worry. They were brought up to regular or frequent
confession, and see their children, good children like Barry,
abandon the practice when they start to take their religious
life into their own hands.

It is not just the children, of course. If adults were going
to confession as they used, the boxes would be busy, which
they are not. In part this is a reaction against what they would
see as an undue emphasis on sin, often leading to

scrupulousness. Thirty years ago, one constantly met Catholics who were crippled or at least unbalanced by worries about sin. Their life was one long guilt trip, and church regulations were so numerous that they could hardly avoid breaking some law or prescription.

As a student I used to be amazed and saddened by the sight of good priests whose celebration of Mass was not a joy but a fear-haunted ritual, charged with anxieties about how they pronounced the Latin words of consecration, or whether they had dropped a minuscule particle of the Host. There was obviously something un-Christlike about a religion that led to such fears. One of the comforts of the last thirty years is the gradual disappearance of that sort of scrupulousness.

Is Barry missing something precious in his abandonment of confession? I think he is. He is quite right in turning directly to God to ask for forgiveness when he has done something wrong. God reaches out to us in pardon whenever we pray, whenever we start the Mass with the penitential service. Confession does something more for us.

Putting words on it, is what makes confession at once so painful and so healing. All of us build up defences against accepting guilt, against facing what is mean or cowardly or cruel in us. In confession we are not looking for counselling or psychotherapy, or for a warm blanket of forgetfulness to be cast over our past. In our own minds we tend towards vagueness about what we have done, and easily condone it. In confession we try to see our meanness as others might see it, putting it in words to an anonymous priest: 'That is what I did, it was bad, and I am sorry.' In all our religious life, there is no act so personal as this. The other sacraments can easily turn into empty rituals. Confession, taken seriously, makes the most intense personal demands on us; and brings a comfort you can feel.

Perhaps that is why there is such an explosion of psychotherapy and counselling of various sorts in Ireland today: a hunger for the comforts of confession, but paid for with fees and without the prospect of God's forgiveness. In *Requiem for a Nun* William Faulkner wrote:

'The maladjustments which they tell us breed the thieves and murderers and rapists... are not really maladjustments but simply because the embryonic murderers and thieves didn't have anybody to listen to them; which is an idea the Catholic church discovered 2,000 years ago.'

Faulkner's history is shaky — the practice of regular confession started much later than he implies. But he puts his finger on something Barry is missing, the palpable blessing that follows when we put into words, before an anonymous priest, the bad things we have done, and feel the Lord lift that burden off our hearts.

## Nora Can No Longer Pray

Thirteen-year-old Nora is upset lately, and has at last admitted that every time God is mentioned, or she is urged to pray for this or that, she feels awful. She does not believe in God, because her prayers are never answered. She has reached the stage where the mention of prayer or God makes her feel evil and wicked, because she doubts God's existence, and questions everything to do with faith.

Nora has something to teach us. She is suffering, but her suffering is a path to wisdom. What has she to teach us? That God is no messenger boy, running errands for us. If that is how we present God to children, the more perceptive of them, like Nora, will see sooner or later that either he is a forgetful and inefficient messenger boy, or he was never there in the first place.

Francis Bacon said: 'It were better to have no opinion of God at all than such an opinion as is unworthy of him.' Jesus' father in heaven was not someone who ran errands for his Son, or whose main job was to listen to prayers. Nora does not look on her own parents as being there just to give her what she asks. They have been cherishing her long before she was able to ask for anything. She loves them, and enjoys just being with them, even without any conversation, much less begging. If sometimes she asks for something and the parents say No, she may grumble, but it does not make her doubt that they are her real parents.

I had a holy and brilliant friend called Róisín, who as a diplomat had to sit through countless formal meals, and would, if conversation was in the doldrums, ask her neighbour (who might be German, Indonesian, Japanese or whatever): 'How do you pray?' It led to some of the liveliest talk and deepest friendships of her life. The question touches the one activity that is totally personal, and at the heart of each person's religion. Even as worldly-wise an interviewer as

John Mortimer found himself constantly gravitating to questions like this when probing for what was central in the distinguished people he met and wrote about.

Obviously we *should* pray. Jesus told us to pray unceasingly; and Saint Paul explained that when we do not know what to pray for, the Holy Spirit within us is constantly speaking to the Father about our needs. When we feel those needs acutely, in moments of desperation or crisis, we pray by instinct. Nothing could stop us. But no matter how urgent our prayers, they are still to a father who knows what we need, and whose mysterious ways are to be found not just in the requests granted, but in the answer No.

I work in a national school, and I know how easily one can confine the mention of God to things we want and pray for: a fine day for the sports, somebody's sick granny, the danger of war or bloodshed, examinations, and so on. We pull God down to the size of our own needs. Our prayers are not so much on the model of asking father or mother for something — when we know the odds are they may say No because they have a fair idea what is best for us — as of leverage on some all-powerful magician in the sky. If that is the way in school, it probably happens in the home as well: a sense of God as the one we turn to in great need rather than as the parent in whom we live and move and have our being, as St Paul put it.

So the God that Nora does not believe in, or doubts and feels bad about, is a god who does not exist. She is right. Why then does she feel so bad about it, tortured and sleepless? I suppose it is because she feels at odds with her parents, and perhaps her school, on a matter (faith) which, however you feel about it, is certainly of great importance. She feels evil, disloyal, wicked.

As a boy I used to think of 'the gift of faith' as a golden casket containing a precious collection of articles of belief, moral commandments, and ways of worshipping God. It was what travel companies would call a package deal. You had to accept the whole casket or you were rejecting the faith. Yet it was hard to know just what belonged inside the casket. Did it include belief in the cures at Lourdes, or in the Thirty Days' Prayer, or eating fish on Friday? If you were on the scrupulous side, you would play it safe. If you had a tough conscience, you might take your chances and then wonder were you putting your faith at risk.

That was of course nonsense. Faith is a personal response to our father in heaven, whom we cannot see or imagine. 'God is not what you imagine or think you understand' said Saint Augustine. 'If you understand him, you have failed.'

Faith is a mixture of darkness and light. The light comes in moments that strengthen us, perhaps in the unchanging ritual of the Mass, or the sparse statements of the Creed, or when we meet truly good and holy people, whose lives would not make sense if God did not exist. God also touches us in our experience, in the sudden realisation of transience, when we feel rootless and alone in this world; or in the ecstasy of love, or the warmth of friendship, or the desolation of abandonment. Faith does not mean feeling good or consoled. Our sense of God can be at its sharpest when we feel lonely and mortal, yet reaching beyond ourselves, knowing we are not mortal.

The darkness and doubt flood us much of the time, when the stories in the media assume that there is nothing worth working for but money and pleasure, and when the wickedness of men makes us wonder where justice has disappeared to. As the Psalmist cried: 'Why do the wicked prosper?'

Nora's darkness must be partly because she has my old notion of faith as an all-or-nothing package, and she cannot square it with what she lives through. For her and her parents, this crisis must be as painful as Gethsemane, where Jesus cried in pain to an apparently empty heaven. There is nothing Nora will suffer that he did not go through first.

That pain and need are the beginning of prayer. At thirteen, Nora is well capable of meditation. God is closer to her than her own thoughts. She can learn, as Christians have learned for centuries, to sit still and silent, moving beyond thoughts and words to quiet awareness. In that state the Holy Spirit prays within us to the Father. Worries bubble up to the surface of our mind, and dissipate themselves as we sit in the loving presence of God. 'Be still and know that I am God.' That is a far cry from the small petitions that often fill our prayers. It is something that children can learn — I have seen this myself — and that can support us through to old age.

## Brian Faces Sex Education

Brian is a well-developed eleven-year-old going into Sixth Class in a city national school. His parents have always answered the questions he and his sisters have asked about birth, sexual development and love. He is naturally interested and asks a lot. Now there is talk of a sex education course running in his class next year, and his parents are concerned about anyone outside the home taking over his education in this matter.

It is a concern common to many parents. The question of sex education in schools has been debated in the councils of the parents, the teachers and the managers of primary schools. Now is the right time to have a debate, while decisions are still pending. We can learn from the experience of other countries, some of which have squandered millions on types of sex education which simply did not achieve what they attempted. In 1971, for instance, the US government set out to reduce the number of teenage pregnancies by giving federal funding to sex education programmes, with an emphasis on methods of contraception. Since then about three billion federal dollars have been spent to promote contraceptives and 'safe sex'.

As a result there was a large increase in the number of teenagers using contraceptives. But the rates of pregnancy and abortion among teenagers not only did not fall, but continued to rise. Since 1970 among US fifteen to nineteen-year-olds, the number of births to single mothers has risen by 61%, the number of unwedded pregnancies by 87%, and the number of abortions by 67%. Sex education with an emphasis on contraceptive methods was an expensive failure, and the price has been paid not merely by the fatherless children, but also by the young people suffering from AIDS and other sexually transmitted diseases.

The failure rate of condoms is highest among teenage users, and raises questions which are politically incorrect and unpopular in Ireland today. The manufacturers themselves admit to a 5% failure rate, but other studies indicate that every fifth use carries the deadly risk of exposure to sexually transmitted disease.[18] So if teachers are slow to impart this skill to their charges, it is because they are reluctant to imply that it is safer to rely on machines than on one's freedom and self-control.

There are two approaches to sex education for adolescents. The first is morally directive, stressing the postponement of sexual activity and the value of long-term fidelity between people who are free of sexually transmitted diseases, The second is morally non-directive and relies on latex barriers; it has been called the 'technofix' approach. In the USA this latter approach has been tried for twenty years at huge expense, and has failed.

It still has strong support among young people in Ireland. Surveys indicate that they have a naive confidence in the use of condoms as a way of allowing sexual activity that will result neither in pregnancies nor in AIDS. Any education by professionals which implies: 'Use contraceptives and you will be safe', is inviting teenagers to Russian roulette, both because of the failure rate of condoms, and because teenagers are careless and spasmodic users of them. They tend to take risks with their bodies, in pot-holing, motor-biking, heavy drinking and physical feats. The same tendency to risk-taking makes them unreliable users of contraceptives, and unless they have established a moral sense about sexual activity, they are at greater risk here than in any other area of danger.

Three developments have made sex education an urgent question in the last few years: the increasingly amoral and explicit treatment of sexual behaviour on TV and film; the revelation of the extent of child sexual abuse; and above all the world-wide plague of AIDS, which is only beginning to show the extent of its menace. As a result children are superficially more knowledgeable, but (like many of their elders) are confused and nervous, and in need of calm and reliable adults who will answer their questions and listen to their confusions.

Who should do this? Obviously the parents. Many parents take it in their stride, make it easy for their children to voice their curiosity when it arises; and will always give an answer to the question that is asked, an answer that satisfies the child — and you know if it satisfied because otherwise he will go on asking.

The few careful surveys we have point to a problem here, and indicate a gap between the parent and child generations on sexual attitudes.[19] The shift has been enormous, and children, even when they are on the brink of adulthood, often feel they cannot air all their questions at home.

These are not merely the questions that used to be under wraps, like masturbation, homosexual relationships, contraception and family planning; but also the perversions and abuses, associating sex with violence and exploitation, that youngsters see on video nasties or in the yellow press. I have come across a pattern of boys using pornographic videos as a warm-up for seduction. Many youngsters have experienced it; but they may well feel their parents are not ready for such horrors.

So where do they turn for advice on sexual matters? To mother or to friends. The Irish mother has carried a great deal over the centuries, and the surveys show that she is still carrying many of the family's worries. Even boys are more likely to talk about sex to mother than to father. In a really serious sexual matter, girls would talk to mother, or both parents, more than to anyone else. It is striking, though not surprising, that the next resource is their friends. Sisters and brothers are consulted quite a bit, and many boys try to sort things out alone or with their partner. The rest of the adult world hardly features.

The sad fact is that many parents funk it, especially fathers with their sons. They cannot face the moment when he looks at you with the spoken or unspoken question: 'Did you do that with Mum?' Dad may compromise by thrusting a pamphlet into the boy's hand and sending him off to read it.

Sex education starts with listening to Brian's fantasies and misinformation, being sensitive to the unspoken questions about his own body. It starts even earlier, with the tenderness and regard parents show towards their children's bodies, with the ability to touch and stroke and caress. That pushes back to the parents' ease and contentment in their own sexuality and their own bodies. Information is only a small part of sex education. Much more important is the person and attitude of the educator, positive towards his or her body, easy in the expression of love, neither prurient nor uptight, and with a deep respect for the privacy of the child.

Because many parents neglect this duty, children sometimes turn to teachers, especially their class teacher in primary school. The teacher may feel unsure of his or her mandate from the parents. At present many schools ask an experienced teacher, often a doctor or nurse, to meet the parents of some classes, discuss sex education with them, and then have one or two sessions with the children. This can work well, although it happens only on one occasion in a child's school life, and does not meet his curiosity when it surfaces (often as a result of a news headline). That is when it is most effectively met. Answers given to live questions are remembered better than information given unasked.

There are other agencies in the wings, awaiting their opportunity: commercial interests, such as the purveyors of sanitary towels and contraceptives, who will organise sex education classes at the drop of a hat, for the sake of getting a toe-hold in this immensely lucrative market. Moreover *some* of the programmes which have been circulated in the name of life-skills or health education, appear to be fiercely manipulative of children, and intrusive on their privacy, asking girls and boys to reveal in class what they would be loath to mention even in their private diary.

If the person and attitude of the educator is the key factor in sex (as in religious) education, then parents are rightly reluctant to share their role in sex education with persons whose training and purposes are not known to them. They should get to know their child's teacher. If they trust her to share the work of Brian's religious education, then they may be happy enough for her to answer children's questions about the facts of life. Many children in Brian's class will not be as easy and curious with their parents as he, and they need to be looked after. Confusion and ignorance about sex are risky for children, and schools have a part to play in overcoming them.

## Sheena Moves Out

Sheena is twenty and has always been close to her mother. She has a job, but still lives at home. She has just announced that she plans to move into a flat with her boyfriend — no question of marriage now. Mother has not reacted much to the news so far, but father is on the point of explosion.

You may remember a *Late Late Show* when Gay Byrne threw out the question: 'What would you do if your daughter started living with her boyfriend?' to a panel of mothers and daughters. A difficult question to handle even with time to reflect, but impossible to answer adequately in the glare of a TV chat show. Those mothers' answers, supportive but embarrassed and uneasy, drew a furious and intemperate roar from a male viewer who phoned in to the programme. Perhaps Sheena's father feels like him.

What the mothers seemed to be saying was: 'Do your own thing, and I will support you.' What they seemed to intend to say was: 'Follow your own conscience.' This latter phrase was not used much in my upbringing, nor probably in that of most older readers. Yet it is one of the key teachings of western philosophy and theology, and was stressed again by the Second Vatican Council, which made such an impact on the Church thirty years ago.

In the old days religion teachers told pupils what they should and should not do. That was what teachers were for, to tell students things they needed to know. Modern Irish literature is thick with stories of authoritarian teaching which allowed no time for questioning, and which sometimes condoned injustice against which there was no appeal.

In the last fifty years we have seen horrible things done in the name of unquestioning obedience: by the SS guards of the concentration camps, by the US soldiers who murdered in My Lai, by the highly placed public servants who condoned burglary and perjury in the Watergate scandal.

The old catechism told us to obey our lawful superiors *in all that is not sin,* implying that everyone should use some personal judgment on whether she is being told to do something evil in the name of authority. Everyone has to account first to her or his conscience. The Second Vatican Council made this clear: God's voice speaks to us first of all through our conscience, i.e. through our judgment of what is right or wrong. If that is true for adults, it is also true for bright and educated teenage boys and girls. They are no longer parroting back the moral instructions of teachers, but are digging within themselves and coming up with value judgments that carry personal conviction.

Does that mean that *sincerity* matters most — I am doing this because I *feel* it is right for me? No, we are not talking about feelings but about judgments, which means that you have to use your head. You are looking not for *your* truth but for *the* truth. It is objectivity that is sought, not sincerity. The Watergate conspirators, or the My Lai murderers, would probably have claimed that they *sincerely* thought they should obey orders. They did not ask about the terrible injustice and violence being done to others.

So Sheena announces that she will move in with her boyfriend for an indefinite period. There are many complex angles to the situation that she faces, especially the prospect of producing a child that either is not wanted or that does not have a stable parental couple to rear it. What worries her parents is their moral position regarding their daughter.

Father is tempted to explosion and coercion, using force either to threaten Sheena or to throw her out of the house. That is not a moral reaction but a physical one. You find it often enough in well-intentioned people who are keenly aware of youth's limitations and who wish to protect them from doing harm to themselves or others.

Another part of them fears confrontation with Sheena. In this situation you can be so afraid of appearing uptight that you tiptoe round areas of disagreement. You fear that if you contradict Sheena you will lose her. You are also painfully aware that in the recent past you warned her against some things which she now considers either harmless or even desirable, and you do not want to send her on any more gratuitous guilt trips.

What position is there between coercion (which in any case seldom works), and *laissez-faire*, which means abandoning any moral stance? You can trust your moral authority, even if you cannot or will not back it with force. 'As a parent, I will never reject you. I am always on your side. But I believe that what you plan to do is potentially destructive and wrong. If you do go that way, you may hurt yourself and others. I do not question your sincerity, and do not want you to stop thinking for yourself. Meanwhile I have a responsibility to myself and to you to stand up for what I believe, and to caution you against behaviour that I consider irresponsible.'

That is a position which springs from love, and can be maintained with love, even if Sheena walks out as she plans. Maybe she will stay. Sometimes a young person, even as old as twenty, unconsciously wants, more than anything else, to have some adult say *No*, to be forthright enough to set the limits they cannot yet set for themselves.

## GOD AND PARENTS

Do parents come closer to God through their children? Saint Thomas Aquinas was asked a similar question at a time when nuns and monks were linking schools with their convents or monasteries. Is caring for children compatible with the search for God? The monks thought of religious life as requiring quiet, the peace of the monastery garden, the opportunity to pray without being interrupted. When children arrived, the peace was shattered. There was noise and constant movement. Things were broken, ink was spilled. Children, unlike roses or cabbages, did not stay where you planted them, or follow instructions. If they didn't like you, they told you so. They demanded so much energy and thought that there was little left for 'religious duties'.

Aquinas considered the question fairly, and his answer made an impact. Educating children was a work of mercy, a giving of oneself. Even if prayer and peace of soul suffered, it was a work of God.

What teachers go through is nothing compared with the experience of parents. The mother of a newborn simply cannot give thought or energy to anything except her child; and the demands on her husband are nearly as great, if he is ready to meet them. A 'retreat' on one's own, such as Religious enjoy, would be an unthinkable luxury for a young mother. If God is to reach such people, who are carrying out *the* most important job in our society, it cannot be through 'spiritual duties', but in other ways.

God touches parents through their children, and in ways that change drastically as the children grow. At first it is a touch that fills you. Kate draws out of you an energy, responsiveness, and love that you did not imagine yourself capable of. She fills your life, changes it. You invest hugely in her, and she rewards you, from the first smile to the day when you stand beside her as a bride or graduate or whatever. She fills your conversation, hangs out of you, wants into your bed in the morning, needs you to think of her body, sleep, food, warmth, clothes, dangers. For her you are larger than life, immortal. You must survive, never get sick. You are the universe for her.

How that changes as she grows into her teens! She reduces you to life-size, then cuts you down still further, takes you off your pedestal. She grows tall, sexy, quick-witted, in touch, feels she can take on the world, doesn't want to know about bedtime, claims she can plan her own life, take her own risks, spar with her friends, share their passions, spurn your advice but quote the same message with awe when it is uttered by some young idiot in her group. She starts to earn money, plan her own holidays, pull away from the family. Once you could do everything for her, now she seems to need you for nothing except bed and board.

Here is the emptying that St Paul placed at the heart of the Christian life. Mary faced it when she found Jesus in the Temple and heard his 'Did you not know I must be about my father's business?' She pondered the words as parents still brood on their daughter's words. Letting go, finding joy in her new skills and independence while holding the limits. Not sharing Kate's grandiose notions of her own power and wisdom, yet neither treating her as a child. Allowing her to make you feel fuddy-duddy, Victorian, three-piece-suited, antediluvian, slow-witted, redundant, *old*, yet remaining what she needs, a parenthood of presence rather than power, setting limits even if they are defied, not living through her, nor trumpeting her triumphs or misdemeanours to your friends.

She needs to know that you have a life of your own without her. Now that she needs you less, she does not want to find that you need her more. When Jesus spoke of 'losing your life in order to find it', he was not talking about exotic martyrdoms, but about the daily life of teenagers' parents. They are asked to love without sensing a return of love, to forgive when they feel their forgiveness is being taken for granted, taken advantage of. Here is a reversal of the joy that young parents feel when they have created a cocoon of love and security for their little ones. Now the cocoon is broken, the umbilical cord is painfully cut, and parents may feel a grief like that of Jesus when the rich young man spurned his invitation and turned away, or even the betrayal as he felt the kiss of Judas on his cheek. In these moments of pain God still touches you.

Sad, disillusioned adults can pray too. Those whose style of prayer has not matured with their years, are like businessmen who still rely on piggy-banks. Nobody can put the words or silence of prayer into our hearts except God, who is touching us even when prayer seems impossible. But some of the concerns of a parent at prayer find voice in these lines from a nameless father:

> I pray that I may let my child live his own life,
> and not the one I wish I had lived.
> Therefore, guard me against burdening him with
> doing what I failed to do.
>
> Help me to see his mis-steps today
> in perspective against the long road he must travel,
> and grant me the grace to be patient with his slow pace.
>
> Give me the wisdom to know when to smile at the small mischiefs of his age
> and when to show firmness against the impulses
> he fears and cannot handle.
>
> Help me to hear the anguish in his heart through the
> din of angry words,
> or across the gulf of brooding silence; and, having heard,
> grant me the ability to bridge the gap between us
> with understanding.
>
> I pray that I may raise my voice more in joy at what he is
> than in vexation at what he is not,
> so that each day he may grow in sureness of himself.
>
> Help me to regard him with genuine affection,
> so that he will feel affection for others.
> Then give me strength, O Lord, to free him
> so that he can move strongly on his way.

## NOTES

17. Andrew Greely, 'A School Report', *Tablet*, London, 27 March 1976

18. Summary of figures and documentation in *Linacre Quarterly*, August 1990, pp. 91-95

19. IMS, op. cit.

# Further Reading

Andrews, Conway, Gaffney, Fitzgerald, *Parenting*, Dublin, Town House and Country House, 1991

P. Ariès, *Centuries of Childhood*, Penguin. 1973

B. Bettelheim, *A Good Enough Parent*, London, Thames & Hudson, 1987

J. Bowlby, *A Secure Base*, London, Routledge, 1988

Corgi Mini-books, London 1969 (14 booklets, *Your 12-year-old, Your Teenager...*)

Tom Crabtree, *Emotional Problems of Children*, London, Unwin, 1981

Eric Ericson, *Childhood and Society*, Peguin, 1965.

Anna Freud, *Normality and Pathology in Childhood*, London, Hogarth, 1966

Michael Paul Gallagher, *Help my Unbelief*, Dublin, Veritas, 1971

Robbie Gilligan, *Irish Childcare Services*, Dublin, I.P.A., 1991

Haim Ginott, *Between Parent and Child*, New York, Avon Paperback, 1965

T. Gordon, *Parent Effectiveness Training*, New York, Peter Wyden, 1974

Penelope Leach, *The Parents' A to Z*, Penguin, 1983

Open University, *Living with Children 5 to 10*, London, Harper & Row, 1982

Open University, *Parents and Teenagers*, London, Harper & Row, 1982

Michael and Terri Quinn, *Parenting and Sex* (and other booklets), Newry, Family Caring Trust, 1991

Michael Rutter, *Helping Troubled Children*, Penguin, 1973

A.C.R. Skynner, *One Flesh, Separate Persons*, London, Constable, 1976

Veritas Parenting Programme, *What can a Parent do?* Dublin, Veritas, 1986

D.W. Winnicott, *The Child, the Family and the Outside World*, Penguin, 1984

# Index

741